LIES THE GOVERNMENT TOLD YOU

Also by Andrew P. Napolitano

*Constitutional Chaos: What Happens When
Government Breaks Its Own Laws*

*The Constitution in Exile: How the Federal
Government Has Seized Power by Rewriting the
Supreme Law of the Land*

A Nation of Sheep

*Dred Scott's Revenge: A Legal History of Race and
Freedom in America*

LIES THE GOVERNMENT TOLD YOU

Myth, Power, and Deception in American History

by

Andrew P. Napolitano

THOMAS NELSON
Since 1798

NASHVILLE   DALLAS   MEXICO CITY   RIO DE JANEIRO

Published in Nashville, Tennessee, by Thomas Nelson. Thomas Nelson is a trademark of Thomas Nelson, Inc.

Thomas Nelson, Inc., titles may be purchased in bulk for educational, business, fund-raising, or sales promotional use. For information, please e-mail SpecialMarkets@ThomasNelson.com.

Library of Congress Cataloging-in-Publication Data

Napolitano, Andrew P.
    Lies the government told you : myth, power, and deception in American history / by Andrew P. Napolitano.
      p. cm.
    Includes bibliographical references.
    ISBN 978-1-59555-266-2
    1. Constitutional history—United States. 2. United States—Politics and government. I. Title.
KF4550.Z9N369 2010
320.520973—dc22   2009051799

Printed in the United States of America

10 11 12 13 14 WC 10 9 8 7

*This book is dedicated
to the memory of
Senator Barry Morris Goldwater,
who, alone among major party
candidates for President,
promised to shrink the federal government,
and who is the father
of the modern American Liberty Movement.*

"'For this I was born, and for this I have come into the world, to bear witness to the truth. Everyone, who is of the truth, hears my voice.' Pilate said to him, 'What is truth?'"

— John 18:37

"[M]en are so simple, and so subject to present necessities, that he who seeks to deceive will always find someone who will allow himself to be deceived."

— Niccolo Machiavelli,
The Prince

"Everything the State says is a lie, and everything it has it has stolen."

— Friedrich Wilhelm Nietzsche,
Thus Spoke Zarathustra

"Their final objective toward which all their deceit is directed is to capture political power so that, using the power of the state and the power of the market simultaneously, they may keep the common man in eternal subjection."

— Henry A. Wallace,
Vice President of the United States
(1941 to 1945)

Contents

Foreword

by Congressman Ron Paul

Andrew P. Napolitano is a true rarity among judges and media personalities: He is a passionate defender of liberty who understands that the United States Constitution puts strict limits on federal power. Judge Napolitano's tremendous knowledge of American law, history, and politics, as well as his passion for freedom, shines through in *Lies the Government Told You*, as he details how throughout American history, politicians and government officials have betrayed the ideals of personal liberty and limited government.

Anyone who knows Judge Napolitano understands that he does not pull his punches or excuse any constitutional violations in order to support any group or political interest. Thus, *Lies the Government Told You* explains how politicians of both parties have routinely disregarded the constitutional limits on federal power and violated our natural rights.

One of the most important lessons Judge Napolitano teaches is how many shared premises there are by advocates of big government from both the right and the left. For example, Judge Napolitano exposes how both the conservatives' war on marijuana and the liberals' war on tobacco are manifestations of paternalism—the idea that government has the legitimate authority to stop adults from doing bad things, like smoking substances that politicians and bureaucrats do not approve of. Of course, smoking, whether of marijuana or tobacco, does have negative health consequences—but respecting the right of individuals to be wrong, as long as they do not interfere with the rights of others, is one of the pillars of a free society.

Lies the Government Told You also avoids the all-too-common error of drawing a distinction between "personal" liberty and "economic" liberty, and focusing on attacks on one type of freedom while ignoring or even supporting attacks on the other category of liberty. When the freedom movement began in the nineteenth century, supporters of liberty, who were then known as "liberals," made no distinctions between government actions that interfered with economic liberties, such as laws infringing upon private contracts, and government actions that restricted personal liberty, such as limits on the freedom of speech. Supporters of liberty were also likely to understand the grave threat posed to liberty and constitutional government by a militaristic foreign policy. Thus, they were also supporters of peace.

However, beginning in the Progressive Era, promoters of big government co-opted the rhetoric of the promoters of freedom, even stealing the label "liberal." Whereas liberal once referred to a supporter of freedom, beginning in the Progressive Era, the term *liberal* began to refer to supporters of the welfare state. The division between supporters of "economic" and "personal" freedoms was accelerated by the Cold War, when many supporters of free markets allowed their (justifiable) loathing of communism to lead them to embrace militarism abroad and limitations on personal freedom at home. Thanks to this division between the supporters of personal and economic liberty, it is not uncommon to find opponents of socialized medicine arguing for the Patriot Act, and opponents of gun control arguing for free speech.

Fortunately, Judge Andrew P. Napolitano is one of a growing number of Americans who support liberty across the board. Thus, *Lies the Government Told You* defends all of our freedoms. Readers of this book will find eloquent defenses of private property, the right to keep and bear arms, and attacks on excessive government regulations along with defenses of free speech, and attacks on unconstitutional wars, the drug war, and the Patriot Act.

One chapter of this book that is particularly important to me deals with monetary policy. Anyone who has followed my career knows that exposing and ending the damage done to our prosperity and freedom by the Federal Reserve's fiat currency system drives much of what I do. While there is substantial literature explaining the myriad ways the Federal Reserve damages our economy, there is not nearly as much writing that explains how the Federal Reserve System violates the Constitution and ties the Federal Reserve to the general assault on liberty waged by Big Government. This book helps fill that gap.

As a congressional representative from a Gulf Coast district who has seen how the Federal Emergency Management Agency (FEMA) fails to live up to its promise to provide assistance to victims of natural disasters in a timely and thorough manner, I particularly enjoyed Judge Napolitano's dissection of the constitutional and practical problems with FEMA.

I have only scratched the surface of the many virtues of this important work. *Lies the Government Told You* will provide those active in the freedom movement with much-needed intellectual ammunition. This book can also help open the eyes of those who are yet to recognize the assaults on our liberty by politicians and bureaucrats. I am pleased to recommend this book to anyone who cares about the direction of this country and wants to understand how we got where we are, and what we need to do to regain our liberties.

—Congressman Ron Paul, M.D. (R-TX)

Introduction

During the 1980 presidential campaign, a joke made the rounds in the Reagan camp. George Washington, Richard Nixon, and Jimmy Carter die and go to Heaven. In a chance meeting about how they got there, Washington boasts, "I never told a lie." Not to be outdone, Nixon proclaims, "I never told the truth." A determined Carter can't resist: "I never knew the difference!"

What is a lie? What is the truth? What is the difference?

One could not begin to count all the words, ink, and paper spent addressing those three questions, even though the answers are implicated in almost every thought and every word and every act that everyone perceives, utters, and engages upon every day of our adult lives.

Truth is identity between intellect and reality. A lie is a knowing and intentional violation of the truth. The difference between the two often depends on whether one is in the governing class or the governed class.

We have all come to expect some lying in our lives and have engaged in lying to some extent; perhaps to avoid or postpone a crisis, or to serve a higher good, or because telling a lie was easier under the circumstances than telling the truth, and the consequences of the lie were harmless. This is all normal human behavior, and it can range from being critical to existence to being innocuous.

If a ship captain is secretly ferrying innocents from slavery to freedom, and his ship is stopped on the high seas by agents of the government that enslaved his passengers, should he lie about their true identities? When a coworker asks how you are during a miserable day, should you lie to avoid a painful but harmless and useless conversation? Can silence be a lie when one has a lawful or moral duty to tell the truth? These are issues with which we wrestle almost every day.

In a free society, we expect the government to wrestle with them as well, but it does not; it is not concerned with truth. The government lies to us regularly, consistently, systematically, and daily on matters great and small, but it prosecutes and jails those who lie to it. For example, a male drug dealer with a heavy foreign accent and minimal understanding of English stupidly tells an FBI agent that his name is Nancy Reagan, and he is arrested, prosecuted, and jailed for lying to the government. Another FBI agent tells the cultural guru Martha Stewart, in an informal conversation in the presence of others, that she is not the target of a federal criminal probe, and she replies that she did not sell a certain stock on a certain day. They both lied, but she went to jail and the FBI agent kept his job.

What is it about the government and its agents and employees that they can lie to us with impunity, but we risk being sent to jail if we lie to them?

Throughout this book, I will suggest answers to these and similar questions. As I do so, you'll see a chip on my shoulder. I am angry that we allow the government to lie to us, that we expect it to do so, and even take comfort in the illusions created thereby. When I told friends about the title of this book, I frequently joked that it would be four thousand pages in length. Most laughed; but none doubted that there have been enough government lies to consume that many printed pages.

When you recall that the Declaration of Independence and the

Constitution of the United States mandate a free and open society, one in which *the government works for us*, you can see where the chip on my shoulder came from. It is morally reprehensible for any government to lie to anyone over whom it has lawful authority. But in a free and open society where *we are the employers, and the government workers are the employees*, every government employee—from a public school janitor to a state governor, from a soldier to an FBI agent, from a cop to the President—has a lawful obligation to be truthful to his or her employers, and it is utterly and completely and unconditionally unacceptable to treat as normal that they should lie to us.

And yet, treat it as normal we do. Just look at the names of the chapters in this book—from "All Men Are Created Equal" to "Congress Shall Make No Law . . . Abridging the Freedom of Speech," from "Innocent Until Proven Guilty" to "Your Boys Are Not Going to Be Sent into Any Foreign Wars" to "We Don't Torture"—and you will see the stuff of which historical myth is made. Every one of those well-known, well-worn, well-stated canards is a goal the government has never reached but claims it has. Each has become a bald-faced lie, a perpetrated myth, a grasp at power, a monstrous deception. And most of us recognize that.

Why do we believe government-generated myths? Why do we allow the use of myth to enhance government power? Why do we condone the government's use of deception to crush our freedom, steal our property, and destroy our lives? And how does the government get away with all this?

These are the questions we will explore in the coming pages, as we tear through American history from 1776 to 2010, and expose the use of myth to seize power and the power of deception to delude the public. When the public is deluded by the very folks it has hired to defend its freedom, the delusion interferes with that freedom by denying us accurate information with which we can decide in whose hands we should repose government power. Would Americans have reelected FDR had they known that he *caused* the attack on Pearl Harbor? Would voters have chosen LBJ, the supposed "peace candidate" in 1964, had they known he was *secretly planning* to ramp up the Vietnam War? Would George W. Bush have been reelected in 2004 if we knew he was illegally spying on us, concocting evidence for war, torturing people, and *lying* about it?

Government lies take on a life of their own since they breed more lies to substantiate the original lies. Government lies induce government lawbreaking, and government lawbreaking means someone is suffering a loss of life, liberty, or property because of some event not caused by the person suffering; and it also means that the lawbreaker walks free in the corridors of power to strike again.

Government lies are a direct assault on freedom because, if believed, if accepted as truth, the lies dupe individuals into making choices they would not make were the truth known. Government lies seduce us into surrendering freedom and accepting unlawful behavior and irretrievable loss as somehow warranted, and they establish a precedent for similar thefts of freedom and personal loss in the future.

In my previous books, I have targeted government excess. In *Constitutional Chaos: What Happens When the Government Breaks Its Own Laws*, I argued that government lawbreaking is a serious, yet hidden problem recognized primarily by those who benefit from or are victimized by it, and if unchecked, will lead to tyranny. In *The Constitution in Exile: How the Federal Government Has Seized Power by Rewriting the Supreme Law of the Land*, I made the case that the feds have systematically stolen power from the States and freedom from individuals, under the guise of interpreting the Constitution, and much of that power and many of those freedoms will be impossible to reclaim. In *A Nation of Sheep*, I showed that government in America hates freedom, that it defends its power and not our rights, even though our rights are natural, come from our humanity, and as Jefferson stated, are "inalienable." In *Dred Scott's Revenge: A Legal History of Race and Freedom in America*, I demonstrated that any government that thinks it can suspend the free will of the innocent is fatal to life, fatal to freedom, and breeds horrors that can last for centuries.

In the pages that follow, I continue with my theme that the government is not your friend. The lies told to us by our own government, and accepted by our grandparents and our parents and our children, have destroyed the lives, stolen the freedom, crushed the God-given rights, and seized the property of those who got in the way of official government deception. Why has our government rejected America's first principles of individual freedom, guaranteed rights, limited government, free enterprise, private property, and the right to be left alone? And why has it denied doing so?

Before you start reading this book, I suggest you flip back to the quotations I have selected as representational themes of this book and reread them. Hold me to these themes, and at the end of the book, decide for yourself if I have supported them.

Come with me now on a tour of myth, power, and deception in America; woven into the fabric of our history, perpetrated even as you read this, and accepted by millions as the norm.

Lie #1

"All Men Are Created Equal"

On July 4th 1776, the thirteen United States of America declared independence from Great Britain and its tyrannical king, George III. The Continental Congress, in the Declaration of Independence, stated that "all Men are created equal, that they are endowed by their Creator with certain unalienable[1] Rights, that among these are Life, Liberty and the Pursuit of Happiness." The delegates to the Continental Congress who signed the Declaration believed that government power is fueled by the consent of the governed, and that its primary purposes are to ensure the people's freedom to pursue happiness and to protect their inalienable rights. King George III had never embraced this philosophy, and the bulk of the Declaration listed the ways in which he had abused his power: Great Britain taxed the colonies without granting them representation, prohibited them from trading with the rest of the world, and broke its own laws to exploit them. According to Congress, the King left the United States no alternative but to sever ties with Great Britain and form a new nation with its own government, one that would keep secure its people's natural rights.

The government that emerged from the American victory in the Revolutionary War, however, did not treat all men equally. The United States Constitution, for example, contained provisions that implicitly and explicitly recognized slavery's legitimacy, protected it as an institution, and insulated it from regulation or interference by the federal government. In fact, the government permitted slavery for almost one hundred years after Thomas Jefferson wrote the immortal "all Men are created equal" language. It was not until recently that the government's behavior matched these words and African-Americans truly became equal under the law.

President Barack Obama stated that it is an American tradition that "all men are created equal under the law and . . . no one is above it."[2] The implication in that statement is false. It may be true that no one is above the law, but for much of American history, African-Americans were below it. The Founding Fathers, as brilliant and courageous as they were, lied to us. Abraham Lincoln, the so-called "Great Emancipator," lied to us. The Supreme Court of the United States, in upholding Jim Crow laws, lied to us. Thankfully, one of the great things about this country is that over time, Americans get smarter. We recognize our transgressions and work to correct them. Some of the greatest advances in human rights have come after some of the greatest assaults on them. After 230 years of exceptional indignity, lawlessness, and bloodshed, we can now say that "all Men are created equal," and mean it. But that was not the case in 1776.

Founding Slave Owners

Upon the signing of the Declaration of Independence, 20 percent of America's population was enslaved.[3] Most of the approximately five hundred thousand slaves living in the United States in 1776 were concentrated in the five southernmost states, where they represented 40 percent of the population.[4] The Founding Fathers owned slaves. In fact, four of the first five American Presidents, including the still-beloved George Washington, Thomas Jefferson, and James Madison, owned slaves.[5]

Thomas Jefferson condemned slavery and vehemently opposed its expansion. In his first term in the Virginia House of Burgesses, Jefferson proposed a law to free Virginia's slaves.[6] In 1774, Jefferson urged the Virginia delegates to the First Continental Congress to abolish the slave trade.[7] According to Jefferson, "[t]he abolition of domestic slavery is the great object of desire in those colonies where it was unhappily introduced. . . ."[8] Furthermore, Jefferson wrote a draft constitution for the State of Virginia that forbade the importation of slaves.[9] Also, in a draft of the Declaration of Independence, Jefferson complained of Britain's introduction of slavery and the slave trade to the colonies.[10]

Jefferson also played an integral role in enacting the Northwest Ordinance of 1787, which quickened the westward expansion of the United States, while also providing that "[t]here shall be neither slavery nor involuntary servitude in the said territory . . ."[11] Later, in 1808, President Jefferson signed a statute prohibiting the Atlantic slave trade.[12]

Jefferson should be admired for instilling in America the democratic and egalitarian principles that we hold so sacred today. The fact remains, however, that Jefferson owned slaves. At the time he wrote that "all Men are created equal," he owned about two hundred slaves, and slavery played an integral role in his life.[13] Slaves constructed his majestic home and even his personal coffin.[14]

According to Jefferson, African-Americans may not have been inferior to whites, but they certainly were different. In his book, *Notes on the State of Virginia*, Jefferson recounted his observations of the physical differences between blacks and whites[15] and wrote negatively and positively about African-American behavior.[16] For example, Jefferson noticed that as compared to whites, blacks required less sleep, but were more adventurous than whites.[17] In analyzing their mental capacity, Jefferson observed that blacks had better memories than whites, but could not reason nearly as well as their white counterparts.[18] From his observations, Jefferson concluded that by nature, African-Americans were not as intelligent as whites.[19] However, with respect to moral capacity (the "heart," as Jefferson called it), Jefferson believed that God did create all men equal.[20] Furthermore, Jefferson wrote that "nothing is more certainly written in the book of fate than that [slaves] are to be free," and he believed that African-Americans had "a natural right" to pursue freedom.

Moreover, according to the historian John C. Miller, in the Declaration of Independence, Jefferson may have intentionally left "property" off the list of inalienable rights to pave the road for placing slaves' human rights above the property rights of their slave owners.[21] Alexander Hamilton, a Founding Father who once owned slaves in New York, and the first United States Secretary of the Treasury, wrote in *The Federalist, No. 1*, written for the People of New York, and more broadly, the citizens of the United States, that signing the Constitution "is the safest course for your liberty, your dignity, and your *happiness*" (emphasis added). However, the Fifth Amendment to the Constitution states, in part, that "[n]o person shall be . . . deprived of life, liberty, or *property* without due process of law" (emphasis added). In ratifying the Constitution, did Congress abandon Jefferson's intent? Did it become less sympathetic to human rights? Did the Founders find no shame in condoning slavery as a property right protected by due process?

Regardless of his ideas on the equality of men, Jefferson believed that blacks and whites could not coexist as equals.[22] He feared that if whites did not treat blacks paternalistically, there would be a race war resulting in the black race overtaking the white.[23] Jefferson stated, "We have the wolf by the ears and we can neither hold him, nor safely let him go. Justice in one scale, and self-preservation in the other."[24] Nevertheless, Thomas Jefferson freed five of his slaves in his will, and even though Virginia law mandated that freed slaves leave the state within a year of their emancipation, Jefferson petitioned the Virginia assembly to permit his freed slaves to remain "where their families and connections are."[25] The Virginia assembly honored Jefferson's request.[26]

George Washington, known throughout the ages as the "Father" of his country, was a Southern planter who owned and relied on slaves.[27] Washington punished his slaves by whipping or selling them, divided their families so they would work more efficiently, and provided them with as little means as tolerable.[28] He also raffled off the slaves of those bankrupt slaveholders who owed him money.[29] Washington's most gruesome act as a slave owner came in 1784, five years before he became President of the United States. In that year, Washington hired a dentist to extract nine teeth from the mouths of his slaves, and implant them into his own mouth.[30]

During his presidency (1789 to 1797), Washington lived at the President's House in Philadelphia. In 1780, Pennsylvania had passed "An Act for the Gradual Abolition of Slavery," which prohibited nonresidents from holding slaves in the state longer than six months. In an attempt to circumvent this law, Washington and his wife, Martha Dandridge Custis Washington, neither a permanent resident of Pennsylvania, rotated their slaves in and out of Pennsylvania so that none of them established continuous residency for six months. This practice violated the Pennsylvania Act, but the Washingtons were never prosecuted under it.

During the Revolutionary War, however, Washington's attitude toward African-Americans was markedly different. Washington recruited free blacks into the Continental Army, and by the time of the Battle of Yorktown, African-Americans constituted 25 percent of the Army.[31] By 1786, Washington promised never to buy another slave. By the time of his death, Washington found slavery morally wrong, and freed his slaves in his will, upon the death of his wife, Martha.[32] He even expressed a desire to have his freed slaves educated.[33]

Like Jefferson, however, Washington, did not seek to abolish slavery swiftly, or with any type of urgency. Despite not purchasing a slave after 1786, and eventually freeing his slaves, Washington believed slavery would be abolished by "slow, sure and imperceptible degrees."[34]

A Less Perfect Union

The Founding Fathers overtly defended slavery and racism in the United States Constitution. Protecting the institution of slavery was necessary to gain the South's support for a new, centralized federal government. It is important to realize that our Constitution legitimized the ownership of some human beings by other human beings. This was, of course, directly opposed to the Natural Law values of the Declaration of Independence, which asserted that the rights of "all Men" come from our "Creator" and are thus "unalienable," absent due process. The Constitution contained express provisions recognizing slavery's existence, protecting it as a legal institution, and insulating it from regulation or interference by the federal government.

Three provisions of the Constitution implicitly recognize the existence of slavery: the Fugitive Slave Clause (Article IV, Section 2, Clause 3), the Importation Clause (Article I, Section 9, Clause 1), and the Three-Fifths Clause (Article I, Section 2, Clause 3). The Fugitive Slave Clause provides that "[n]o Person held to Service of Labour in one State" shall be discharged from such labor if he or she escapes into another State. This clause essentially required the States to return fugitive slaves who escaped into their territory. The courts interpreted this clause as providing slaveholders with a right to their slave property that no state where slavery was prohibited could qualify, control, or undo.

The Importation Clause in the Constitution forbade Congress from outlawing the "importation of such Persons as any of the States now existing shall think proper" until 1808. This clause permitted the international slave trade until at least 1808. The United States discontinued the international slave trade in that year when President Jefferson signed legislation prohibiting it.

The "Three-Fifths Compromise" was the clearest example of the delegates who wrote the Constitution abandoning ethical and moral standards, and even core values, in order to construct a new federal government. The Northerners wanted apportionment for the House of Representatives to be based solely on the population of free persons living in each state, whereas the Southerners wanted their slaves to count as whole persons, thus increasing Southern representation in Congress. The infamous and despicable Three-Fifths Clause emerged from the debate. It provides that apportionment be determined by the "whole number of free Persons" in each state, minus the number of "Indians not taxed," plus "three fifths of all other Persons." Therefore, the Constitution counted slaves ("other Persons") only as 60 percent of free, white persons.

In Their Defense . . .

Regardless of their faults, many of the Founding Fathers did *not* own slaves and recognized slavery's inherent immorality. Benjamin Franklin, for example, called slavery "a source of serious evils" and "an atrocious debasement of human nature."[35] In 1774, two years *before* signing the Declaration of Independence, Franklin and his fellow Founding Father, Benjamin Rush, formed the Pennsylvania

Society for Promoting Abolition of Slavery.[36] John Jay, an author of *The Federalist Papers* and President of a comparable society in New York, as well as the first Chief Justice of the United States, declared that "[t]he honour of the states, as well as justice and humanity . . . loudly call upon them to emancipate these unhappy people. To contend for our own liberty, and to deny that blessing to others, involves an inconsistency not to be excused."[37]

James Madison owned slaves, yet deemed slavery "the most oppressive dominion ever exercised by man over man."[38] Madison noted that the delegates to the Constitutional Convention "thought it wrong to admit in the Constitution the idea that there could be property in men."[39] In *The Federalist, No. 54*, Madison stated that "we must deny the fact, that slaves are considered merely as property, and in no respect whatever persons."[40]

The Founders seemed to believe that slavery would meet its natural demise in the United States. At the Constitutional Convention, a Connecticut delegate, Roger Sherman, stated, "The abolition of slavery seemed to be going on in the United States. . . . The good sense of the several states would probably by degrees complete it."[41] George Washington, in a draft of his first inaugural address, expressed the desire for the country to "reverse the absurd position that the many were made for the few."[42] Just before his death, Thomas Jefferson, referring to slavery, asserted that "[a]ll eyes are opened, or opening, to the rights of man."[43]

The prominent abolitionist Frederick Douglass actually believed that the Constitution created an "anti-slavery government."[44] In 1864, Douglass wrote, "It was purposely so framed as to give no claim, no sanction to the claim, of property in man. If in its origin slavery had any relation to the government, it was only as the scaffolding to the magnificent structure, to be removed as soon as the building was completed."[45] Technically speaking, Douglass was absolutely right. The Thirteenth Amendment to the United States Constitution states that "[n]either slavery nor involuntary servitude . . . shall exist within the United States, or any place subject to their jurisdiction," yet none of the original text was in any way altered.

It is interesting to note that William Lloyd Garrison, another great abolitionist and editor of *The Liberator*, a radical abolitionist newspaper, believed that the Constitution was actually a *pro*-slavery document. He called the Constitution a "pact with the devil." Frederick Douglass[46] had admired Garrison, but when Douglass, in 1851, stated his belief that the Constitution could be used to *fight* slavery, Garrison and Douglass engaged in a vicious debate in which they communicated through newspapers and letters.

Slavery was a tradition embedded in the culture of the South and played a key economic role there. Its economic importance was the key factor impeding abolition. Nevertheless, slavery is morally reprehensible, and completely indefensible,[47] and the fact that many Americans, including the Founding Fathers, recognized that it was wrong, in a way makes us even more responsible for the crimes committed against the African-American race. Frederick Douglass may have been right when he said that the Constitution paved the road for abolition, but it took the United States nearly one hundred years to take serious action.

Preserving the Union

President Abraham Lincoln, known as the "Great Emancipator," is widely regarded as a defender of black freedom who supported social equality of the races and led us into the American Civil War to free the slaves. According to Lincoln, "If slavery is not wrong, nothing is wrong."[48] Lincoln did, in fact, view slavery as an evil institution, but did not seek to abolish slavery because it was morally despicable. Rather, he only supported an end to slavery when he felt it became necessary to win the war.

Lincoln's *first* action as President was to persuade the States to ratify a constitutional amendment that would have *legalized* and *preserved* the institution of slavery. The proposed amendment, "The Corwin Amendment," stated the following: "No Amendment shall be made to the Constitution which will authorize or give Congress the power to abolish or interfere, within any State, with the domestic institutions thereof, including that of persons held to labor or service by the laws of the State." Slavery, to Lincoln, was a "domestic institution" under this Amendment. The Amendment, of course, was never formally adopted, as Southern legislatures were already prepared to secede from the Union to express their discontent with federal dominion over their interests.

Lincoln opposed slavery's expansion into America's new territories not based on any moral duty to uphold the Natural Law, or the need to right inherent wrongs. Instead, Lincoln simply wanted to keep African-Americans out of the West and keep the white and black races separate. In 1857, prior to becoming President, Lincoln expressed his opposition to the Kansas-Nebraska Act, which would have admitted Kansas into the Union as a slave state: "There is *a natural disgust* in the minds of nearly all white people to the idea of indiscriminate amalgamation of the white and black races . . . *A separation of the races is the only perfect preventive* of amalgamation, but as an immediate separation is impossible, the next best thing is to keep them apart where they are not already together"[49] (emphases added). Lincoln went on to state that "if white and black people never get together in Kansas, they will never mix blood in Kansas."[50] Moreover, to alleviate racial tension in the United States, Lincoln favored the deportation of the African-American population to settlements in either Africa or Central America. According to Lincoln:

> Racial separation must be effected by colonization of the country's blacks to foreign land. The enterprise is a difficult one, but where there is a will there is a way . . . Let us be brought to believe it is morally right and, at the same time, favorable to, or, at least, not against, our interests, to transfer the African to his native clime, and we shall find a way to do it, however great the task may be.[51]

When the South began seceding from the Union, Lincoln met with leaders from Missouri, Kentucky, Maryland, and Delaware, using slavery as a bargaining device. Lincoln promised that the federal government would not interfere with slavery in those states as long as they remained in the Union. Some border states, albeit temporarily, agreed to remain in the Union. Therefore, it is quite clear that Lincoln was willing to support the existence of slavery so long as his federal government stayed intact.

Lincoln was reluctant to issue the Emancipation Proclamation. He feared that it would conflict with his goal of "saving the Union," or rather, expanding the size of the federal government. In fact, Lincoln actually issued a "Preliminary Proclamation" to the Confederacy on September 22nd 1862, warning the Confederate States that if they continued in rebellion, he would end slavery in the South on January 1st 1863 (the date on which the Emancipation Proclamation was issued). *Therefore, if the slave states had rejoined the Union, Lincoln would have permitted them to keep their slaves.* After issuing the Proclamation, Lincoln declared:

> My paramount objective in this struggle is to save the Union, and is not either to save or destroy slavery. If I could save the Union

without freeing any slave, I would do it, and if I could save it by freeing all the slaves, I would do it; and if I could save it by freeing some and leaving others alone, I would also do that. What I do about slavery and the colored race, I do because I believe it helps to save the Union.[52]

Furthermore, Lincoln saw the Proclamation as a wartime measure to weaken the South, not as a step toward the abolition of involuntary servitude. If the slaves were freed, Lincoln believed that they would revolt against their masters and bolster the Union Army. Lincoln publicly announced that the Emancipation Proclamation was "sincerely believed to be an act of justice, warranted by the Constitution *upon military necessity*" (emphases added).

Moreover, the Emancipation Proclamation was rather limited in its scope, and had very little effect by itself. The Proclamation applied *only* in the Confederacy, and had no legal justification, as the Confederate states had already seceded. Even after the Proclamation, eight hundred thousand African-Americans were still enslaved in the border states of Kentucky, Missouri, Maryland, Delaware, and West Virginia, as well as in the North, with the blessings of the Great Emancipator. In essence, the Proclamation supported slavery after its issuance.

The Union Army forced emancipated African-Americans to enter into yearly labor contracts with their masters to avoid "vagrancy" and "idleness." Once they were under contract, the blacks were not allowed to leave their respective plantations without permission. This system of forced free labor spread throughout the parts of the South that were dominated by the American Army, and lasted until the end of the Civil War.

Lincoln's Emancipation Proclamation, therefore, achieved little in terms of African-American freedom. The federal government did not officially recognize emancipation until Congress enacted the Thirteenth Amendment to the United States Constitution on December 6th 1865. By that time, slavery had been abolished in Missouri, Maryland, Louisiana, and Arkansas; and Tennessee and Kentucky were both in the process of ending slavery.

Supreme Racism

The Union won the Civil War, and the slaves were emancipated, but African-Americans were far from equal to whites in the United States during the Reconstruction Era and beyond. The Southern state and local governments enacted Jim Crow laws, with the purpose of segregating blacks and whites, and institutionalizing the idea that African-Americans are morally and legally inferior to whites. Sadly, the United States Supreme Court supported Jim Crow through various troubling and openly racist decisions.

The Supreme Court ruled unconstitutional the Civil Rights Act of 1875, which stated in part,

> [t]hat all persons within the jurisdiction of the United States shall be entitled to the full and equal enjoyment of the accommodations, advantages, facilities, and privileges of inns, public conveyances on land or water, theaters, and other public places of public amusement; subject only to the conditions and limitations established by law, and applicable alike to citizens of every race and color regardless of any previous condition of servitude.

This Act was passed pursuant to the Fourteenth Amendment to the United States Constitution, which states, in relevant part: "No State shall make or enforce any law which shall abridge the privileges or immunities of citizens of the United States; nor shall any State deprive any person of life, liberty, or property, without due process of law; nor deny to any person within its jurisdiction the equal protection of the laws." Furthermore, Section 5 of the Fourteenth Amendment grants Congress the power to enforce the Amendment by "appropriate legislation." According to the Supreme Court's majority opinion in the *Civil Rights Case*, decided in 1883, the Civil Rights Act of 1875 was unconstitutional because it was not passed in reaction to discriminatory *state* legislation.[53] The Court held that the Equal Protection Clause applies only to *state* action, not discrimination perpetrated by private businesses. Through this decision, the Court essentially condoned private discrimination, providing African-Americans with no recourse against racist state and local governments that forced white business owners to separate the races.

The case of *Plessy v. Ferguson*, decided in 1896, was an example of state action.[54] In 1890, the State of Louisiana passed the "Separate Car Act," a law requiring separate, but "equal" accommodations for African-Americans and whites on railway cars. Homer Plessy, who was only one-eighth black, but was classified as an African-American under Louisiana law, was convicted under the Act for sitting in a "white" railway car. Plessy challenged the law as a violation of the Fourteenth Amendment, but the Supreme Court disagreed, in a 7 to 1 decision.

According to the majority, Plessy's argument *falsely* assumed that "the enforced separation of the two races stamps the colored race with a badge of inferiority."[55] As far as the majority was concerned, Louisiana was permitted to pass such a law, so long as the separate accommodations were "equal." The Supreme Court also stated that the Constitution does not protect against social differences between the races, declaring that "[i]f one race be inferior to the other socially, the Constitution of the United States cannot put them on the same plane."[56]

The lone dissenter, Justice John Marshall Harlan, wrote a passionate dissent in which he declared: "[T]here is in this country no superior, dominant, ruling class of citizens. There is no caste here. Our Constitution is color-blind, and neither knows nor tolerates classes among citizens. In respect of civil rights, all citizens are equal before the law."[57]

Unfortunately, Justice Harlan's opinion did not represent the prevailing view in this country until well after the case of *Brown v. Board of Education of Topeka*, decided in 1954, in which the Supreme Court held that segregation of public school students violates the Equal Protection Clause of the Fourteenth Amendment.[58] Separate facilities for blacks and whites, according to the Court, are inherently unequal. Until 1954, the States, with the Supreme Court's permission, were free to discriminate against African-Americans who attempted to be accepted as equals in American society. The Supreme Court, through its decisions in the latter part of the nineteenth century, gave strength to the idea that there existed a color barrier between blacks and whites, and defied Jefferson's supposed self-evident truth that "all Men are created equal."

Toward a "Post-Racial" Era

The United States of America, after a long, dark history of legal slavery and legal racial discrimination, is moving closer and closer to a "post-racial" era, a time when Americans move beyond racial differences. Nevertheless, as much as politicians would like to believe that we have transcended race, the race issue is still prevalent in American society. We are still judged on what makes us different from one another, and not as much on what unites us.

The affirmative action debate is important to explore because it is a current example of distinguishing people based on race and reflects a modern-day obstacle to Jefferson's truism. "Affirmative action" is the term describing government policies that take race into account in order to foster racial equal opportunity, or to right past wrongs. Affirmative action policies are widespread in education, as well as in employment.

In the 1978 case of *Regents of the University of California v. Bakke*, the Supreme Court held that affirmative action policies in publicly owned college admissions are constitutional, but institutions cannot employ a "quota system" based on race.[59] That is, colleges cannot set aside a certain amount of seats for students solely for minorities, but they can take race into account as one factor in determining whether an applicant should be admitted. The Supreme Court recently upheld this decision in 2003, in *Grutter v. Bollinger*, when asked to assess the University of Michigan Law School's conceded racially discriminatory admissions procedures.[60]

Justice O'Connor, writing for the majority in *Grutter*, surmised that "25 years from now the use of racial preferences will no longer be necessary to further the interest [in achieving a diverse student body] approved today."[61] Justice O'Connor's weird articulation of the Court's position on affirmative action raises many questions. It is clear from her statement that racial inequality still exists in this country; that is not disputed. It is also evident that Justice O'Connor believes that affirmative action policies are not the ideal way to conquer these differences, yet according to her, some form of affirmative action is presently necessary. No matter how we look at affirmative action, it is a form of racial discrimination; it is government making decisions based on race. Affirmative action consists of the government, which is supposed to be color-blind, helping some (who could use the help) and harming others (who harmed no one themselves) *based solely on race*. It has survived because it is not the typically historical brand of racial discrimination. It seeks to *correct* past discrimination against African-Americans, and put them on a level playing field with whites.

However, Supreme Court Justice Clarence Thomas believes that affirmative action amounts to a "reverse-racism" tool. In *Adarand Constructors, Inc. v. Pena*, an affirmative action case decided in 1995, Justice Thomas, in his concurring opinion, stated that "[i]t is irrelevant whether a government's racial classifications are drawn by those who wish to oppress a race or by those who have a sincere desire to help those thought to be disadvantaged."[62] Therefore, according to Justice Thomas, all affirmative action programs violate the Equal Protection Clause. Furthermore, in his dissent in *Grutter*, Justice Thomas responded directly to Justice O'Connor, and stated that if Michigan's affirmative action system will be illegal in 25 years, it must be "illegal now," for the Constitution "means the same thing today as it will in 300 months."[63]

Justice Thomas is correct. The government has no power to make decisions based on race, just as it has outlawed innkeepers, schoolteachers, landlords, shopkeepers, and even Presidents from doing so. I am loath to endorse the federal regulation of private behavior for reasons I have articulated elsewhere;* essentially because the Constitution has never given Congress the power to do so. But it can certainly assure that the States as States, as sovereign governments, respect the Natural Law, which is color-blind. Isn't it ironic that it took a black man on the highest court in the land to point this out?

---

* See my previous books: *Constitutional Chaos: What Happens When the Government Breaks Its Own Laws; The Constitution in Exile: How the Federal Government Has Seized Power by Rewriting the Supreme Law of the Land; A Nation of Sheep; Dred Scott's Revenge: A Legal History of Race and Freedom in America.*

What is it about "all Men are created equal" that we still struggle to implement that statement 235 years after it was written? Do we really understand today—after a Civil War, constitutional amendments that were popularly adopted in some states and compelled by force of arms in others, Reconstruction, Jim Crow, official segregation, and now a biracial President—any better just what Jefferson meant?

Lie #2

"All Men . . . Are Endowed by Their Creator with Certain Inalienable Rights"

Wilhelmina Dery, an elderly woman who had lived in her house since her birth in 1918, was planning to stay there with her husband, Charles, until she died.[1] That was her plan, at least, until the City of New London decided it would take her house, and the entire neighborhood, away from the homeowners so it could build a development on the land. By the time they lost the case, *Kelo v. New London*, in the Supreme Court, Wilhelmina and her husband, at age eighty-seven and eighty-six years old respectively, were about to be kicked to the curb by the State of Connecticut.[2] Yet, after the Court's unfavorable ruling, many of the plaintiffs, including the Derys' son, were able to delay the government's confiscation of their homes. In the meantime, Wilhelmina got her wish and died in the house she had been born in eighty-eight years earlier.[3]

Susette Kelo, the named plaintiff in *Kelo v. New London*, stated, "There is no amount of money that could replace our homes and our memories. This is where we chose to settle, and this is where we want to stay. This is America, the home of the free, isn't it?"[4] Kelo's poignant words make a very meaningful point: What ever did happen to the freedom to enjoy happiness on your own property?

That right to enjoy your own property derives from Natural Law, and Natural Law teaches that human freedom extends from human nature, which originates with God. So under Natural Law, legislatures have unwritten limitations imposed on them because human gifts that come from God are greater than government powers based on consensus, whim, fear, or force.

Under Natural Law, our fundamental rights—like freedom of speech, freedom to travel, freedom of religion, etc.—cannot be taken away by the government, unless it follows procedural due process. Due process means that we knew before we violated the law that the government would prosecute, that we were fully notified by the government of the charges against us, and that we had a fair trial with a lawyer before a neutral judge and jury. It also means that we can challenge the government's evidence against us by summoning persons and evidence that support our case, that the government must prove its accusations against us beyond a reasonable doubt, and that we are given the right to appeal to another neutral court. Under the Natural Law, only by following procedural due process can the government deprive us of our Natural Law rights.[5]

Numerous intellectuals throughout history have espoused the Natural Law. Sophocles, Aristotle, and Cicero; Augustine, Aquinas, and Locke; Jefferson, Martin Luther King, Jr., Justice Clarence Thomas, and Pope John Paul II, all recognized the existence and immutability of Natural Law. As Aristotle put it, "one part of what is politically just is natural, and the other part is legal." If you fast forward a little bit, transcendental thinker Henry David Thoreau argued in his famous essay, *Civil Disobedience*, that people should follow their own consciences over what the government purports to be right. *Civil Disobedience* was published in the mid-1800s, a time when slavery was legal and America was in the midst of a war with Mexico. Throughout the text Thoreau emphasized that through the refusal to accept passively what the government actively tells us, the individual chooses to obey his own morality.[6]

The underlying message of these philosophers still holds true today within the context of Natural Law. Certain rights are inalienable and implicit within our humanity, regardless of whether they are written down on paper. Among these natural rights are the right to life, to self-expression, to worship, to the use and enjoyment of one's own property, the ability to contract, and the right to reap the benefits of one's own labor; and the right to be left alone.

Not only is the right to your own property implicit through the doctrine of Natural Law, but it is also a concept closely tied to the achievement of the American Dream. The familiar white picket fences, lawns, and cars in the garage are the material things and the consequent set of values that the government threatens through infringing upon our natural rights. If I own the brain inside my head and the fingers on the ends of my hands, then I own what they together have conceived, created, and built, be it a book or a house.

Despite Natural Law rights, the government skulks its way into our homes, businesses, kitchens, and even our backyards (literally). However, courageous people have struggled to keep a grasp on their personal liberties in spite of the government's powerful encroachment upon them.

Your Home Is Your Castle

You may think that once you pay for your house, it is actually yours, and no one can take it away from you. But, guess what? The Takings Clause of the Fifth Amendment to the U.S. Constitution specifies that the government may take private property for "public use," so long as the government pays the private owner "just compensation" for it, otherwise known as using eminent domain. The Jeffersonians argued that any use of eminent domain should not be permitted under any circumstance; namely, that only by mutual consent and a fair bargain, but never against your will, could the government end up owning your property. Conversely, the Hamiltonians argued that the government could take any land it wants for free, just like the British kings at one time could and did.

In one New Jersey Supreme Court decision, taking the Hamiltonian position to the extreme, Chief Justice Robert N. Wilentz stated, "The basis for the constitutional obligation is simple: the State controls the use of land, *all* of the land"[7] (emphasis in original). This alarming use of state power discussed by the late Chief Justice is exactly the type of action the Constitution was expressly meant to limit. The New Jersey governor who appointed Wilentz as Chief Justice (and who also appointed me to the Superior Court of New Jersey) called this opinion "socialist."[8]

Traditionally, a government taking has meant that if someone's house stood where the government planned a roadway or a post office or a school, the person would be forced to move in order to accommodate the public project, and the government would pay the owner for the market value of the vacated property. The only issues between the government that coveted the private property and the owner of the private property traditionally have been "when" will the government get the property and "how much" will the government pay. Since Jefferson lost the argument in which he asserted that a taking must be fully consensual, the "whether" the government can get the property has rarely been in dispute. Originally, these "public use" and "just compensation" requirements were put in place by the drafters of the Constitution in order to limit governmental power and protect personal property rights. The Fifth Amendment, which addresses government takings, was drafted with the lingering memory of British soldiers taking the colonists' property and was therefore put in place to ensure that these indiscriminate takings would not continue to occur.[9] Let's take a look at the way the government has perverted this meaning.

Over time, courts have morphed the public *use* requirement into something much broader, called public *benefit*. In fact, the public use requirement has all but been obliterated. While it had previously meant that the use was "in common and not for a particular individual," cases whittled the requirement down to basically whenever the court thought the public could benefit from the taking.

The drafters' intention has been almost completely abandoned. As I wrote about in the beginning of this chapter, most recently, the Supreme Court of the United States, in a 5 to 4 opinion in the case of *Kelo v. New London* (2005),[10] took the limiting term "public use" and expanded it to permit the City of New London, Connecticut, to take over a nine-acre residential neighborhood and give it to a *private* developer.[11] The City created the New London Development Corporation to buy the land and find a developer that would build an "urban village" to attract shoppers and tourists to the City.[12] The City used this proposed plan along with financial incentives to entice Pfizer, a giant pharmaceutical company, to build a headquarters in New London.[13]

The idea that a city government, or any government for that matter, can justify a taking of one's private property to give to another private entity for the local government's economic benefit is one that utterly obscures the distinction between takings for private and public use, and one that visits instability on all property owners and omnipotence on any government that has jurisdiction over the real estate. It also suggests that the government can take private property if it believes that the land can be put to *better* use. Justice O'Connor's dissent in *Kelo* rightfully took a frightened tone toward that possibility. She wrote, ". . . [The Public Use Clause] has no realistic import. For who among us can say she already makes the most productive or attractive possible use of her property? The specter of condemnation hangs over all property. Nothing is to prevent the state from replacing any Motel 6 with a Ritz-Carlton, any home with a shopping mall, or any farm with a factory."[14] If only the "highest and best use" of a particular property is honored, the *Kelo* Court essentially fostered a type of slavery where a landowner is forced to labor over property against his will.

Justice Thomas also dissented in *Kelo*, pointing to both the short and long-term consequences of the Court's ruling. He discussed the immediate loss that property owners feel when they are displaced from their homes and uprooted from their communities. Furthermore, he stated that this is not something for which the government can realistically provide compensation because a "subjective value" is involved. Thomas then articulated some of the daunting long-term consequences involved when the government allows takings for economic development. Harkening Jefferson, he noted, "Allowing the government to take property solely for public purposes is bad enough, but extending the concept of public *purpose* to encompass any economically *beneficial* goal guarantees that these losses will fall disproportionately on poor communities"[15] (emphases added). Justice Thomas's dissent touches upon one of the most sorrowful themes underlying the *Kelo* case: by choosing to hand the land over to the developer, the Court rejected the homeowners' personal values in favor of the government's economic value; the choice of personal values is protected by the Natural Law.

The choice of personal values (a book or a TV, a car or a bicycle, early to bed or up all night) is absolutely immune from government interference unless the exercise of that choice substantially and unfairly interferes with another's natural rights. The use to which one puts one's real estate (cottage or mansion, grass or Astroturf, indoor or outdoor plumbing) is a personal value. Moreover, the traditional bundle of rights encompassing, and even defining personal ownership of real estate are the right to use, the right to alienate, and the right to exclude; the last of these encompassing even *the right to exclude the government*.

In *Kelo*, Uncle Sam is saying that the government can take away your land, simply because it doesn't value the way you use it. *Kelo* also gives the government an easy target, by allowing the government to infringe unduly upon the rights of poor people. Many of these people worked very hard to buy these homes, to achieve their own version of the American Dream. Who is the government to take it away?

(We) Give, and (They) Take

Although the *Kelo* case signaled the most drastic expansion of government power under the Takings Clause, the government had been testing the water for decades. In the 1954 U.S. Supreme Court case *Berman v. Parker*, the federal government razed a local store so that a private company could build a redevelopment project. In that case, the Court paid little attention to the "public use" requirement, and instead decided that the Washington, D.C., area where the store was located was blighted, even though the store itself was not blighted. *Kelo* took a further leap because there was no accusation that the Connecticut neighborhood was blighted; the city merely felt that government-approved developers could improve the area economically.

In *Poletown Neighborhood Council v. City of Detroit* (1981), the Supreme Court of Michigan permitted the government of the City of Detroit to wipe out a community in order to let General Motors build an assembly plant. (*Wow*, the government helping out GM? Who would've thought!? But more on this later . . .) As a result of this massive taking, 3,468 people were ousted from their homes. In that case, the Court justified the taking based on the number of jobs that would be created by the plant (6,000) and the assurances that it would be for "public use."[16] The City of New London did not even bother to make this type of assurance. It just asked the Court to take its word for it, and five justices listened.

You Can't Make This Stuff Up!

On November 9, 2009, to add insult to injury, Pfizer announced that it would *leave* New London in 2011, moving most of its New London employees to nearby Groton, Connecticut.[17] Pfizer's exit proves that the New London City Council, shockingly, is not as intelligent as it originally thought. The "urban village" was never built, and the land that the City took remains barren.[18] According to Scott G. Bullock, senior attorney at the Institute for Justice, the New London debacle "really shows the folly of these plans that use massive corporate welfare and abuse eminent domain for private development. They oftentimes fail to live up to expectations."[19] Tell me about it.

Thankfully, the *Kelo* saga wasn't a total loss. Legislators in forty-three states, in response to New London's abuse of power, passed statutes prohibiting similar exercises of the eminent domain power.[20] Regardless, governments should not have to pass laws requiring themselves to operate within the Fifth Amendment. Americans are under the impression that obeying the Constitution is part of the government's job.

A Man's Word Is His Bond

The freedom to contract is another right derived from Natural Law. One law review article noted:

Freedom of contract, together with the right to own property, were core elements in the American vision of personal liberty . . . The American constitutional scheme places contract liberty well above common law status; it is a guaranteed personal right. Liberty of contract is recognized not as power delegated by the sovereign, but as power originating in and guaranteed to the people.[21]

In other words, it is a natural right. You agree to pay me X dollars for this book, and I agree upon receipt of the X dollars to deliver you the book. The right to enter into that agreement is a natural right; the right to have that agreement enforced is one of the aspects of human freedom that governments exist in order to protect. At one time in our history, these rights—to enter into a binding contract and to use the government to enforce the contract—were *guaranteed*. Sadly, now that is no longer the case.

In a way, people who enter into contracts with each other make law for themselves because the government is constitutionally restrained from interfering unless there is a breach of the contract or the essence of the contract is unlawful. Yet, like our right to private property, our natural right to contract, as well as the rights defined in the Contracts Clause of the Constitution (Article I, Section 10, Clause 1), have repeatedly been violated *by the government*.

One of the greatest cases of government assaults on the right to contract was in *Home Building & Loan Association v. Blaisdell* (1934), where the U.S. Supreme Court upheld as constitutional a Minnesota law prohibiting banks from foreclosing upon mortgages that were in default. John and Rosella Blaisdell had borrowed money from Home Building & Loan to buy a house. The agreement, which was freely made between the Blaisdells and the bank, specified that if the Blaisdells defaulted on the loan, the bank could foreclose on the house, sell it, pay itself back the unpaid loan, and then turn over any remaining amount, what lawyers and economists call equity, to the Blaisdells. But the "government-knows-best" attitude in the State of Minnesota would have none of this freedom. It chose the value of people living for free over the value of enforcing freely entered contracts. It imposed a moratorium on home foreclosures, and the Blaisdells, preferring to live for free, took advantage of that.

Yet, the U.S. Supreme Court held that it was constitutional if Minnesota stopped the banks from foreclosing on mortgages when the borrower defaulted. So, what was the Court's justification for this blatant disregard of both our natural rights and the Contracts Clause? Was there a justification? In *Blaisdell*, the Supreme Court tore the Constitution's Contracts Clause to shreds by allowing state interference with private contracts (those as to which the government is not a contracting party) whenever state legislatures found a "valid police purpose"[22] that interfered with the remedy (foreclosure), not the contract (the promise to repay a loan). So, in truth, the State can butt into our personal right to contract, whenever it feels like it,[23] so long as it doesn't blatantly outlaw contracts, just their remedies. The Blaisdells still owed the bank the money they borrowed; the bank just couldn't get the money back until the State of Minnesota said it could.

Justice Sutherland wrote in his dissent:

> [W]hether the legislation under review is wise or unwise is a matter with which we have nothing to do. Whether it is likely to work well or work ill presents a question entirely irrelevant to the issue. The only legitimate inquiry we can make is whether it is constitutional. If it is not, its virtues, if it has any, cannot save it; if it is, its faults cannot be invoked to accomplish its destruction. *If the provisions of the Constitution be not upheld when they pinch as well as when they comfort, they may as well be abandoned.*[24] (emphases added)

Obviously Justice Sutherland understood not only the nature of the Contracts Clause, but the natural right to contract and the spirit of the entire Constitution. The Constitution is the supreme law of the land. The oath to enforce and uphold it is taken by everyone in the government. They are charged with enforcing its terms—upholding the liberty *it guarantees*—whether that liberty pinches or comforts. The *Blaisdell* result is not the way the Framers intended the Constitution to be used.

The buck did not stop at *Blaisdell*. Today, in the wake of the Chrysler bailout, we see the current establishment's utter carelessness when it comes to the contract rights of Chrysler's bondholders. The bondholders are secured creditors, which means by law they hold a higher ranking than shareholders or unsecured creditors in a reorganization or bankruptcy. Outrageously, though, the government—which has inserted itself into this private bankruptcy by virtue of its massive loans to Chrysler—is completely ignoring this rule and is instead awarding majority ownership to the United Auto Workers, and only a small part of ownership to bondholders.

When the bondholders tried to get a larger stake in Chrysler, President Obama publicly referred to them as "vultures," and they eventually backed down.[25] Since when are you a "vulture" just because you ask that the contract you agreed to be enforced? And since when does the President interject himself into the fray when a lender wants a loan repaid? When contracts don't mean what they say; that's when.

While it may be reasonable for the court to step in when a person was deceived or actually forced into a contract, it is quite another circumstance when the Court enters into a perfectly fair agreement between the parties. This often paternalistic nature of the Court does more than take away our personal liberties; it also destroys the value of the contract itself. If the Court can actually dismiss the terms of a contract, allowing a party to breach, what is the point of making an agreement in the first place? If the use of contracts is put into question, a cloak of doubt is cast on our whole way of doing business in America.

Aren't You Entitled to the Fruits of Your Labor?

You would think that if you grew something in your own backyard, for your own personal use, the government would not meddle. Guess again! In 1940, the federal government fined Roscoe Filburn, an Ohio farmer, for producing an excess amount of wheat on his farm. The government's act of limiting the amount of wheat Filburn grew and then actually punishing him for it, seems like a gross restriction on individual liberty in itself. But the situation gets downright ridiculous when you consider that Filburn was not selling this wheat, not bartering with it, not leaving the State with it; poor Filburn was just growing the wheat for himself and his family to use. Now imagine how outraged you would be if the government regulated the parsley you grew in your backyard garden, or the summer tomatoes you planted. You get the picture. This ruling is simply a violation of the natural right to the fruits of one's lawful labors.

The Supreme Court used and abused the power of the Commerce Clause against Filburn in this case. The Commerce Clause gives the federal government the right to regulate commerce with foreign nations, among the states, and with the Native American tribes. While the Court's interpretation of "among the states" has varied over the years, one of the main reasons for the clause was to prevent excessive competition between the states. The original meaning of the word *regulate* was "to keep *regular*." Its sole purpose was to prevent states from creating state tariffs to be used to the detriment of other states.

So, basically, the Commerce Clause was intended to empower Congress to keep interstate commerce regular, that is, devoid of tariffs imposed on the movement of goods over interstate borders by the states. Such tariffs had severely hampered commerce under the Articles of Confederation and were a major impetus for drafting the U.S. Constitution. Some of the broader interpretations of the Clause have included intrastate commerce that could have an effect on interstate commerce. Yet, who would have guessed that the government could regulate something that goes from your backyard to your kitchen table and is never actually bought or sold or moved more than a few feet?

The government's argument was that through the cumulative effect of Filburn's use of his own wheat, and others' potentially similar use of theirs, there *might* or *could* be an effect on interstate commerce, and that these activities were therefore subject to federal regulation. This means that *if* lots of people started to overproduce wheat in their backyards and consume it, it could affect the amount of bread or cereal that is being bought (or not bought) in stores. But, that is a big *if*. Also, the act of growing crops to provide for your own family has been going on much longer than the government itself. This harebrained reasoning employed by the government and accepted by the Supreme Court, paired with the destruction of the personal property rights conferred through Natural Law, make *Wickard v. Filburn* one of the more truly absurd and highly dangerous federal power trips.

Commerce Clause: No Rationality Required

Not only has the government regulated the remedies for defaulting on loans, not only has it regulated the amount of wheat grown in our backyards, it has also regulated the number of hours per day bakers can spend turning that wheat into bread. An 1897 New York State law pertaining to this, stated: "No employee shall be required or permitted to work in a biscuit, cake, or bread bakery or confectionary establishment" for more than ten hours per day. New York tried to rationalize the law by stating that the measure was meant to protect the health, safety, welfare, or morality of bakers in New York.[26] Huh? Since when can the government tell people that they cannot voluntarily work more than ten hours per day? And why would bakers need to be protected from these long hours; is it particularly dangerous work?

When the Supreme Court heard this case, it looked at whether there was a legitimate need for the State of New York to regulate workers' hours because of the nature of baking. The Court said that given the nature of certain types of work, like mining or working with coal, it may be appropriate for the state to regulate, yet there was no genuine health issue present in baking. Consequently, the Supreme Court decided in *Lochner v. New York*, that New York had no right to make such a law. The opinion states:

> It is a question of which of two powers or rights shall prevail—the power of the State to legislate or the right of the individual to liberty of person and freedom to contract . . . The act must have a more direct relation, as a means to an end, and the end itself must be appropriate and legitimate, before an act can be held to be valid which interferes with the general right of an individual to be free in his person and in his power to contract in relation to his own labor.

This poorly reasoned opinion did the right thing (uphold freedom of contract) for the wrong reason (the state's claim of right to interfere was not strong enough). The state is without *any* right to interfere in freely negotiated for contracts. But sadly, *Lochner* is no longer the law. Since the days of *Lochner*, the defense of natural rights has fallen into disrepute with courts. If individuals know that the government can step in and nullify the contracts they enter into, what purpose do they serve? The post-*Lochner* era challenges both the sanctity and meaning of contracts themselves, taking another one of our fundamental rights with it.

We Are Free to Work as Much (or as Little) as We Want

Flash forward. What do cases like *Wickard v. Filburn, Home Building & Loan Association v. Blaisdell*, or *Lochner v. New York* mean today? While there may not be too many cases involving backyard wheat production in recent memory, the right to keep the fruit of our own labor is still in peril. Between the current economic downturn and the Big Government crowd still in power, it would not seem unlikely for the government to put constraints on our freedom to work. A *New York Times* article suggests that the federal government should force workers to take extended vacations, days off, or restrict their weekly hours, in order to reduce the number of layoffs.[27] The suggestion is to adopt a policy similar to European countries like France, where the law dictates the number of hours workers are allowed to clock in per week, thereby reducing the amount of overtime individuals are able to receive and, essentially, the amount of money they are able to make. In *Blaisdell*, the Supreme Court opened the door to exactly this type of government assault on our right to enter into and enforce binding private contracts.

While longer vacations never fail to sound appealing, mandates like this from the government are patently un-American. We have always been a self-made, individualistic people who pick ourselves up by the bootstraps and work as hard, and for as many hours as needed to reach our intended goals. And the bottom line is, this is a democracy whose government is by law restrained by a Constitution that guarantees enforcement of the Natural Law, and it should be our choice to work as much or as little as we please.

One of the reasons why people come to America is that there are fewer speed bumps to the top of the ladder in comparison with other countries. People from a variety of backgrounds can toil and sweat their way up the ladder here. If sanctions were put on the number of hours we were allowed to work, there would be fewer avenues open to reach the top, and only certain people would be able to make it (likely those with the best educations, most social and family connections, the most money, and in favor with the government). This is not what America is about, and this is certainly not freedom in a broad sense.

All of the natural rights discussed in this chapter deal with subject matter that is exceedingly personal. The private decisions we make about where we want to raise our families, the agreements we make with other parties, and the amount of work we decide to do, are all choices that have an effect on our personal health, wealth, and happiness. As individuals, we make decisions that are varied. What is good for one may simply not be good for another. It is time for the government finally to recognize the American people as individuals and hand us back our natural rights.

Lie #3

"Judges Are Like Umpires"[1]

President Barack Obama, in an interview conducted less than two months into his presidency, was asked about the toughest decisions he had to make as president. He responded by stating that "[b]y the time an issue reaches my desk, it's a hard issue. If it was an easy issue, somebody else would have solved it and it wouldn't have reached me."[2] The same goes for Supreme Court justices, and to a lesser extent, appellate judges. The Supreme Court is mainly faced with the hard cases in which the law is unclear, or lower federal courts or state supreme courts have ruled differently or inconsistently on federal issues. In deciding these cases, the Supreme Court justices must essentially state what they believe the law to be. By doing so, the majority of the Court, in clarifying the meaning of the law, makes policy.[3]

One of the main concerns that politicians in the legislative and executive branches of government have with the federal judiciary is that judges will engage in "judicial activism." According to *Black's Law Dictionary*, a source universally accepted in the American and British legal communities, *judicial activism* is "[a] philosophy of judicial decision-making whereby judges allow their personal views about public policy, among other factors, to guide their decisions."[4] Judges espousing this philosophy tend to "find constitutional violations and are willing to ignore precedent."[5] This definition implies that judicial activists are biased judges who intentionally disregard the true meaning of the law to further their own policy agendas, and essentially legislate from the bench. Given these characteristics, judicial activists have no place on any court, let alone the United States Supreme Court.

Recent Supreme Court confirmation processes have revolved around the concept of judicial activism. President George W. Bush made it perfectly clear that he would nominate judges who would "exercise not the will of men, but the judgment of law."[6] When nominating Judge John G. Roberts to be Chief Justice of the United States Supreme Court, President Bush vowed that Roberts would "strictly apply the Constitution and laws, not legislate from the bench."[7] At his Senate confirmation hearing on September 12th 2005, then-Judge Roberts told the Senators, "Judges are like umpires. Umpires don't make the rules; they apply them. The role of an umpire and a judge is critical. They make sure everybody plays by the rules. But it is a limited role. Nobody ever went to a ball game to see the umpire."[8]

President Bush later stated, when nominating my Princeton classmate, Judge Samuel A. Alito, that then-Judge Alito "understands that judges are to interpret the laws, not to impose their preferences or priorities on the people."[9] Senator Jeff Sessions, a Republican from Alabama, who interviewed Roberts prior to voting to confirm him, criticized "[a]ctivist rulings not based on statutes or the Constitution."[10] Senator Tom Coburn, a Republican from Oklahoma, echoed Sessions's complaint, stating that "[d]ecades of judicial activism have created . . . huge rifts in the social fabric of our country."[11]

During the debate over the nomination of Supreme Court Justice Sonia Sotomayor, conservative senators and commentators were troubled with comments Judge Sotomayor repeatedly made in speeches outside of the courtroom. Senator Sessions voted against Sotomayor's confirmation, fearing that she lacks "the deep-rooted convictions necessary to resist the siren of judicial activism."[12] Senator John McCain, a Republican from Arizona, also opposed Sotomayor's confirmation, stating that while he had "great respect" for her, she had a "long record of judicial activism."[13]

The senators' reservations about confirming Sotomayor are mainly derived from a lecture she gave at the University of California–Berkeley, in 2001. Her lecture was entitled "A Latina Judge's Voice." In the speech, Sotomayor focused on her heritage and her gender, and concluded that her background and personal experiences influence her judging. Toward the end of the speech, Sotomayor stated that she "would hope that a wise Latina woman with the richness of her experiences would more often than not reach a better conclusion than a white male who hasn't lived that life."[14] Sotomayor reiterated this sentiment in later speeches. Furthermore, at a conference at Duke University in 2005, Sotomayor stated that "the court of appeals [the court on which she was sitting at the time] is where policy is made."[15] Taking these out-of-court statements at face value, it may appear that Sotomayor feels that her personal experiences and biases will directly influence her decisions, that she seeks to develop policy from the bench, and that she harbors legal views based on nationality or race.

Yet, Judge Sotomayor's decisions as a federal district court judge, and as a judge on the Second Circuit Court of Appeals, indicate that she is far from an activist. I do not agree with all of her decisions, but it is clear that she is highly intelligent, has a tremendous respect for the law and precedent, and exercises judicial authority well within the present-day parameters of American legal thinking. She will likely be an intellectual asset to the Supreme Court.

It is dangerous for judges actively to make policy, and there are structural constraints in place to prevent them from doing so. The judicial power of the United States is outlined in Article III of the United States Constitution, which states, "The judicial Power shall extend to . . . *Cases* . . . arising under this Constitution and the Laws of the United States . . . [and] to *Controversies* between two or more States. . . ." (emphases added). Section 2 goes on to define the types of cases that federal court judges can hear. This Section limits a federal judge's power by requiring that a federal court must be presented with a case or controversy over which it has jurisdiction in order to act. Furthermore, when a case reaches an appellate court, the legal issue at hand becomes so specific and fine-tuned that there is very little room for a judge drastically to affect the law.

Nevertheless, judges at the Court of Appeals level, and justices of the Supreme Court, are not judicial umpires who merely "officiate" disputes between parties. They are not moderators whose sole purpose is to keep order while the parties resolve their disagreements. They are legal scholars often faced with serious decisions about uncertain areas of the law.

The Supreme Court's behavior in defining the law does not make its members "judicial activists." In fact, the Framers *wanted* the Supreme Court to perform this function. They envisioned the federal judiciary as a branch of government independent of the legislative and executive branches, and one that would preserve the Constitution.

In *The Federalist, No. 78*, Alexander Hamilton* wrote that given our "limited constitution" (one that identifies certain specified exceptions to legislative authority), the courts must be independent in order to check legislative action.[16] According to Hamilton:

---

* I am loath to cite Hamilton for any purpose because he is the father of Big Government and devoted the last years of his wretched life to undermining the Constitution and the Bill of Rights. But, just like a stopped clock twice a day, on this point he is correct.

Limitations [on legislative authority] can be preserved in practice no other way than through the medium of the courts of justice; whose duty it must be to declare all acts contrary to the manifest tenor of the constitution void. Without this, all the reservations of particular rights or privileges would amount to nothing.[17]

James Madison agreed with Hamilton, stating that the job of the judiciary is to act as an "impenetrable bulwark" to protect our constitutional liberties against the political branches of government.[18] There is no serious dispute that the Framers envisioned judges engaging in what I'd like to call "constitutional activism," whereby judges interpret the Constitution, preserve its legitimacy, uphold the Natural Law, and restrain the power of all governments to take away our individual liberties.

The Birth of "Judicial Activism":
Marbury v. Madison

Chief Justice John Marshall's opinion in *Marbury v. Madison*[19] mimicked the Framers' views on the federal judiciary. On February 27th 1801, a week before the end of President John Adams's term in office, Congress adopted an act permitting the president to appoint forty-two justices of the peace.[20] Adams and the Federalist Party had been turned out of office and lost the presidency to Thomas Jefferson and the anti-Federalists (sometimes called by the odd-to-contemporary-ears name, Democratic-Republican Party), but the Federalists' terms in office had not yet expired. Adams submitted his nominations on March 2nd, and the Senate confirmed his nominees on March 3rd, the day before Jefferson took office.[21]

John Marshall had begun serving as Chief Justice of the United States on February 4th 1801, but had been Secretary of State of the United States since June 6th 1800. He served as both Chief Justice and Secretary of State until Jefferson took over the presidency. As Secretary of State, he was charged with signing the new justices' commissions. After signing them, Marshall called upon his brother, James Marshall, to deliver them.[22] Unfortunately, a few of the commissions, including William Marbury's, were not delivered until after Jefferson's inauguration. Jefferson, a Democratic-Republican and anti-Federalist, instructed James Madison, his Secretary of State, to withhold the commissions. Marbury filed suit in the Supreme Court of the United States seeking a *writ of mandamus*, which would have compelled Madison to deliver his commission. The commission was the formal document naming Marbury, who had validly been appointed by President Adams and validly confirmed by the Senate. In an era before personal identifications, photographs, and other means of identifying and recognizing someone, a judge, especially a newly appointed judge, needed to show his commission to court authorities before taking the bench.

Chief Justice Marshall, writing for the Court, broke the case down into three issues: (1) whether Marbury has a right to the commission; (2) if he has a right to the commission, whether he has a legal remedy for the failure to deliver it; and (3) if he has a legal remedy, whether the Supreme Court of the United States can provide him with such a remedy. Since Adams nominated Marbury, and the Senate confirmed him, Marshall held that Marbury did have a legal right to the commission. Marshall went on to state that "where there is a legal right, there is also a legal remedy."

It is necessary, in every case, for a court to determine whether a legal right has been violated before it can act. In the case of *Baker v. Carr* (1962), the plaintiffs, Tennessee citizens and urban dwellers, argued that the Tennessee Legislature violated the Fourteenth Amendment to the United States Constitution by not reapportioning (altering voting-district lines) to account for population changes in the state. By not acting, the plaintiffs argued that the Tennessee Legislature gave the less-populated rural areas more influence than the urban areas. The Supreme Court held that it could hear reapportionment cases, and found that the Tennessee Legislature violated the Fourteenth Amendment, and the means to remedy that violation was a federal lawsuit, filed with a federal district (trial level) judge.

Justice Felix Frankfurter, however, dissented in *Baker*, arguing that the Legislature had not violated a *federally* protected legal right. All Tennessee citizens maintained the right to vote, and their votes were counted. Frankfurter stated that the plaintiffs were simply "dissatisfied" with their current degree of representation, and argued that it is not the job of the federal courts to give them more political power. According to Frankfurter, "there is not under our Constitution a judicial remedy for every political mischief, for every undesirable exercise of legislative power. The Framers, carefully and with deliberate forethought, refused so to enthrone the judiciary." In *Baker*, Frankfurter reiterated his plurality opinion in *Colegrove v. Green* (1946), in which he stated that "Courts ought not to enter this political thicket."

In *Marbury v. Madison*, unlike in *Baker*, Marbury did, in fact, have a legal right and a remedy. The problem for Marbury was that the United States Supreme Court could not provide the remedy Marbury deserved. Marbury filed his case *directly* in the Supreme Court because Section 13 of the Judiciary Act of 1789 stated that the Supreme Court had "original jurisdiction" over the matter. That is, the statute stated that the case could be filed *directly* with the Supreme Court; it did not need to make its way through lower federal courts or through a state court system first, as is usually the route, and as was the route in *Baker v. Carr*.

Article III, Section 2, of the Constitution, however, states that "[i]n all Cases affecting Ambassadors, other public Ministers and Consuls, and those in which a State shall be Party, the supreme Court shall have original jurisdiction." This clause clearly did not cover Marbury's predicament. The question for Chief Justice Marshall, then, was whether the constitutional provision at issue represented an exhaustive list, or whether Congress could expand the Supreme Court's original jurisdiction through legislation. Marshall held that Article III does, in fact, create a ceiling on the Supreme Court's original jurisdiction, and therefore declared Section 13 of the Judiciary Act of 1789 unconstitutional. Unfortunately for Marbury, he had filed his case in the wrong court because he had followed a law that was the very first in history to be declared unconstitutional.

This case is significant because it established the Supreme Court as the authoritative interpreter of the Constitution, and asserted the Supreme Court's power of judicial review. The concept of judicial review permits the federal judiciary to review and to strike down as unconstitutional acts of the legislative and executive branches (and eventually of state governments as well). According to Marshall, "It is emphatically the province and duty of the judicial department to say what the law is."

Chief Justice Marshall clearly engaged in a form of policymaking, or "activism." Marshall held that Article III limits the Supreme Court's original jurisdiction. More importantly, he advanced the policy that the Supreme Court, and neither of the other two branches, is the final authority on "what the law is." Therefore, it had the power to strike down executive and legislative acts repugnant to the Constitution. The Constitution, however, is silent on the role of the judiciary, aside from the rules that judges will "hold their Offices during good Behavior," receive compensation, and hear certain types of cases.

Who, then, was Chief Justice Marshall to create unilaterally a role for the federal judiciary not envisioned in the Constitution? Or was it envisioned? Don't the members of the popular branches also take an oath to uphold the Constitution? What's so special about judges? If the branches of government are *equal*, how can one branch *invalidate* the official behavior of the other two?

The answer to these questions, simply, is that it is dangerous to leave constitutional questions up to the branches of government that are actually making the laws, and the Framers understood that. If Congress and the President had the power to make laws *and* interpret the Constitution, there would essentially be no check on their power. The Constitution would be toothless, and the popular branches would work systematically to restrict our liberties. (We know this because Congress and the President still try to take away our freedoms.)

According to Harvard Professor Laurence Tribe, a renowned American attorney and constitutional law scholar, "The whole *point* of an independent judiciary is to be 'antidemocratic,' to preserve from transient majorities those human rights and other principles to which our legal and political system is committed"[23] (emphasis in original). Tribe went on to state that "[w]ithout this role there would be nothing to stop a bare majority of our citizens from deciding tomorrow that the minority should be enslaved or required to give up its belongings for the greater good of the greater number."[24] Tribe reminds us that without an independent judiciary with the power of judicial review, persons in our republic would have no recourse against popular government policies that infringe upon their natural rights.

It is important to note, though, that Chief Justice Marshall did not argue that the judiciary was in any way superior to Congress. Rather, his opinion echoed Hamilton's statement in *The Federalist, No. 78*, which he did write (but could not have sincerely intended):

"The Constitution is superior to all; the judiciary is just acting to preserve its legitimacy."

Judicial Passivity

There have been many Supreme Court opinions throughout history in which the Court should have acted in a more activist way, but failed to stand up to government abuse.

A great example of judicial inaction was the Supreme Court's decision in *Plessy v. Ferguson*.[25] The conflict in *Plessy* resulted from government-mandated racism, not from private behavior. In 1890, the State of Louisiana enacted a law that *required* racial segregation in public accommodations, including on railroads. African-Americans despised this law because its goal was to maintain white supremacy. The railroad companies also vehemently opposed it because it forced them to add more railroad cars and more employees, and thus incur more costs, so as effectively to segregate blacks and whites.

On June 7th 1892, Homer Plessy, who was seven-eighths white, and only one-eighth African-American, boarded a railroad car that was designated for whites only, with the purpose of violating the law. After refusing to move to the "colored" car, Plessy was arrested and jailed for violating the Louisiana statute. Before the Supreme Court of the United States, Plessy argued that the Louisiana law violated his rights under the Fourteenth Amendment's "privileges and immunities" and "equal protection" clauses. According to the Fourteenth Amendment, "No State shall make or enforce any law which shall abridge the privileges or immunities of citizens of the United States; . . . nor deny to any person within its jurisdiction the equal protection of the laws."

Today, about a half-century since the Civil Rights Movement, the decision in this case seems like an easy one. Racial segregation commanded by the government, by definition, treated whites differently from blacks, and therefore deprived blacks of equal protection. Under today's notion of equality, therefore, the Louisiana law would be struck down as blatantly unconstitutional.

In 1896, however, the United States was not too far removed from the Civil War and the institution of slavery. The Thirteenth, Fourteenth, and Fifteenth Amendments were the so-called "Reconstruction" Amendments, geared toward promoting racial equality. However, these amendments, while abolishing slavery, did not explicitly abolish legally enforced segregation.

Nevertheless, the Supreme Court should have engaged in "constitutional activism" and struck down the Louisiana law. First, it is obvious that in a society where blacks had been considered inferior for so long, a law *compelling* the segregation of the majority white race and the numerically inferior black race cannot under any circumstances be considered equitable. These laws were passed with the *sole purpose* of maintaining African-American cultural inferiority.

Second, the Supreme Court had already laid the groundwork for overturning these race-based laws. In 1883, in the case of *Strauder v. West Virginia*,[26] the Supreme Court struck down a West Virginia law prohibiting African-Americans from serving on juries. According to the Court in *Strauder*, the Fourteenth Amendment's Equal Protection Clause protected African-Americans "from unfriendly legislation against them distinctively as colored" and shielded them from "legal discriminations, implying inferiority in a civil society."[27]

Plessy was a bit different in that blacks were not excluded from riding the railroad, as they were excluded from serving on juries in *Strauder*.

There is no way to get around the clear fact, however, that the Louisiana law, while slightly more friendly than the West Virginia law in *Strauder*, was enacted to promote African-American inferiority. It was the government using its power to make decisions based on race. It was the government preventing the free choice of railroad owners and customers. It was the government interfering with freedom of contract and freedom of travel. It was the government, by forcing the railroads to spend their money on equipment they did not want or need, taking property from the railroad owners.

The Supreme Court made a huge mistake in *Plessy*, creating the "separate but equal" doctrine, and thus providing shelter to segregationists that lasted until *Brown v. Board of Education* was decided, fifty-eight years later. This was a Supreme Court that probably feared being labeled "activist," or worse, that agreed with the ramifications of its decision.

The case of *Korematsu v. United States* is another case in which the Supreme Court dropped the ball and deferred to a federal government that was openly persecuting people of Japanese descent, including many Japanese-Americans. I will not go too far into the details of this case, as it is discussed in later chapters, but basically, after the Japanese attack on Pearl Harbor, the federal government freaked out and started setting curfews for Japanese-Americans living in this country, displacing them from their homes, and placing them in internment camps. The government claimed that since some Japanese-Americans were "disloyal" to the United States and could not be trusted, we might as well round up all of them to play it safe. The first problem with this twisted notion is that in America, you cannot be convicted of a crime only because you have the same heritage as others who commit crimes. In the United States, only individuals are guilty of crimes. The second problem with the government's program was that it was blatantly racist.

The Supreme Court in *Korematsu*, in truly amazing fashion, *acknowledged* that the United States was infringing on the fundamental rights of Americans *based on race*. Nevertheless, during World War

II, the impression of safety was more important to the Court than the reality of individual liberties. Instead of reversing the government during a time of war, the Court was silent, passive, and weak, and allowed the persecution to continue.

In the case of *Kelo v. New London*, decided in 2005 (also discussed in Chapter 2), the Supreme Court stood idly by (or at least five of its members did) as the City of New London violated the Constitution. In an effort to rehabilitate the New London economy, the City developed a plan to create jobs and refurbish the downtown and waterfront areas. The City intended to build a waterfront hotel, a park and river walk, restaurants and retail stores, new residences, marinas, and office and research facilities on ninety acres of land in the Fort Trumbull area. Some of this land was already privately owned. Some of the private landowners voluntarily sold their land to the government, and others were informed that the City would use its eminent domain power to take their land. This threat prompted private landowners to sue the City, arguing that the development plan was an abuse of the power of eminent domain.

State and local governments have the power to seize private property, but that property, according to the Fifth Amendment's Takings Clause, must be "taken for public use" and the private owners must be provided "just compensation." The plaintiffs in *Kelo* argued that their land was not taken for "public use" because the City's plan was to be carried out by a *private* developer, much of the developed land would not be open to the general public, and under the plan, some of the benefits the City sought to reap were economic benefits such as increased tax revenue.

This case was a relatively difficult one because the Fifth Amendment does not define "public use." The Framers could have meant that the land taken must be exclusively open to the general public. But they could not have meant that the government could essentially evict

people from their homes so that the city in which they live will benefit economically. It seems clear that the City of New London's plan
worked to evict its private landowners, and allowed the government
to benefit much more than the "public." Unfortunately, in a 5 to 4
decision, the Supreme Court upheld the plan when it should have
invalidated it.

The fact is that the Supreme Court has been tweaking the "public
use" requirement for some time, and allowing the government to
violate the Constitution as a result. In the eighteenth and nineteenth
centuries, the phrase "public use" simply meant "a use by the public."
Over the last century, though, the government and the courts have
turned the Takings Clause on its head. Today, "public use" has
morphed into "public benefit," a softer requirement whereby the
government can steal our land, give it to their corporate cronies, and
claim that the developer's use "benefits" the public. This is exactly
what happened in *Kelo*.

Justice Sandra Day O'Connor realized this atrocity and wrote
an inspired dissenting opinion in *Kelo*. O'Connor conceded that
the Court defers to legislative judgments about what government
actions will help the public. However, O'Connor feared that by
allowing the political branches to be "the sole arbiters of the public-
private distinction, the Public Use Clause would amount to little
more than hortatory fluff." O'Connor, like Chief Justice Marshall
in *Marbury v. Madison*, stressed that some form of judicial review
is necessary for the Takings Clause to have any meaning at all.
According to O'Connor, "An external, judicial check on how the
public use requirement is interpreted . . . is necessary if this con-
straint on government power is to retain any meaning."

Constitutional Activism

The Supreme Court of the United States has often addressed constitutional issues head-on, standing up to government actions, and making policy that reflects the sentiment of the Constitution and the Natural Law.

In *Brandenburg v. Ohio*, for example, the Supreme Court struck down the Ohio Criminal Syndicalism statute, which made it a crime to "advocate . . . the duty, necessity, or propriety of crime, sabotage, violence, or unlawful methods of terrorism as a means of accomplishing industrial or political reform" and to "voluntarily assemble with any society, group or assemblage of persons formed to teach or advocate the doctrines of criminal syndicalism." Clarence Brandenburg, an Ohio Ku Klux Klan leader, was convicted under the Act after a rally he held in Hamilton County, Ohio. At the rally, Brandenburg alluded to the idea that "there might have to be some revengence [*sic*] taken" against the federal government. One participant expressed his bitter hatred for African-Americans and Jews, stating, "Personally, I believe the nigger should be returned to Africa, the Jew returned to Israel."

After many years of yielding to onerous government restrictions of the freedom of expression, the Supreme Court finally decided "to say what the law is." In unanimously overturning the oppressive Ohio law, the Supreme Court created a rule that is still very much alive today. According to the Court, "the constitutional guarantees of free speech and free press do not permit a State to forbid or proscribe advocacy of the use of force or of law violation *except* where such advocacy is directed to inciting or producing imminent lawless action *and* is likely to incite or produce such action" (emphases added). It essentially held that all innocuous speech is absolutely protected; and all speech is innocuous when there is time for more speech to challenge it. This was an example of constitutional activism by a rarely unanimous Court determined to uphold the natural right to speech, even offensive speech.

In the case of *Shapiro v. Thompson* (1969), the Supreme Court decided a matter concerning the right to travel. Vivian Marie Thompson was nineteen years old and had just moved from Massachusetts to Connecticut. She had a child and applied for government assistance under the Aid to Families with Dependent Children (AFDC) program in Connecticut. Connecticut denied Thompson's request, citing its one-year residency requirement.

This was yet another hard case for the Court because the right to travel, or the right to move between states, is listed nowhere in the Constitution. Yet, the Supreme Court held that the "right of interstate movement" is a *fundamental* right. Notice how the Court described the right as "fundamental" and not "natural." This is because natural rights are rights that are God-given rights, those received by virtue of our humanity. The Supreme Court is a secular body, however, causing some justices to conclude that it is inappropriate for the Court to refer to a right as "natural." Nevertheless, the "right of interstate movement" is in fact a natural right, also known as a fundamental right, and is therefore a constitutionally protected right.

Due to the significance of the right, regardless of the way in which the Court described it, the Court stated that for a regulation restricting the right to travel to be acceptable under the Fourteenth Amendment, it must serve a compelling state interest. That is, it must pass the Court's "strict scrutiny" test. According to Justice William J. Brennan, Jr., writing for the Court, Connecticut's goal of preventing indigents from moving into states did not serve a compelling state interest.

True Judicial Activism

Judges have exercised true judicial activism in many cases throughout history. A classic example of judicial activism is the United States Supreme Court's decision in *Roe v. Wade* (1973), arguably the most controversial Supreme Court decision in modern times. In this case, Jane Roe challenged a Texas law making it a crime to "procure an abortion," except under circumstances in which the life of the mother is at stake. On January 22nd 1973, the Supreme Court, in a 7 to 2 decision, held that the right to an abortion falls under the "right of privacy . . . founded in the Fourteenth Amendment's concept of personal liberty and restrictions upon state action. . . ."[28]

The Court also characterized the abortion right as "fundamental," and thus stated that a state could only restrict it if it had a "compelling state interest" that outweighed the right. The Court outlined three state interests that could potentially justify restrictions on abortion: the interests in (1) discouraging illicit sexual behavior, (2) protecting pregnant women from the risks of the abortion procedure, and (3) protecting prenatal life. The Court reasoned that since the Texas statute outlawed abortion at *all times* during the pregnancy, except when the health of the mother was at stake, the Texas law could not outweigh a pregnant woman's right to privacy.

Regardless of one's opinion on abortion, the seven-justice majority in *Roe* blatantly legislated from the bench. The Court created a new right, and was not ashamed to admit it. Justice Harry A. Blackmun, writing for the majority, conceded that "[t]he Constitution does not explicitly mention any right [to an abortion]." Furthermore, it is highly unlikely that the drafters of the Fourteenth Amendment recognized, or even were aware of an abortion right.

According to then-Justice William H. Rehnquist, who dissented in *Roe*, the first state law limiting abortion was enacted by the Connecticut Legislature in 1821, forty-seven years prior to the passage of the Fourteenth Amendment. Texas passed the statute in question in *Roe* in 1857, and by the time the Fourteenth Amendment was ratified in 1868, there were at least thirty-six laws in states or territories limiting abortion. Rehnquist went on to state that when the Fourteenth Amendment was ratified, no one publicly questioned the validity of any abortion law. Moreover, Rehnquist believed that the nationwide debate on abortion at the time *Roe* was decided was evidence that the right was not by any stretch fundamental and protected by the Constitution. (After all, how often do we debate the validity of the freedom of speech, or the freedom of religion?) Therefore, the Court in *Roe* clearly created a new right.

In addition, the Court, trying to play the role of "Supreme Legislature," announced rules governing a state's ability to restrict the right to abortion. The Court declared that a state's interests in restricting abortion only become "compelling," and thus, able to outweigh a pregnant woman's right to privacy, after certain checkpoints during the course of the pregnancy. A state's interest in the health of the mother is "compelling," according to the Court, at approximately the end of the first trimester. A state's interest in protecting prenatal life is "compelling" only at the point of viability (the time when the baby can survive outside the mother's womb). These rules are arbitrary. What expertise did the Supreme Court have in this field, and since when did the justices acquire the power to make these types of judgments?

The Supreme Court's decision in *Roe* also had a profound effect on the rest of the country. It not only invalidated the Texas statute, but also forced twenty-one states to amend their abortion statutes. *Roe v. Wade* is a prime example of how a little judicial activism can certainly go a long way. Due to the tremendous impact of the Supreme Court's opinions, it is important to prevent this utter disregard for the Constitution.

A less popular, yet exceedingly ridiculous example of judicial activism occurred in the case of *Missouri v. Jenkins*, a case that dragged on for eighteen years. In this case, beginning in 1977, United States District Judge Russell G. Clark, sitting in the Western District of Missouri, acted as a legislator and school superintendent in handling the case before him. Judge Clark held the Kansas City School District liable for segregating its schools, and created a plan for the District to revamp its schools, through which he greatly overstepped his judicial power.

The District spent $61 million to respond to the desegregation order, but Clark was not satisfied.[29] Clark developed a scheme to improve the school system at a cost of *$1.6 billion!*[30] To pay for the improvements, Judge Clark *ordered* the city to increase property taxes on its citizens by *91 percent!*[31] He also *ordered* the State of Missouri to increase income taxes by *25 percent!*[32] A court of appeals panel struck down the income-tax increase, but unfortunately did not find anything troubling about the property-tax hike.[33]

Clark's improvement program was also extremely unnecessary, in addition to being wildly unconstitutional. His plan called for drastic remodeling to the schools, Olympic-sized swimming pools, zoos, gymnasiums, and "learning resource" centers.[34] Judge Clark also required that the schools fund salary increases and remedial education programs. Luckily, in 1995, after nearly two decades of Judge Clark's abuse, the Supreme Court of the United States, by a slim, 5 to 4 margin, decided that mandating increased salaries and funding for remedial programs was an abuse of power.

Wake Up!

During the recent recession in the United States, the Supreme Court was too soft in analyzing government actions that were surely against the law. For example, at the end of President George W.

Bush's second term in office, and at the very beginning of President Barack Obama's first term, the federal government decided that it would take an extremely active role in bailing out companies that were deemed "too big to fail."

One of the industries that got special treatment, particularly during the Obama administration, was the auto industry. In June 2009, the government dashed to complete Chrysler's bankruptcy court proceedings so that it could merge with Fiat, an Italian auto company.[35] The bankruptcy blatantly wronged Chrysler's secured creditors who, under settled law, are first to be paid in the event of a bankruptcy.[36] The secured creditors in this bankruptcy, however, received less per dollar than the United Auto Workers, an unsecured creditor that also gained 55 percent ownership of Chrysler.[37] The Supreme Court approved the bankruptcy, taking a time-out from its function of defending freedom, property, contracts, and other good stuff that the Constitution keeps from the government's grasping hands.

Conclusion

It is clear that judges should not act as "judicial activists" and bring their legislative agendas to the bench. However, there are many instances where judges can act as "constitutional activists," to uphold the Constitution and our freedoms. As former Supreme Court Justice William O. Douglas stated in his autobiography, "The Constitution is not neutral. It was designed to take the government off the backs of the people." Only a constitutionally activist Supreme Court can assure that it does so.

Lie #4

"Every Vote Counts"

The 2000 American presidential election will be remembered as one of the most glaring examples of the federal judiciary infringing upon the fundamental right to vote. The Supreme Court of the United States, in *Bush v. Gore*, took the election out of the hands of the Florida voters and, in a 5 to 4 decision, essentially decided the election in favor of then-Texas Governor George W. Bush. Some have gone so far as to call the decision criminal.[1] How did it happen? We have a very complex history of voting rights in our country.

The United States government is not a direct democracy, in which the majority of its citizens have the right to govern, but a democratic republic in which the people exercise only some degree of influence on government decision making. Article IV, Section 4, of the United States Constitution requires that "[t]he United States shall guarantee to every State in this Union a Republican Form of Government." According to James Madison, in *The Federalist, No. 57*, "The elective mode of obtaining rulers is the characteristic policy of republican government."[2] Today, it is widely accepted that a necessary component of this republican form of government, and a basic human right, is the right of the people to vote for their representatives. In fact, the people's right to vote is the most effective mechanism to hold government officials accountable and ensure that they act in a manner consistent with their constituents' freedom.

The right to vote is so important to us that we use it as a primary criterion in grading other democratic governments. The new Iraqi Constitution, the text of which was influenced by the United States, highlights the right to vote. Among other references to voting and the rights of voters, Article 20 of the Iraqi Constitution states that "[t]he citizens, men and women, have the right to participate in public affairs and to enjoy political rights including the right to vote, to elect and to nominate."[3] The right to vote is so central to the Iraqi government that it permitted its people to ratify the Constitution by direct vote.[4] President George W. Bush viewed elections in Iraq as an essential step in achieving stable, democratic government. After the first Iraqi elections, Bush stated that by voting, Iraqis were "exercising their rights as citizens."[5] According to Bush, the relatively high voter turnout showed Iraq's "commitment to democracy" and its rejection of "the anti-democratic ideology of the terrorists."[6]

President Obama, apparently adopting Bush's stated purpose for U.S. military action in the Middle East, also considers legitimate elections vital to the success of the new government in Afghanistan, and fears the consequences of fixed results. In June 2009, on the eve of the Afghan elections, Obama vowed to work with the "Afghan electoral authorities and the United Nations to help Afghans ensure a credible, secure and inclusive election process."[7]

In America, the right to vote is protected throughout the United States Constitution:

- Article I, Section 2, Clause 1, provides that "[t]he House of Representatives shall be composed of Members chosen every second Year by the People of the several States."

- The Fifteenth Amendment, ratified in 1870, states that the right to vote "shall not be denied or abridged by the United States or by any State on account of race, color or previous condition of servitude."
- The Seventeenth Amendment, ratified in 1912, provides for the direct election of United States Senators by the people of the States. (Article I, Section 3, had provided that each state's legislature selects that state's senators.)
- The Nineteenth Amendment, ratified in 1920, states that the right to vote "shall not be denied or abridged . . . on account of sex." (It should have stated ". . . on account of gender.")
- The Twenty-Sixth Amendment, ratified in 1971, grants the right to vote in all elections, federal and state, to all American citizens "eighteen years of age or older."
- The Fourteenth Amendment protects the right to vote by preventing the States from infringing on individual liberties without due process, and guaranteeing all persons equal protection of the laws.

The Constitution prevents the government from restricting the right to vote based on age, race, or gender. Surprisingly, however, neither the original United States Constitution, nor the Bill of Rights, explicitly grants or recognizes a *federal* right to vote. Rather, the Constitution, as it stands today, protects the right to vote *only when* it is granted by the States. Voting privileges, therefore, extend only as far as our respective state legislatures permit.

This chapter describes unfairness in the American system of selecting representatives, as well as discrimination perpetrated against voters, to show the many ways in which the government has taken the future of this republic out of the hands of the American voter.

Empowering the Majority, Assaulting Federalism

The Seventeenth Amendment does not violate the literal proposition that "every vote counts," in that all eligible voters can directly elect their U.S. Senators. The direct election of senators dilutes the people's strength, however, by constricting the States' power to protect themselves against the massive power of the federal government.

First things first: The Framers did not vest our state legislatures with the power to select their U.S. Senators because they distrusted our ability to make decisions, or because they desired to withhold voting power from us. Rather, they sought to give the States a voice in the federal government, and thus provide a structural check on the power of the federal government. The United States government was founded on the principles of checks and balances and of federalism. One such check and balance is bicameralism, which instructs that the legislature be divided into two chambers. In the United States, Congress is divided into the House of Representatives and the Senate. According to Article I, Section 2, Clause 1, of the United States Constitution, "The House of Representatives shall be composed of Members chosen every second Year by the People of the several States. . . ." Every two years, all eligible voters may vote to elect one congressperson to represent them in the lower house, with no intervention from their respective state legislatures. The House of Representatives, therefore, is often referred to as the "People's House."

On the other hand, Article I, Section 3, Clause 1, of the Constitution states that "[t]he Senate of the United States shall be composed of two Senators from each State, *chosen by the Legislature thereof*, for six Years; and each Senator shall have one Vote" (emphases added). James Madison, among other Framers, supported a two-chambered Congress. In *The Federalist, No. 51*, Madison stated that "[i]n republican government, the legislative authority, necessarily predominates." According to Madison, "[t]he remedy for this inconveniency is, to divide the legislature into different branches; and to render them by different modes of election, and different principles of action, as little connected with each other, as the nature of their common functions and their common dependencies on the society, will admit." The Framers also believed that the bicameral Congress would prevent the influence of special interests on government policy, and allow the federal legislature to satisfy smaller voting districts on the one hand, and entire states on the other.

In another check and balance, the Framers insisted that the U.S. Senate, whose members were to be selected by the state legislatures, would preserve the federal society they created. Federalism is a system in which political power is divided between a central government and sovereign states, and each may check the other's exercise of power. The Framers believed that the Senate would protect the States' power. *The Federalist, No. 62*, states that even though the Constitution enumerates federal powers, mere "parchment barriers" will not prevent a central government from abusing its power. Therefore, the Framers believed that certain structural barriers, or "forms," were necessary to hold federal power in check. One of these barriers is the U.S. Senate, and the method by which its members are selected.

Even Alexander Hamilton, the father of Big Government, believed that the election of senators by state legislatures would preserve the States' power by providing an "absolute safeguard" against federal government tyranny. George Mason opined that the election of senators by state legislatures would provide the people with "some means of defending themselves against encroachments of the National Government."

Simply put, U.S. Senators were intended to be "ambassadors of the states,"[8] as States, not representatives of the people in them. Recall that the *States*, through their delegates at the Constitutional Convention, formed the federal government and ceded power to it. President Ronald Reagan highlighted this fact in his First Inaugural Address, stating that "[a]ll of us need to be reminded that the Federal Government did not create the States; the States created the Federal Government." It only made sense, then, that in the upper house of Congress, the States, as States, would be represented. The preamble of the Constitution begins with, "We the People . . . ," but this is misleading, for the "People" did not cede power to the Constitution. Rather, "We the *States* . . ." did so.

For some time, state legislatures held their U.S. Senators accountable and instructed them on how to act. The Virginia and Kentucky Resolves of 1798, for example, instructed those States' senators to oppose the Sedition Act, which effectually criminalized the uttering of statements critical of the federal government.[9] The Resolves would not have been possible without the influence of state legislatures.[10] State legislatures also played an integral role in forcing their senators to support President Andrew Jackson's crusade against the Bank of the United States.[11] Senator Pelog Sprague of Maine, for example, was forced to resign in 1835, after disregarding his state's instruction.[12] Seven other senators suffered the same fate.[13]

The direct election of senators was a popular idea until the end of the nineteenth century. The very first resolution calling for direct election was introduced in the House of Representatives on February 14th 1826, eighty-six years before the Seventeenth Amendment was ratified.[14] In the interim, 187 comparable resolutions were introduced in Congress, 167 of which were introduced after 1880.[15] Concern over the original selection of senators increased as the methods by which the States chose their U.S. Senators proved cumbersome for the U.S. Senate, which, pursuant to Article I, Section

4, is entrusted with determining whether its members have been appropriately chosen.[16]

Since Article I, Section 3, does not specify the manner in which state legislatures must select their U.S. Senators, the States' selection methods were not uniform. Some senate elections resulted in "legislative deadlock," where no candidate received a majority of the state legislature's vote.[17] To avoid having to review elections, the Senate, with approval by the House of Representatives, passed legislation in 1866 exercising greater control over senate elections.[18] The legislation, which is a clear example of federal imposition on states' rights, also proved to be highly ineffective, as legislative deadlocks increased drastically.[19] It was also unconstitutional.

Charges of bribery and corruption stemmed from the deadlocks that the 1866 legislation created.[20] Between the passage of the 1866 act and 1900, the Senate investigated potential bribery in nine senate election cases, and had investigated five more cases by 1912.[21] Corruption was found in a very limited number of cases, but the investigations were highly publicized, and supported the notion that state legislatures could not be trusted.[22]

Furthermore, the development of Populism and Progressivism— two demons that have only destroyed individual liberty—pushed for a change in the way senators were selected.[23] The Populists characterized the Senate as a "millionaires club" that was "too far removed from the people, beyond their reach, and with no especial interest in their welfare."[24] Progressivism, a movement that developed as Populism declined, supported a democracy in which the people directly chose all of their representatives.[25] Despite the Founders' ideas, Progressives believed that Americans had become "a new people living and acting under an old system."[26] Progressivism was, and is, based on what I like to call the Gang theory and the Robin Hood theory of government.

The Progressives believe that all power goes to the gang that gets the most votes, and thus all structural efforts to temper that power—like federalism, states' rights, even natural rights—must give way to the majority's will. Progressives also believe that somehow, from somewhere, from some source other than the Constitution, they can use the power of government to steal from those who have and give to those who do not. Woodrow Wilson led the Progressives in the Democratic Party, and Theodore Roosevelt led the Progressives in the Republican Party. By promoting and enacting just two amendments to the Constitution—the Sixteenth, which purported to permit taxes on personal incomes; and the Seventeenth, discussed herein—these pernicious little tyrants destroyed many property rights, much federalism, and a great deal of personal freedoms.

The Seventeenth Amendment was approved by Congress on May 12th 1912, and ratified by three-quarters of the States on May 31st 1913. The Amendment states, in part, that "[t]he Senate of the United States shall be composed of two Senators from each State, elected by the people thereof. . . ." This Amendment is a mortal blow to the concept of federalism, as it prevents state legislatures from having any influence in the federal government. Sure, the Amendment ensures that all members of Congress are elected by the people, but the people of an entire state are unable to affect the actions of their U.S. Senators; they can only vote them out of office after their lengthy, six-year terms. Furthermore, the people of every State are not trained to influence federal government policy, and would not know what to do even if given the opportunity to communicate with their senators.[27]

We live in a representative democracy, not a true democracy, and we trust our representatives to look out for our best interests. The original Constitution provided our state legislatures control of our U.S. Senators, but the Seventeenth Amendment took the power out of their hands, rendering the States defenseless against federal government abuses. It is no coincidence that the size of the federal government has grown exponentially since 1913 and U.S. Senators have been controlled by special interests often exercising their influence from outside the States that the senators represent.

Repealing the Seventeenth Amendment would not attract the same problems that led to its passage in 1913. Today, we can protect ourselves against corrupt state legislatures through term limits and campaign disclosure statements.[28] Also, information on our government officials is highly visible.[29] Moreover, to protect against deadlocked state legislatures, the governor of a State could appoint a U.S. Senator if the State's legislature does not elect a senator or fill a vacancy within thirty days.[30]

If any amendment is unconstitutional, it is this one. Can an amendment to the Constitution be unconstitutional? I submit it can, even if lawfully adopted, if it strikes at the core values of the Constitution. Removing the representation of the States as States in the central government was a direct and impermissible assault on federalism; more tyranny of the majority. It undermines the premise that the people *and the States* would have a place at the federal table. It also undermines the States' check on federal corruption of states' rights. This amendment, along with the Sixteenth (which permitted federal income taxes), has contributed more to *1984*-style Big Government than any other. It is a direct repudiation of the framework the Founders set up. If anyone tells you that this Amendment enfranchises voters, tell that person that the Amendment disenfranchises the States.

The Fifteenth Amendment, Voting Rights Act, and Racial Gerrymandering

In 1870, the United States ratified the Fifteenth Amendment, which prohibits voting discrimination "by the United States or by any State on account of race, color, or previous condition of servitude."[31] The governments in the South did not adhere to this amendment and did much to prevent blacks from voting.[32] Literacy tests were administered to disqualify the substantial black population that could not read or write.[33] Property requirements were also implemented to prevent blacks from voting.[34]

Furthermore, Southern governments used various districting techniques to dilute the African-American vote. One of these techniques is "cracking," in which the legislature split a large number of black voters among several majority-white voting districts.[35] The same governments also engaged in "packing," in which a significant number of African-Americans were placed in one district, thus limiting black representation in that part of a State to that district only.[36]

The Southern States continued to disobey the law, and the federal government permitted them to do so until Congress finally passed the Voting Rights Act of 1965. Section 2 of the Act, as amended in 1982, states that "no voting qualification or prerequisite to voting or standard, practice or procedure shall be imposed or applied by any State or political subdivision in a manner which will result in a denial or abridgement of the right of any citizen of the United States to vote on account of race or color."

Therefore, according to the Act, complainants need only prove that a voting plan had the *effect* of discriminating against minorities, not that it was devised with the *intent* to discriminate.

Today, the concern is not whether African-Americans actually have the right to vote, but whether they are adequately represented.[37] To ensure adequate representation for African-Americans (and other minorities), many States have redrawn congressional district lines based on race, through a process called racial gerrymandering, to create "majority-minority" districts.[38] In this way, States can guarantee representation for minorities. But isn't this a government decision based on race; and was not the Fourteenth Amendment written to abolish that? In *Shaw v. Reno* (1993), the United States Supreme Court held that redistricting based on race is subject to the highest standard of judicial scrutiny under the Equal Protection Clause of the Fourteenth Amendment, but the States still may take race into account to comply with the Voting Rights Act.[39]

Shaw v. Reno tells us that racial gerrymandering is constitutional if the plan is "narrowly tailored to serve a compelling state interest." Could any racial gerrymandering plan, regardless of its lawfulness, be constitutional today? Majority-minority districts are unnecessary, particularly due to the advances African-Americans have made in this country.[40] Conservative whites do not vote for black candidates, particularly in the South, not because they are racist, but because the liberal views associated most with African-Americans are not attractive to conservative whites, regardless of the candidate's color.[41] Furthermore, the existence of majority-minority districts reinforces racial differences, when the goal of the Voting Rights Act and Civil Rights Movement was to achieve color blindness and equality.[42]

The 2008 presidential election is further evidence that racial gerrymandering is unnecessary.[43] Barack Obama did not win an overall majority of white votes, but no Democrat since Lyndon B. Johnson in 1964 has won the majority of the white vote.[44] Obama captured 43 percent of the white vote, a slightly *higher* percentage than that of Al Gore (42 percent) in 2000, and John Kerry (41 percent) in 2004.[45] In Iowa, which has a negligible black population, 5 percent of voters said that race was the most important factor in the election.[46] However, 54 percent of Iowans voted for Obama.[47] Obama achieved similar results in Minnesota and Wisconsin, states that are also predominantly white.[48] This data shows that black candidates can win elections, even in majority-white areas. In fact, as early as

1990, 40 percent of the black members of Congress did *not* come from majority-black districts.[49]

Another major problem with racial gerrymandering is that it involves blatant government manipulation of people. Legislators redistrict all the time to achieve desired results. They group people together based on how they think they will vote. There is something fundamentally wrong with this tactic; it is unconstitutional, it is manipulative, it is patronizing, and it infringes upon all citizens' right to vote.

Collectivism is a political theory that favors the group over the individual. It is a philosophy diametrically at odds with the American concept of individual liberty and limited government. According to Ayn Rand, "[c]ollectivism holds that man must be chained to collective action and collective thought for the sake of what is called 'the common good.'" By engaging in racial gerrymandering, legislatures are operating under the false and dangerous premise that all members of a particular race will support a similar candidate, and promoting collectivist ideals, thus "chaining" individuals to their respective races.

The right to vote in America is an *individual* right, not a collective one; one may vote because one is a citizen, and at least eighteen years old, not because one belongs to a group the membership in which is some immutable characteristic of birth. On Election Day, we select our representatives by secret ballot, and we choose our candidates based on their ability to protect our individual rights, not the rights of the group of people with which we most closely identify. (Though surely, many voters are more interested in voting for a Robin Hood than a Thomas Jefferson.) Most of us choose not to reveal the candidates we voted for, and it is considered rude to ask another directly how he or she voted.

Racial gerrymandering takes the individual out of the voting process, and divides large groups of individuals into smaller voting blocs based on race. Legislatures create "majority-minority" districts to ensure that the African-American community, or the Hispanic community, or the Italian-American or Irish-American or Jewish-American communities receive fair representation, not the individual African-American or Hispanic or Italian-American or Irish-American or Jewish-American voter. It is true that certain groups typically vote the same way, but it is not a government's job to assume that the "common good" will be served if it artificially groups people so as essentially to rig election results. *Individuals* should decide, and let the chips fall where they may.

If the purpose of the Fourteenth and Fifteenth Amendments was to remove race from the government's weapons, racial gerrymandering has nullified that purpose.

An "Unpopular" Decision

I opened this chapter with one of the most contentious voting events of our history, where the Supreme Court essentially decided the result of the 2000 presidential election. The Supreme Court's decision in *Bush v. Gore* is so disheartening not because Vice President Al Gore received over 539,000 more popular votes than Governor Bush, but because the Supreme Court disregarded not only the fundamental right to vote, and in turn kept us from discovering the true winner (whoever it may have been),[50] but it assaulted federalism by denying the State of Florida the ability to manage its mechanisms of voting and interpreting its own laws.

The contested 2000 presidential election involved a series of legal proceedings. For the purpose of this discussion, we'll pick up the story in early December 2000. At this point, the Secretary of State of Florida, Katherine Harris, had certified the election for Governor Bush. On December 4th 2000, in the case of *Gore v. Harris*, a local judge in Tallahassee, Florida, upheld Harris's certification, and rejected any further recounts, concluding that a recount would make no difference. Gore appealed to the Florida Supreme Court, which on December 8th, ordered a manual recount of all "undervotes" that had not yet been counted. An "undervote" in the context of this case was a ballot where the counting machine failed to register a preference in the race. Approximately 60,000 Florida undervotes were outstanding at this time. Bush then appealed to the United States Supreme Court, asking the Court to stay the recount. The Court, ruling by 5 to 4, granted the stay and heard oral arguments on the merits of the case on December 11th. On December 12th, the Supreme Court decided, again 5 to 4, to stop the recounts because the standards applied in the recounts were not uniform across the state, and would result in unequal treatment of votes and thus fundamental unfairness.[51]

The Court's decision to hear this case stemmed from the majority's political affiliation; their self-interest in the election cannot be denied. Each of the five justices in the majority, to different extents, was affiliated, or had been affiliated, with the Republican Party. Justice Sandra Day O'Connor, a native Arizonan, is a Republican who typically referred to Republicans as "we" and "us."[52] She served three terms in the Arizona State Senate and also served as co-chairperson of the Arizona state committee to elect Richard Nixon president.[53] O'Connor was also an old friend of the Bush family.[54] She played tennis with Barbara Bush, and admired George W. Bush.[55] In fact, she spent election night at a party hosted by Republicans, and was heard saying, "This is terrible," when the networks had called the election for Gore.[56] According to her husband, Sandra was ready to retire to Arizona, but did not want to give up her seat to a Democratic president.[57]

Chief Justice William Rehnquist campaigned for Barry Goldwater in 1964, and in 1962, provided legal advice to Republicans working to challenge Democratic voters' credentials at a Phoenix, Arizona, polling station.[58]

Justice Anthony Kennedy was considered a "Sacramento lawyer-lobbyist," who voluntarily traveled the State of California campaigning for then-Governor Ronald Reagan's anti-tax initiative.[59]

Justice Clarence Thomas's wife worked for the Heritage Foundation, a conservative organization, to manage Bush's transition to the White House.[60]

Two of Justice Antonin Scalia's sons worked for law firms representing George W. Bush.[61] I mean this thumbnail personal, political history not as an assault on the Republican members of the Court, some of whom—at this writing—I am privileged to call personal friends. And I cannot overlook the pre-judicial Democratic political activities of Justice Ruth Bader Ginsburg and Justice Stephen Breyer. And I am mindful of the incendiary admission of Justice William O. Douglas that "up there [at the Supreme Court] no one is neutral."[62] Nevertheless, whether the justices' intentions were good or bad, pure or impure, constitutional or political, *Bush v. Gore* was an assault on federalism and freedom.

The justices' political motivation was also evident from the decision itself. Conservative judges typically claim to have a strong belief in the concept of federalism, and want us to believe that they will exercise deference to state governments when applicable. They also tend to assail liberal "activist" judges for not practicing judicial restraint and essentially legislating from the bench. Here, however, the conservatives acted out of character. Until *Bush v. Gore*, neither the Supreme Court, nor any other federal court, had ever enforced a uniformity rule in the counting of ballots.[63]

Furthermore, every State has varying methods of casting and counting votes; this issue was not unique to Florida. Florida election law required that the votes be counted to determine the "intent of the voter." The Florida Supreme Court, perhaps somewhat hap-hazardly, ordered manual recounts to ascertain voter intent. (You may recall the "hanging chad" and "pregnant chad" news stories of that time.) The United States Supreme Court, however, essentially overruled the Florida Supreme Court's determination, claiming the recount process violated the Equal Protection Clause.

The more disturbing part is that the Supreme Court did not seek to remedy the Equal Protection violation. According to the Court, uniform standards could not be set before the federal deadline for Florida to certify its results. The deadline happened to be December 12th, the date on which the decision was rendered. Therefore, the Supreme Court deemed the recounts unconstitutional, yet in the end proceeded to ignore the 60,000 undervotes, rather than allow the Florida Supreme Court to attempt to resolve the situation.

As icing on the cake, the Supreme Court further stated, in its opinion: "Our consideration is limited to the present circumstances, for the problem of equal protection in election processes generally presents many complexities."[64] The Court, however, is not supposed to decide complex issues that involve politics, especially when the State involved in the suit has already made a decision.

Furthermore, no Supreme Court decision is "limited to the present circumstances." It is true that the Supreme Court decides cases, and does not actively make law, but its decisions establish precedent applicable to future cases. Moreover, even if the Court's decision did not extend to future circumstances, it did damage to its own legitimacy and the legitimacy of the 2000 presidential election, and disenfranchised 60,000 American voters. And the winner of that election certainly did not confine his exercise of presidential power "limited to the present circumstances." *Bush v. Gore* literally had limitless effect on the lives of six billion human beings; and the Court ought to have known that.

But Who Really Cares?

The Supreme Court's decision in *Bush v. Gore* was a travesty, but even if we had discovered the true winner, the two-party system would still dominate American politics, limiting voter choice and the development of third parties.

No matter what they say, Democrats and Republicans in the United States do not control the government because they are best able to serve us and meet our needs. In fact, both parties couldn't care less about us. The United States government, as stated earlier, is not a democracy. In fact, some would argue that it is not even a republic, since our leaders do not actually work for us. Some believe that the United States government is actually an oligarchy in which just a few thousand people, "mostly in government, finance, and the military-industrial complex, run this country for their own purposes."[65] These powerful people seek to preserve their power by manipulating the mainstream media, controlling campaign finance money, and thus nominating candidates who will work for them, regardless of their party affiliation.

Democrats and Republicans, controlled by powerful interests, work to preserve their power. Both parties promote "changing Washington," but in reality, they like Washington just the way it is: little gets done that they don't like, and none of our officials are truly held accountable. If we don't seek to change the system, the Republican Party will always be the party that *claims* it does not want to govern, and the Democratic Party will always *pretend* to govern.

The 2008 presidential election is a great example of the two-party monopoly putting forth two candidates who were substantially the same. Senator John S. McCain, a "Republican" from Arizona, and Senator Barack Obama, a "Democrat" from Illinois, spoke *ad naseum* about the "fundamental disagreements" between them.

After following the campaign closely, listening to the speeches, and watching the debates, it was still difficult for me to come up with issues on which the two candidates truly disagreed. Both candidates oppose gay marriage, at least so long as they are politicians. Obama hoped that the Iraq War would end during his presidency, while McCain ran on the idea that the "surge" was working. President Obama currently has plans to shift American involvement in Iraq to Afghanistan.

Both candidates supported bigger and more powerful government; not just Obama. McCain stated that he supported "smaller" government, but chose to "suspend" his campaign in September 2008 (He did no such thing; it was a PR stunt) after the fall of Lehman Brothers, Fannie Mae, and Freddie Mac, to go to Washington and vote for the first of many massive, bailout packages. That package authorized the borrowing or printing and spending of over one trillion dollars on the same government-motivated, get-rich-quick schemes that produced the crisis.

Both Obama and McCain thought that it would be nice to decrease the national debt, and both viewed lower taxes as better for Americans than higher ones. Moreover, I do not think the Federal Reserve Bank was discussed publicly even once by either candidate during the campaign, let alone plans to audit, reform, or abolish it.

They both approved TARP funds for struggling companies and supported the federal takeover of education, Medicare prescription drug benefits, and the burdensome Sarbanes-Oxley Act.

Moreover, Obama and McCain *still* endorse the unconstitutional, liberty-restricting Patriot Act, which, while not making us safer, invades our natural rights. Both candidates opposed the legalization of marijuana, although Obama stated he was open to the use of marijuana for medicinal purposes.

On abortion, Obama and McCain seemingly disagreed. Obama is

pro-choice, and believes that having an abortion is "one of the most fundamental rights we possess."[66] McCain claims to oppose abortion. Throughout the campaign, he denounced the Supreme Court's decision in *Roe v. Wade*, and vowed to nominate Supreme Court justices who would overturn it. Yet, in August 1999, McCain stated, "[C]ertainly in the short term, or even in the long term, I would not support repeal of *Roe v. Wade*, which would then force X number of women in America to undergo illegal and dangerous abortions."[67] I do not doubt that McCain is personally pro-life, but his stance against abortion is not nearly as realistic as his campaign made it out to be.

In selecting their running mates, both Obama and McCain chose candidates whom they hardly knew. John McCain asked then-Governor Sarah Palin of Alaska to be his running mate just six months after meeting her for the first time.[68] Before inviting her to his home in Sedona, Arizona, to offer her the job formally, McCain had only spoken to Palin once on the phone about the position.[69] Obama, who had only been a Senator for two years prior to the start of his presidential campaign, chose veteran Senator Joe Biden as his running mate. The two colleagues appeared to be good friends, but it is clear that Obama picked the experienced Biden merely to counter his image as a young, naïve candidate.

We did not hear about the similarities between the two candidates, however, because the campaign was not about real issues that matter to people. I think we will remember Reverend Jeremiah Wright much better than Obama's proposed healthcare plan. At one point during the campaign, it seemed for a moment that William Ayers was Obama's running mate. We will all remember that John McCain has more than one house, but most likely fewer than ten.

When it was all said and done, America voted for Obama not because of where he stood on the issues, but because he was not a Republican, and he had the ability to captivate his audiences. America voted for change, but neither Obama nor future Democratic or Republican candidates will disrupt the current two-party monopoly in this country. In the end, the ruling parties preserved their power.

Campaigns do not have to be about real issues because the colossal Democratic and Republican Parties have adopted them all. It may help to think of them as huge superstores that have everything you could ever want. They cover all the issues, but just frame them a bit differently. In the end, no matter how you slice it, the two-party system in this country ensures that we more or less maintain the status quo.[70]

The people getting shut out of the system are candidates who limit their campaigns to the issues, and the voters, who more often than not choose the lesser of two evils. Due to the two-party monopoly, third parties, like the Libertarian and Green Parties, are perceived as radical, fringe groups with no chance of success. Ralph Nader was ostracized by the Democrats for helping George W. Bush win the 2000 election, rather than commended for opposing the "Republocrat"[71] regime.

Congressman Ron Paul is a "Republican" for the purpose of running for office because it would be unwise for him to label himself a "Libertarian." Paul ran for president in 2008 as a Republican, even though he shares little in common with the present Grand Old Party. People around the country have come to know Ron Paul as a libertarian and constitutionalist because he, unlike mainstream politicians, speaks his mind truthfully, understands our financial systems dutifully, and follows the Constitution faithfully.

Congressman Paul also suffered from an institutional preference for mainstream candidates. The last major presidential candidate who loved the Constitution and ran offering to shrink the federal government was Senator Barry M. Goldwater (R-AZ) in 1964. Even though Ron Paul raised more campaign dollars in one day— over five million dollars on November 5th 2007—than any other candidate, the Republican Party establishment and much of the national media labored mightily against him.

The only chance for a third-party or independent candidate to achieve electoral success is if he or she is a well-known and powerful politician, has a boatload of money, or both. Senator Joseph I. Lieberman of Connecticut was a lifelong Democrat who switched his political affiliation to "Independent" after losing his last Democratic primary. Due to his popularity and influence in Connecticut, Lieberman then defeated his Democratic opponent in the general election.

Governor George Wallace of Alabama ran as an "American Independent" in 1968, on a segregationist platform. Due to the racism then prevalent in the South, Wallace carried five States, won forty-six electoral votes, and received 14 percent of the popular vote, but fell far short of victory.[72]

Ross Perot is the most notable independent candidate of the recent past; a wealthy businessman who spent an exorbitant amount of money to make Governor William Jefferson Clinton and President George H. W. Bush nervous during the 1992 presidential election. Perot recorded nearly 19 percent of the popular vote, but won no electoral votes.[73] Clinton won the election with only 43 percent of the popular vote.[74] Perot's minor success relative to the money he spent shows that in the current system, there is little hope for third-party candidates—even fabulously wealthy ones.

The limited success of third parties has produced a feeling in this country that it is foolish to vote for nonmainstream candidates. People are said to be "wasting" their votes on candidates who cannot win. Voting for third-party candidates is like buying store-brand potato chips when Doritos are staring you right in the face, or like purchasing hybrid cars before they were cool. Voting on the issues needs to become popular again. We must move beyond the emptiness of major party candidates and vote for candidates based on their stances on the issues, and what they are going to accomplish for us while in office.

It is evident that as Americans, we have very little influence on the political process. The federal government and state governments have gone to great lengths to leave the impression that our votes count, but have continuously diluted our power. If exercising the right to vote were truly effective, the government would not be so eager to promote it.

Lie #5

"Congress Shall Make No Law . . . Abridging the Freedom of Speech"

The First Amendment to the United States Constitution, enacted on December 15th 1791, states, in part, that "Congress shall make no law . . . abridging the freedom of speech. . . ." It is the opening line of the Bill of Rights. It is the most famous phrase in the Constitution. It is the historical and moral equivalent of "All Men Are Created Equal." The right to freedom of speech is one of the most fundamental rights protected in the United States of America, and one that separates us from other nations. It is also a natural right in that we have it by virtue of our existence as humans. We know this because the Founders refer to it as *the* freedom of speech. This language implies that free speech was not a new concept, but a natural right that must be safeguarded.

The freedom of speech preceded the existence of the United States, and the Constitution recognizes that. The First Amendment is essential to American government because it ensures that "debate on public issues . . . [is] . . . uninhibited, robust, and wide-open."[1] Differences of opinion and conflict result in informed decisions.

Furthermore, the freedom of speech is invaluable to our personal autonomy because it removes constraints on our ability to think what we want to believe, and say what we want to think; to exchange ideas at will. The freedom of speech is, in a word, liberating.

Taken word-for-word, the First Amendment prohibits only *Congress* from abridging the freedom of speech. However, the First Amendment also applies to the States via the Fourteenth Amendment, which prohibits the States from making or enforcing any law that abridges the privileges or immunities of citizens of the United States.

Although the First Amendment applies to all levels of government, it does not apply to all speech. No one would argue that speech involved in a criminal conspiracy should be protected, nor can using a megaphone outside someone's home at 3:00 a.m. be justified. Nevertheless, our federal and state governments have seriously sought to undermine the value of the First Amendment by smothering dissent, influencing how we act, or censoring the material we can utter, publish, view, or hear. Thankfully, the Supreme Court has kept Congress, the President, and state legislatures in check, but that has not stopped lawmakers from continuing their attack on this natural and sacred freedom.

Thou Shalt Not Frighten the Government

On June 15th 1917, about two months after the United States entered World War I, which President Wilson claimed would be the "war to end all wars," Congress enacted the Espionage Act of 1917, with the stated purpose of eliminating espionage and protecting military secrets. Title I, Section 3, of the Act makes it a crime for any citizen, during wartime, (1) willfully "to make or convey false reports or false statements with intent to interfere with the operation or success of the military or naval forces of the United States or to promote the success of its enemies"; (2) willfully to "cause or attempt to cause insubordination, disloyalty, mutiny, refusal of duty, in the military or naval forces of the United States"; or (3) willfully to "obstruct the recruiting or enlistment service of the United States." Violators of this Section face a fine of up to $10,000, or imprisonment of up to twenty years, or both. *That's twenty years in jail for the utterance of government-prohibited political speech.*

The Act, on its face, the government maintained, was somewhat legitimate. Especially during a war as complex as World War I, actual physical interference with the American military effort would have posed a grave threat to our country's safety. *Sticks and stones can break my bones, but names will never hurt me.* In his Virginia upperclass youth and at Princeton University, Woodrow Wilson probably never heard this nursery rhyme truism. The Wilson Department of Justice exploited the Act's vague language, using it to prosecute roughly two thousand Americans who engaged in constructive verbal criticism of America's involvement in the Great War.[2] In the process, the government made a mockery of the First Amendment by suppressing dissent, and seriously undermining the fundamental right to freedom of speech, which it claimed it was fighting the war in order to preserve.

Remarkably, in 1919, the United States Supreme Court *unanimously* upheld Charles T. Schenck's conviction under Section 4 of the Espionage Act, for conspiring to violate Section 3 of the Act.[3] Schenck, Secretary of the Socialist Party, supervised the distribution of a leaflet that likened the draft to slavery, and called involuntary conscription a crime against humanity. The leaflet urged those subject to the draft not to "submit to intimidation" and to exercise their right to oppose it.

Justice Oliver Wendell Holmes Jr., writing for the Court, declared that the relevant inquiry in cases of this type is "whether the words used are used in such circumstances and are of such a nature as to create a clear and present danger that they will bring about the substantive evils that Congress has a right to prevent." In analyzing the *Schenck* Case under this framework, Holmes reasoned, literature that may be appropriate in peacetime may be an impediment to the military during wartime, and may pose a clear and present danger of obstructing the ultimate military goals. He also held that the evidence permitted the conclusion that Schenck's goal in distributing the leaflets was to incite potential draftees to obstruct the draft, as obstruction was the only effect that could feasibly be expected. The Court, therefore, concluded that Schenck conspired to violate the Espionage Act.

What makes the *Schenck* decision so disturbingly fascinating is that it admits that the First Amendment is toothless in times of war and at other times when the context in which speech is uttered causes an impact on society that the government dislikes, hates, or fears. The opinion also states that a court can find that a defendant willfully violated the Act based on the speech's *potential* to cause a clear and present danger, not on whether the speaker actually intended to obstruct the military; much less whether he even succeeded in doing so. On the other hand, a speaker who blatantly attempts to obstruct the military can sidestep the Act if his statements do not present a clear and present danger. What sense does that make?

On the same day as the Court rendered its decision in *Schenck*, it also decided two other cases, *Frohwerk v. United States* and *Debs v. United States*.[4] The Court made no mention of "clear and present danger" in those opinions, but echoed the theme from *Schenck* that speech can be restricted based on its potentially inflammatory effect. In *Frohwerk*, Jacob Frohwerk and Carl Gleeser were convicted under the Espionage Act of conspiring to cause "disloyalty, mutiny, and refusal of duty in the military and naval forces of the United States."

Frohwerk and Gleeser had made the foolish mistake of publishing in the *Missouri Staats Zeitung*, a German periodical, articles condemning World War I and exposing the hardships faced by draftees. Justice Holmes, again writing for a unanimous Court, upheld the convictions, stating that the articles had been circulated "in quarters where a little breath would be enough to kindle a flame."

In *Debs*, the famous Eugene Victor Debs, national leader of the Socialist Party and 1912 presidential candidate, was convicted of disrupting the recruitment service with a speech he gave criticizing the war and the draft, and telling his audience that it was "fit for something better than slavery and cannon fodder." The Court, again via Justice Holmes, unanimously upheld the conviction.

Holmes was the ultimate legal positivist, believing that law is solely man-made. He argued that rights not written down do not exist. Remarkably, he did not believe that Natural Law established, protected, and mandated *the* freedom of speech, nor did he believe that Natural Law existed in the first place.

Believe it or not, prosecutions under the Espionage Act got more ridiculous. The Reverend Clarence H. Waldron was sentenced to *fifteen years* in jail for distributing literature stating, "If Christians [are] forbidden to fight to preserve the Person of their Lord and Master, they may not fight to preserve themselves, or any city they should happen to dwell in."[5] The government, in this case, argued that Waldron's statements had obstructed the recruitment service, and the Court agreed.

The case of Robert Goldstein is perhaps the most shocking, however. Goldstein produced a film entitled *The Spirit of '76*, a historical film that happened to have portrayed the Wyoming Valley Massacre, in which British soldiers abused and killed women and children. Goldstein was sentenced to *ten years* in prison because the government satisfied a federal judge and jury that his factual account could promote mutiny in the military because it "negatively" portrayed Great Britain, an American ally in World War I.[6]

So, the government saw fit to prosecute someone who accurately reported on a 150-year-old event in which the British committed atrocities against *American* women and children, because it believed that Goldstein's film would somehow jeopardize the American war effort almost 150 years later.

Unfortunately, the many horror stories of this time period are not made up, nor would it be possible to fabricate credibly such absurdity. During this era of fear, the government simply sought to smother dissent, and cleverly used the Espionage Act to shield itself.

Woodrow Wilson, the President of the United States during this period, was a racist who openly supported segregation and did everything in his power to preserve it.[7] When he took office, one of his associates stated that "Negroes should expect to be treated as a servile race."[8] He also worked to prevent women's suffrage, even though his efforts ultimately failed. He opposed even legal immigration.[9] It is not at all shocking that someone with such a track record on human rights would sign a bill limiting the freedom of speech, and prosecute those who challenged him.

Getting Smarter

Over time, the Supreme Court of the United States came to its senses, ultimately rejecting federal and state government efforts to quash the freedom of speech. In *Abrams v. United States* (1919), the Supreme Court, in typical fashion, upheld the convictions of Russian, socialist immigrants prosecuted under the Sedition Act of 1918, a law similar to the Espionage Act of 1917.[10] Justice Holmes, however, in an impressive about-face, wrote an inspired dissenting opinion in which he introduced into First Amendment discourse the element of the "free trade" or "marketplace" of ideas.

According to Holmes's new theory of free speech (he must have been searching for new theories), the search for truth, knowledge, and wisdom is more likely to end successfully if the government refrains from trying to control the debate. Holmes also instructed that Americans "should be eternally vigilant against attempts to check the expression of opinions that we loathe and believe to be fraught with death." Holmes believed that speech should be punishable *only if* it creates, and is intended to create, immediate harm before there is time or opportunity for counter-speech to avert such harm. Therefore, Holmes would have reversed his earlier opinions that upheld convictions of those denouncing the war, because the literature and speeches at issue had no chance of causing immediate harm. Stated differently, only if the speech being prosecuted *failed in its purpose* could it be entitled to constitutional protection.

Later, in *Whitney v. California* (1927), the Supreme Court upheld the constitutionality of California's Criminal Syndicalism Act, which made it a crime knowingly to become a member of any organization that advocates "the commission of crime, sabotage, or unlawful acts of force and violence or unlawful methods of terrorism as a means of accomplishing a change in industrial ownership or control, or effecting any political change."[11] The law was enacted during the Red Scare of the 1920s, when fear of Communism was widespread. The Court held that the Act was neither an unreasonable nor an arbitrary exercise of California's police power. In a concurring opinion, however, Justice Louis Dembitz Brandeis echoed Holmes's "imminence-of-danger" idea, and stated his belief that free speech promotes active self-government, helping us to fulfill our role as citizens. Repression of ideas, according to Brandeis, was a sign of weakness or panic.

What makes the outcome in this case even more frightening is that Charlotte Anita Whitney, a political activist, did not come close to violating the California statute.[12] At a convention in Oakland during which Whitney hoped to organize a California branch of the Communist Labor Party, Whitney supported a resolution calling for the achievement of the party's goals through *political* means.[13] Not once did Mrs. Whitney advocate violent action. She actually *voted against* a radical, militant platform that the Party ultimately adopted. Since the platform advocated violent action, Whitney was charged with belonging to a group that advocated criminal syndicalism, even though Whitney herself never advocated violence.

Saving the First Amendment . . . for Real

In 1969, in the case of *Brandenburg v. Ohio*, the Supreme Court of the United States finally came full circle, and unanimously overturned what was left of *Schenck* and *Whitney*.[14] Clarence Brandenburg, an Ohio Ku Klux Klan leader, was convicted in an Ohio state court under the Ohio Criminal Syndicalism statute of "advocat[ing] . . . the duty, necessity, or propriety of crime, sabotage, violence, or unlawful methods of terrorism as a means of accomplishing industrial or political reform" and of "voluntarily assembl[ing] with any society, group or assemblage of persons formed to teach or advocate doctrines of criminal syndicalism."

Brandenburg conducted a Klan rally in Hamilton County, Ohio, in which members wore hoods, burned a cross, and made several vicious speeches expressing their hatred for nonwhites. As noted in "Lie #3," one participant at Brandenburg's rally actually stated, "Personally, I believe the nigger should be returned to Africa, the Jew returned to Israel." The Klan members also discussed participating in a march on Washington to fight for the white race, and threatened to take "revengence." While the Klan's speech was utterly despicable, a unanimous Court held that the Ohio Act was unconstitutional because it punished "mere advocacy" of unlawful action.

According to the Court, the United States Constitution does not allow the federal government or a state government to proscribe advocacy of the use of force or unlawful action, *"except* where such advocacy is directed to inciting or producing imminent lawless action *and* is likely to incite or produce such action"* (emphases added). This opinion cemented the rule that neither the states nor the federal government can pass laws to silence offensive or inflammatory statements that are not likely to result in imminent lawless action.

The new rule on free speech from and after *Brandenburg*—and still the law today—is that all innocuous speech is absolutely protected, and all speech is innocuous when there is time for more speech to neutralize it before the sought-for result can come about. Therefore, if *Brandenburg* had been applied during World War I, or during America's preoccupation with the evils of Communism, all of the aforementioned cases would have come out differently. Unfortunately, Clarence Schenck, Eugene Debs, Charlotte Whitney, Clarence Waldron, and Robert Goldstein, who spent their adulthood as prisoners for their speech, were dead by the time the Court came to its constitutional fidelity in *Brandenburg*.

Brandenburg is still good law for good reason. As Americans, we are brought up under the impression that we live in a "free country," where we can say whatever we want, with very limited repercussions. *Brandenburg* reestablished this view, while also protecting against unthinking, reflexive violence. The *Brandenburg* decision ensures lively debate on key public issues, but also guarantees exposure to all kinds of opinions, no matter how disgusting or irrational. We do not enjoy hearing about Ku Klux Klan rallies, or any type of hate speech.

Mahmoud Ahmadinejad, the current President of the Islamic Republic of Iran, has called homosexuality an abomination, denied the Holocaust, and hopes someday to blow Israel off the face of the Earth. Nevertheless, Columbia University President Lee C. Bollinger invited Ahmadinejad to speak at his school on September 24th 2007. Bollinger introduced Ahmadinejad as a "petty and cruel dictator," and Ahmadinejad's speech was met with strong opposition from the audience, as well as protestors outside the event. At first, one might ask, "Who would welcome such a lunatic?" Looking back on the event, Bollinger's goal was clear: he wanted to expose his students to Ahmadinejad's views, so as to educate them and show them that such ideas cannot gain much traction in America, but the speaker of them has as much right to advance them as does any other speaker to seek to repel them.

The Court in *Brandenburg* essentially conveyed the same message. That is, all American governments must permit all speech, whether offensive, harmful, incendiary or not, and trust that a consensus of freedom will prevail.

Did You Get the Message?

The government frequently tries to regulate "commercial speech," or speech that proposes a commercial transaction. After deciding that commercial speech is afforded at least some First Amendment protection in *Virginia State Board of Pharmacy v. Virginia Citizens Consumer Council* (1976),[15] the Supreme Court of the United States developed the modern, speech-protective rule governing restrictions on commercial speech in the case of *Central Hudson Gas v. Public Service Commission of New York* (1980).[16] In *Central Hudson Gas*, the Commission issued an order banning electric utility companies from engaging in promotional advertising intended to encourage the use of electricity. The Court invalidated the order, outlining a four-part test used to determine the validity of similar restrictions.

First, the Court determines whether the speech at issue is true and nondeceptive, and whether it promotes a lawful product or service. Second, the Court determines whether the government has a substantial interest in regulating the speech. (How can any government in America have any legitimate, lawful, constitutional, national interest in regulating speech?) Third, the Court determines whether the regulation directly advances the government's interest. Fourth, the Court determines whether the government's restriction is more extensive than necessary to serve the interest. The fourth prong of the test is the most crucial, as it is the most difficult for the government to satisfy.

In *Central Hudson*, the Court found that the ban on *all* promotional advertising was more extensive than necessary, because no exception was made for promotional advertising of electric products that would actually *reduce* total energy use. Furthermore, the Commission did not demonstrate that its interests could be satisfied in a more limited way.

The Supreme Court, in the last twenty years, has used the *Central Hudson* test in a very speech-protective manner. In *Edenfield v. Fane* (1993), the Court bolstered the *Central Hudson* test, placing the burden on the government to demonstrate that its restriction *directly* advances the state's interest.[17] In the case of *44 Liquormart, Inc. v. Rhode Island* (1996), the Court was faced with a Rhode Island statute prohibiting *all* advertising of the price of alcoholic beverages in the State, except for price tags or signs located within liquor stores and not visible from the street.[18] The Court invalidated the statute.

While some of the justices simply held that the law violated the fourth prong of the *Central Hudson* test, Justice Stevens went one step further in his plurality opinion. According to Stevens, "[bans] against truthful, nonmisleading commercial speech [usually] rest solely on the offensive assumption that the public will respond 'irrationally' to the truth."[19] This statement could not be more accurate. The government cannot rob persons from saying whatever they want nor keep information or opinions away from consumers. Why is the government opposed to persons making informed decisions for themselves by recognizing their natural right to think, speak, publish, and hear whatever they wish about whatever they wish?

Unfortunately, the government does not seem to get the message. In *Lorillard Tobacco Co. v. Reilly* (2001), the Massachusetts attorney general issued regulations banning outdoor advertising of tobacco products within one thousand feet of a public playground or elementary or secondary school.[20] The Supreme Court held that the regulations violated the First Amendment. Justice Sandra Day O'Connor delivered the opinion of the Court, in which she conceded that the State has an interest in preventing underage tobacco use, but stated that "[tobacco] retailers and manufacturers have an interest in conveying *truthful information* about their products to adults, and adults have a corresponding interest in receiving truthful information about tobacco products"[21] (emphases added). The requirement of truthful information is antithetical to "Congress shall make no law abridging . . . the freedom of speech." Is the government, which has stolen everything it owns and has lied about everything it does, institutionally capable of ascertaining the truth? Only if the truth will enhance or confirm its power; otherwise, I think not.

Despite Massachusetts' failure to control tobacco use, the federal government found it wise to give similar regulations a shot. On June 22nd 2009, President Barack Obama signed the Family Smoking Prevention and Tobacco Control Act.[22] The word *control* is actually built into the title of the law! The Act restricts retail stores and many forms of print advertising to black-and-white text.[23] In step with the unconstitutional Massachusetts regulations, the Act also bans outdoor advertising within one thousand feet of schools and playgrounds.[24] According to opponents of the law, the ban on outdoor advertising would essentially ban tobacco advertising in many cities.[25] Furthermore, the ban on colorful ads will undoubtedly restrict tobacco companies' communications to adults.[26]

This law is filled with even more First Amendment problems than the regulations in *Lorillard*, and will undoubtedly face constitutional challenges. I have an idea: If the government hates or fears certain speech, why not combat it with more speech rather than making it criminal? If government derives its power from the consent of the governed, and if we the governed cannot ban the speech we hate or fear, how can we authorize the government to do so?

The government also tries to protect its citizens from indecency and nudity. In *Erznoznik v. Jacksonville* (1975), the Supreme Court of the United States struck down a Jacksonville, Florida, ordinance characterizing nudity in films displayed at drive-in movie theaters as a public nuisance.[27] Specifically, the ordinance banned movies "in which the human male or female bare buttocks, human female bare breasts, or human bare pubic areas are shown, if such motion picture[s] [are] visible from any public street or place." Such "selective exclusion" is not only odd, but blatantly reveals the government's attempt to regulate some types of speech "on the ground that they are more offensive than others." According to the Court, these types of restrictions violate the First Amendment. The Court also opined that the Jacksonville ordinance is "over-inclusive" in that it disregarded the context in which the nudity was portrayed. Therefore, the ordinance worked to restrict nonobscene material.

In 1989, the Supreme Court struck down a ridiculous law banning the interstate transmission of "dial-a-porn" services that communicated "indecent" telephone messages.[28] Justice Byron White wrote the opinion of the Court, in which he stated that the government cannot ban messages that individuals must take "affirmative steps" to obtain. Justice White understood the government's interest in protecting children, but reasoned that the federal statute amounts to censorship "limiting the content of adult telephone conversations to that which is suitable for children to hear."[29]

The foregoing examples represent just the tip of the iceberg. Fortunately, however, the Supreme Court has generally resisted government efforts to circumvent the First Amendment and control people.

The "Fairness" Doctrine and Censorship

"Fear of ideas makes us impotent and ineffective."

– Supreme Court Justice William O. Douglas

The so-called Fairness Doctrine debuted in 1949, as a Federal Communications Commission (FCC) rule requiring that licensed broadcast stations discuss public issues and present both sides of any debate.[30] The Doctrine stemmed from the FCC's fear that due to the limited number of radio frequencies available, and the overwhelming number of applications for licenses, broadcasters could simply report a limited number of perspectives, shutting out most other views.[31] The Doctrine worked in tandem with Section 315 of the Communications Act of 1937, which mandated that radio stations offer "equal opportunity" to all legal candidates for specific offices if it permitted one candidate to use its airwaves.[32]

In 1969, the Supreme Court of the United States expressed its approval of the Fairness Doctrine in *Red Lion Broadcasting Co., Inc. v. FCC*, which involved a Pennsylvania radio station that had aired a "Christian Crusade" program attacking author Fred J. Cook.[33] Exercising his right under the Fairness Doctrine, Cook requested time to rebut the program's attacks. Red Lion, however, did not grant Cook's request. The FCC prosecuted Red Lion's infraction, and the Supreme Court upheld the Fairness Doctrine, ruling against the broadcast company.

The Court ruled that it made sense that with the limited

spectrum on which to broadcast, it was only "fair" that stations be obligated to represent both sides of issues. The Fairness Doctrine, however, had the effect of censoring speech because it induced stations to steer clear of controversial topics that may be reported to the FCC.[34] It also *forced* speech, a concept as antithetical to freedom as suppressed speech. As a result, very few stations did opinion pieces, and talk radio was relatively bland.[35]

By the 1980s, with the rise of cable television and the growing number of channels available, many more voices could be heard in the "marketplace of ideas."[36] Seeing little reason to continue the Fairness Doctrine, the FCC, in 1985, issued its "Fairness Report," recognizing the Doctrine's chilling effect on free expression.[37] In 1987, the FCC voted unanimously to cease enforcement of the Doctrine, stating that "[t]he Fairness Doctrine, on its face, violates the First Amendment and contravenes the public interest."[38] So, the government is in essence admitting that it created and implemented an unconstitutional doctrine for *decades* and now it just says, "Oops, my bad"?

Especially now, there is no place for the Fairness Doctrine in talk radio. Today, news and opinions are literally everywhere. There are six cable news stations representing a plethora of political views. The Internet is a treasure trove of information and perspectives. There are hundreds of blogs and news Web sites specifically geared toward every possible political persuasion. In today's world, the Fairness Doctrine also runs contrary to the idea of the "marketplace of ideas." Markets are supposed to be "free," not artificial. "Free" can only mean free from regulation by the government.

The great part about the freedom of expression is that it sparks debate among competing viewpoints without restriction. By forcing a radio station to represent both viewpoints, a station cannot take a solid position on the issues. The Fairness Doctrine essentially dilutes the station's opinions, rather than providing fair coverage.

Furthermore, commercial radio stations are in business to make money; they get no outside funding. They must attract listeners so that they can attract advertisers and turn a profit. If talk radio stations do not give the people what they want, listeners will likely shop elsewhere. Liberals may want to hear conservative viewpoints, and vice versa, but they do not want opposing ideas to drown out their own views. Put another way, a New York Yankee fan may want to know what's going on in Boston, but won't necessarily want to be exposed to Red Sox propaganda on a New York-area radio station.

The First Amendment—which everyone in government has sworn to uphold—mandates that individuals be free to listen as well as free to speak.

It is important to realize the hazardous effects of the Fairness Doctrine and understand that its implementation is violative of the First Amendment and will only weaken the level of debate in this country.

Caution!

Another potential form of censorship, outside of the Fairness Doctrine, is a new bill that President Obama signed into law on October 28th 2009. This law, the Hate Crimes Prevention Act, contains very troubling language.[39] According to the Act:

Whoever transmits in interstate or foreign commerce [radio, TV, Internet] any communication, with the intent to coerce, intimidate, harass, or cause substantial emotional distress to a person, using electronic means to support, severe, repeated, and hostile behavior, shall be fined under this title or imprisoned not more than two years, or both.

This potential law can lead to "thought crimes" committed by radio or television hosts, or even Internet bloggers who are intentionally hostile toward *any* person, but do not actually intimidate or cause substantial emotional distress to the intended audience.

Part of First Amendment doctrine states that speakers cannot be prosecuted because they say things that merely offend people. This law, however, can be used to violate the First Amendment by permitting the federal government to prosecute people for simply *intending* to be offensive. The Hate Crimes Prevention Act can cause disastrous results and seriously restrict the freedom of speech. Victims of hate crimes, as well as potential victims, must be protected, but the protection cannot criminalize offensive speech. *Change the channel, move the dial, boycott the products, but leave speech alone.*

Conclusion

The government has historically attempted to undermine the First Amendment, and it is a foregone conclusion that it will continue to do so. We have learned over the years that Congress *will* abridge the freedom of speech. It is up to the courts and more importantly, we the people, to notice government invasion of this sacred right and to fight to eliminate it.

Lie #6

"The Right of the People to Keep and Bear Arms Shall Not Be Infringed"

After the Constitution of the United States had been enacted and the issue of the Bill of Rights rose to the forefront, the Second Amendment was "passed [by] the House by a voice vote without objection and hardly a debate."[1] The debate that did exist was centered on whether or not the right to keep and bear arms actually needed to be articulated in the Constitution, since many saw it as a natural and thus fundamental right that could not be taken away by any government, absent due process. George Washington called the Second Amendment the teeth that gave the Constitution its bite.

Essentially, the right to keep and bear arms is a restatement of the ancient natural right to self defense; it recognizes not only the right to protect oneself from criminal conduct, but also from a tyrannical state or federal government. That is why the Founding Fathers placed it second in the Bill of Rights, following behind only the right to freedom of expression and worship. And for almost one hundred and fifty years, the federal government did not interfere with this fundamental liberty.

During the early twentieth century, the federal government's benign attitude began to change. The progressives in the federal gov-ernment began to erode this natural right, as they did many others, always with "good reason" for the "safety and security of the people." Their descendants today argue that without gun control the U.S. will turn to anarchy; that, if armed, people will shoot each other on the streets during minor disagreements like traffic disputes. Yet when you ask those who make such claims whether *they* would shoot another person, the response is always, "Well, no; *I* wouldn't do that."

Each time the government creates new laws that regulate and limit our access to firearms, we are one step closer to being a dis-armed and defenseless people, the very state of affairs the Founding Fathers feared and sought to prevent. Yet the government—while obtaining more power for itself—continues to deceive us, claiming that it is not trying to strip the people of the right to bear arms and that anyone can arm herself; she just needs to follow the rules. And it justifies these rules, claiming that guns cause violence and death and that gun control results in lower crime and safer streets.

But one must ask, safer for whom? Safer for the criminals who rob, assault, and rape, all the while knowing that the probability of their victim being armed is slim and thus they do not have to fear a fight that they cannot win? Safer for a tyrant who fears an armed citizenry? Safer as opposed to freer? If things continue this way, lib-erty's tombstone will read, "This was for your own good."[2]

If constitutional guarantees are dependent upon the goodwill or benign intentions or untyrannical nature of future governments, while presently allowing the "good" government slowly to abridge our Second Amendment rights, then the Constitution becomes noth-ing more than a piece of paper, defenseless and easily destructible.[3] And we can listen to those who deride even the mention of the tyrannical and disastrous results of other national disarmaments, claiming, "Not in America" as they roll their eyes.

If the road to hell is paved with good intentions, then the road to tyranny is paved by believing the government. Even if it had the best of such intentions, the government's infringement of the people's right to defend themselves, their homes, their families, and most importantly their liberties, is an asphalt truck paving such a road at an ever-increasing rate.

Shortly after the repeal of Prohibition, the progressives in the federal government decided that we were in need of gun control legislation, and Congress passed the National Firearms Act of 1934. Since Congress recognized that it did not have the authority to regulate guns, it snuck what was in essence the first gun control law through the back door, claiming it as a revenue-raising measure under the taxing power of Congress.

Surprisingly, Congress recognized that it could not ban guns outright, so instead it overtaxed them. This is the reason why until recently the Bureau of Alcohol, Tobacco, and Firearms was under the authority of the Treasury Department. The 1934 Act regulated and taxed the transfer of certain types of firearms and required the registration of such arms[4] and was to be enforced by the Treasury agents who were looking for work due to the happy end of Prohibition. Looking for work, or looking for targets?

Justification for enactment of the legislation centered around the gang wars during Prohibition and especially the Valentine's Day Massacre in Chicago in 1929, when Al Capone had seven of George "Bugs" Moran's men executed with machine guns. The argument, though moot considering that Prohibition was at an end, claimed that if assault weapons had been regulated, then the violence of Prohibition would not have occurred. The gang violence that had proliferated as a result of Prohibition became the perfect excuse for the federal government, but also another of its lies, considering that gang violence slowed to a crawl once Prohibition was repealed.

Did anyone actually believe that mobsters, who stole, maimed, and killed on a daily basis, would hand over their guns because the federal government said they should? Even more egregiously, the 1934 Act regulated other weapons, like short-barreled rifles, which were not associated with any gang activity. But, as usual, once the government was able to gain an inch, it decided to take a mile.

Disarming the Poor

The core of the National Firearms Act was the price people were expected to pay. In order to register a shotgun, payment of a $200 tax was required, an exorbitant amount when considering that it is equal to $3,056.11 at today's values.[5] It is even more excessive when one considers that, according to the Sears catalog in 1938, a *brand-new* shotgun could be purchased for $6.95. So why would anyone in his right mind pay a tax of $200 for a $7.00 gun? It is government theft to place a tax on an item that is greater than the value of the item itself, but even more incredible when the tax is *twenty-eight times* the value of the item. The equivalent theft today would be a tax that forced us to pay $200 to the federal government for a paperback novel or a cheeseburger.

Even more shocking is that the Supreme Court upheld the Act, holding that the $200 tax was a constitutionally valid exercise of the taxing power of Congress. The Court refused to look beyond the face of the Act, which was cited as a revenue raiser, not a prohibitory measure, to condemn it as a regulation of matters beyond the power of Congress.[6]

Stranger still, just a few years earlier, in the *Child Labor Tax Cases*, the Court held that imposing a 10 percent tax on the net profits of employers who employed child laborers was "an act of Congress which clearly, on its face, is designed to penalize and thereby to discourage or suppress, conduct . . . *cannot be sustained* under the federal taxing power by calling the penalty a tax."[7] Was that not the exact intention of the Firearms Act, to regulate and prohibit certain firearms? If charging 10 percent of earnings is considered penalizing, then what else but a penalty is a tax that is more than twenty-eight times the value of the taxed item? The Court apparently did not see this incongruence, noting that the Act did not expressly state the intention to prohibit certain firearms.

And so the government learned that as long as it lied convincingly about its intentions, no matter how unbelievable its claims, and couched the lies in constitutional verbiage, the Court would sanction its actions. And thus began the era of lies and deceit by the government in order to diminish slowly but surely that right the Founding Fathers saw as so fundamental, the right to self-defense.

Supreme Mistake

On the afternoon of June 22nd 1938, Frank Layton and Jack Miller were driving through Arkansas when Treasury agents stopped them. The agents, somewhat bored without booze smugglers to hunt, were hoping to make a bootlegging bust, but encountered a problem when they realized that Miller's truck contained no illicit bootlegging equipment. Fortunately for the agents, all was not in vain, as the two men were in possession of an unregistered sawed-off shotgun, prohibited under the new laws. So, though no violent or criminal acts had been committed by the men, who were carrying Miller's beat-up shotgun for protection as they traveled through lonely back roads, they were summarily arrested.

Unbeknownst to them—and to the joy of the agents—the shotgun was required to be registered under the new "revenue-raising" National Firearms Act. The two men therefore faced substantial fines and up to five years in jail, all for driving across a state border *without* an extra two inches of steel. They faced a long prison sentence for carrying a gun that was *slightly too short*. Of course, even if they had known about the legislation, it is doubtful that Miller and Layton would have registered their weapon, as the price of registration, as we have seen, was astronomical.

The implications of this case and the National Firearms Act on the Second Amendment were not lost on the federal district judge presiding over the criminal case against Miller and Layton in *United States v. Miller*. Dismissing all charges, the judge noted that charging a $200 tax on a $6.95 firearm was so expensive that it was in effect a direct infringement on the Second Amendment right to keep and bear arms. Miller and Layton were freed and continued with their lives, content in the knowledge that their fundamental rights were protected by the courts.

Unfortunately, the federal government was not willing to accept this condemnation of its convoluted legislation and appealed to the United States Supreme Court. When the case reached the Supreme Court, Miller and Layton were not available, while their counsel, having represented them for free, could not spare the expense of further litigation. The result was that neither briefs nor oral arguments were presented on their behalf. This was in itself a shocking result as it is unheard-of for the Supreme Court to hear and consider only one side of a case. But hear it and consider it the Court did.

Undisputed, uncontested, and undeterred, the government was able to argue that firearms with a barrel shorter than sixteen inches were not used in the military, that the Second Amendment only granted protection to arms that were used by the militia, and that the militia could only be armed with weapons used by the military. The government remembered its earlier lesson well, and knew that as long as it lied and lied well, the Court could be seduced. And that is exactly what occurred. The Supreme Court of the United States did not investigate the truth of the statements and accepted each false claim by the government with no scrutiny.[8]

Justice McReynolds simply stated that "certainly it is not within judicial notice that this weapon is any part of the ordinary military equipment or that its use could contribute to the common defense." Of course it was not within judicial notice; how could it have been, when the only people providing information to the Court were law-yers for the federal government? Typically, in order to have a fact be taken into judicial notice, it must be so notoriously well-known that it is almost irrefutable. Yet here, the Court chose to turn the rule on its head, and accept something as fact because no other evidence had been brought to the Court to refute it. The Supreme Court in essence chose to ignore basic rules of evidence and accept an assertion to be fact with no evidentiary presentation and only the contention of the government. And unfortunately, there was no one to object or complain.

With little fanfare, the Supreme Court held that since there was *"no evidence tending to show* the possession or use of a 'shotgun hav-ing a barrel of less than eighteen inches in length' at this time has some reasonable relationship to the preservation or efficiency of a well-regulated militia, we cannot say that the Second Amendment guarantees the right to keep and bear such an instrument." Neither providing a historical analysis of the right to bear arms nor acknowl-edging that a militia historically consisted of a citizenry armed with their own guns rather than those of the military, the Court upheld the constitutionality of the National Firearms Act of 1934. Sadly, the Court's flawed and convoluted reasoning was the precedent that would govern Second Amendment jurisprudence and legisla-tion for almost seventy years.[9]

A Rose by Any Other Name
Would Not Smell as Sweet

The reign of *United States v. Miller* allowed both the state and federal governments to infringe continuously upon the fundamental right of the people to keep and bear arms. In 1968 came the Gun Control Act and the Omnibus Crime Control and Safe Streets Act, which prohibited firearm ownership by certain individuals, including those under eighteen years of age, and most importantly prohibited the private sales of guns between the residents of different states, as well as establishing a national gun licensing system. Of course, the Acts were aptly named, the government having incorporated the most beneficent of motives in the title. Who would not want the streets of their neighborhoods to be safer?

The Acts also created the "sporting use" test, which required that any imported firearms "be generally recognized as particularly suitable for or readily adaptable to sporting purposes, excluding surplus military firearms." The subjectivity of such a test permitted the government to choose what was sport and resulted in a ban on firearms used for popular gun sports not recognized by the law enforcement agencies. Eerily enough, large portions of the Gun Control Act were almost identical to those of the Control Acts of Nazi Germany, which resulted in the disarming of an entire population of Jews.[10]

The Gun Control Act of 1968 spawned a variety of similar state regulations, which resulted in an increasing frequency of rebellious grumblings from those who believed that Second Amendment rights guaranteed to the people were being trampled. As a result, the United States Senate Committee on the Judiciary formed a Subcommittee on the Constitution, which was to examine the rights granted by the Second Amendment.[11] The committee at the time consisted of some very familiar names, including Orrin Hatch,

Bob Dole, Ted Kennedy, and Arlen Specter, as well as the current vice president, Joe Biden. In February 1982, after extensive historical research and hearings, the subcommittee issued its report, and stated that

> the conclusion is thus inescapable that the history, concept and wording of the second amendment to the Constitution of the United States, as well as its interpretation by every major commentator and court in the first half of the century after its ratification, indicates that what is protected is an *individual right of a private citizen to own or carry firearms* in a peaceful manner. [emphases added]

Partially as a result of the remarkable findings of the subcommittee, Congress enacted and President Reagan signed into law the Firearm Owner's Protection Act of 1986, which was billed as an attempt to return back to the people their Second Amendment rights. But of course, as in the past, the claim made by the title of the Act was a falsity. Instead of protecting personal rights, the Act banned the manufacture, transfer, and civilian use of machine guns not manufactured as of the date of the Act; except, of course, for law enforcement officials. The justification was once again that this was for the prevention of violent crime. Even Ronald Reagan, who claimed he believed in the original meaning of the Second Amendment as articulated by the Senate Judiciary Committee's Subcommittee on the Constitution, fell for this.

Of the 175,000 licensed automatic firearms in existence at the time, *none* had been used to commit a violent crime.[12] Considering this information, maybe Reagan should have thought to name the Act more appropriately, rather than being complicit in pulling the wool over the eyes of the people and assaulting their Second Amendment rights.

Federal regulations became more frequent, including an Executive Order by President George H. W. Bush banning the importation of machine guns. Then the Brady Handgun Violence Prevention Act followed five years later, creating a national background check system and requiring a waiting period before a gun could be purchased. Though the Act mandates that all paperwork received by the BATF be automatically destroyed, quite often the BATF will find excuses to keep the records on file for extended periods.[13] Of course, this was another well-crafted title by the government, continuing the deception that its actions were all for our own good, even though no evidence was ever found to illustrate the effectiveness of gun control on violence prevention. Maybe a name like "Make It So Difficult to Get a Gun That No One Does" Act would have been more truthful.

Finally, the federal government gave us the Violent Crime Control Act of 1994, which it actually subtitled with some truth as the Federal Assault Weapons Ban. In essence, this Act was a prohibition on the sale to civilians of specified semiautomatic firearms, which were defined as "assault weapons." The Act designated nineteen weapons by name as assault weapons and then provided a definition of assault weapons that was based on certain combinations of a senseless variety of features.

Especially interesting to note is the fact that while the term "assault weapon" sounds threatening and brings to mind rapid-fire machine guns, in reality "the weapons outlawed by the ban function the same as any semiautomatic and legal hunting rifle. They fire the same bullets at the same speed and produce the same damage. They are simply regular deer rifles that look on the outside like AK-47s."[14] These guns do not fire multiple rounds; only one bullet is ejected each time the trigger is pulled.

The federal government chose to ban weapons on appearance

rather than utility and all under its ever-popular guise of crime control. When the ban was set to expire in 2004, there was a hue and cry by politicians that its expiration would facilitate a bloodbath in the streets. Thankfully, the Act was not extended, and, not surprisingly, nothing happened. The lifting of the ban was heralded by no increase in crime. Rather, a study on the assault weapon ban by the federal government's own Centers for Disease Control and Prevention was unable to find sufficient evidence to illustrate the effectiveness of the ban on violence prevention.

Six months after the ban ended, the FBI reported a 3.6 percent *drop* in violent crime, the first in five years. And those states that continued to have assault weapons bans actually saw the lowest drops in murder rates.[15] Of course, the public is never made aware of these statistics, and the government still claims that we were safer with the ban.

The reason the government continues to get away with these lies and deceptions is the absurd willingness of the people to believe that by disarming the general public and law-abiding persons, we will also effectively disarm criminals. Rational thought dictates the opposite effect: By disarming law-abiding persons, the government effectively gives criminals more firepower for their crimes. Yet a study that cross-referenced the FBI uniform crime report with concealed weapons laws in every state found a very high correlation between laws banning concealed weapons and high crime rates. But it was a different correlation than the government expected, because rather than having lower crime in those areas where gun control was most stringent, there was the opposite effect: The states with the most lawfully concealed weapons had the lowest rates of crime.[16]

Vermont is the state most famous for its permissive gun carry laws, and it has one of the lowest crime rates in the Union. Compare the District of Columbia, with the highest gun murder rate, at almost 57 out of 100,000 persons to a city across the river, Arlington, Virginia. Arlington has much more permissive guns law, but its gun murder rate is 1.6 per every 100,000 persons. One could argue that this is due to a different city landscape, but if it does not prove that access to guns lowers crime, it at least illustrates that gun control does not help lessen crime and violence. And if it cannot do that, then what is its use? Might it have something to do with the lust of those in power to dominate us?

Fewer than 2 percent of handguns and 1 percent of all guns in this country will ever be used to commit a violent crime, so the all-encompassing gun laws aimed at the entire population, when only a small subset of it is involved in crime, is like burning a haystack to get at a needle.[17] On the other hand, it is law-abiding citizens who are often successful in warding off crime, and studies have shown that assailants armed with guns will typically flee when their victim draws a weapon.[18]

Guns are used defensively more than two million times per year, which means that more armed citizens successfully defend themselves and reduce criminal activity each year.[19] Benjamin Franklin once stated that democracy is two wolves and one lamb voting on what to have for dinner, while liberty is a well-armed lamb contesting that vote. Slowly but surely, the lambs are being disarmed while the wolves continue to sharpen their teeth.[20]

But of Course Law Enforcement Officers Deserve to Be Armed

But then we should consider who the wolves in the scenario are. The government looks us in the eyes and tells us that it is acting with our best intentions at heart. There is one name, Ken Ballew, that is not familiar to many of us; but it should be. He is just one example of the atrocities that have been perpetrated during the fraud that is gun control.

On a balmy night in June 1971, Ballew was in the middle of his shower when he heard a banging on his back door as if someone was trying to break it down. Worried about the safety of his live-in girlfriend, who was sleeping in bed, he ran and grabbed his gun and whirled toward the door. At the same time, about twelve men spilled into his home, dressed in ratty clothes and carrying weapons. Naked and terrified, Ballew instinctively drew his weapon up, ready to protect his home and loved one. At that moment, one of the men breaking into his home yelled *"Gun!"* The next thing Ballew knew, he was lying on the ground, bleeding from a gunshot wound to the head while his girlfriend was being dragged from her bed, naked, and thrown into a hallway. Ballew managed to survive but was paralyzed for the rest of his life.[21]

The home invaders were not criminals, but rather a combination of BATF and local law enforcement officials. Ballew was not a hardened criminal who had just committed heinous crimes. Actually, he had not committed any crime at all. Unfortunately for him, a so-called reliable confidential informant provided "information" to the police that Ballew had live hand grenades in his home. Even though the law enforcement officials noted that there were no grenades registered under his name, as required by an obscure provision of the National Firearms Act, the BATF felt that a night raiding party of twelve men was the appropriate reaction. And their reactions led to Ballew's permanent paralysis. Of course, after an investigation, the reality was that all the grenades in Ballew's home were deactivated and so did not have to be registered.

This is just one of the reasons that a subcommittee of the Senate Committee on the Judiciary attacked the Bureau of Alcohol, Tobacco, and Firearms, stating that it was apparent that the "enforcement tactics made possible by current federal firearms laws are *constitutionally, legally and practically reprehensible*" (emphases added). The subcommittee noted that about "75 percent of BATF gun prosecutions were aimed at ordinary citizens who had neither criminal intent nor knowledge, but were enticed by agents into unknowing technical violations. In one case, the Bureau's acting chief admitted that the individual was being prosecuted for completely lawful behavior."[22] Innocent citizens who choose to be prepared to defend themselves often get caught in the cross fire of convoluted and undecipherable legislation.

If you think that it would never happen to you, consider the case of Wanda Boley, a music teacher of twenty-one years. Wanda carried a gun in her car, which was legal in Virginia as long as the weapon was easily visible. Unbeknownst to her, the federal government had recently passed the School Safety Zones Act in 1990, which prohibited weapons near school zones, and which was eventually declared unconstitutional by the Supreme Court. Since she was following Virginia law, her gun was in view of a passerby who reported it to the BATF. Boley was then arrested during the middle of a girl's choir class. Though she had never been violent and had done her best to obey the law, she became a "criminal" facing up to five years in prison.[23] She was initially suspended from her teaching job, but the support she received from students, parents, and the school—combined with an unusually rational district attorney—resulted in a probationary period of six months with good behavior, at which time she was able to return to the school.

The subjectivity of the provisions in the Act granted broad latitude to the BATF to enforce the gun regulations. The Bureau of Alcohol, Tobacco, and Firearms is the chief enforcer of all federal regulations with regard to guns. But, unlike most other enforcement agencies that are under the Department of Justice, the BATF originally began as a part of the Internal Revenue Service, then was shuffled to the Department of Treasury, then the Department of Justice, then back to the IRS, until finally, after the creation of the Department of Homeland Security, it returned to the Department of Justice.

The government's own confusion as to where to place these jack-booted thugs stemmed from its initial lie with regard to the National Firearms Act; that it was a revenue-raising measure, not a means of gun control, and therefore fell under the auspices of the IRS. Yet, if all the gun control regulations are considered revenue-raising measures, why do agents of the BATF raid homes for the most minor of offenses that carry small fines; fines that, if assessed, bring in less revenue than the cost of the raid?

One Small Step Forward: The Right to Bear Arms Is a Fundamental Individual Right

The spawn of gun control regulations at the state and federal levels resulted in a situation in which it was almost impossible for a law-abiding citizen to obtain a handgun permit, even for his own home. The District of Columbia, for example, criminalized the act of having an operational handgun in one's own home. Imagine that, even if you were able to obtain a permit for your firearm, the law in essence prohibited you from being prepared to use it for the constitutional purpose of self-defense. You might have a slim chance to own a handgun legally, but get no chance to use it legally.

One man in the District of Columbia wanted to be able to use his gun. Dick Heller owned his handgun, a 1911 single action Colt .22, bought in 1976. It was the gun from *Gunsmoke*.[24] Unfortunately for Heller, this was the year that the District of Columbia passed its infamous gun ban. Having learned from Germany's past history with gun registration, Heller decided not to register his gun, fearing that it would be confiscated. Soon, Heller began working as a security guard for the Federal Judicial Center. While on the job, he was required to carry a handgun in order to protect himself and his federal workplace. Heller was a federal police officer with a federal license to use his federally issued gun at his federal workplace.

Until 2002, things went along famously. But Heller lived in a high-crime area, and one day he noticed bullet holes in his town house. This motivated him to action, and he decided to request a permit for his Colt. Unfortunately, his *"Gunsmoke"* weapon was no longer acceptable. Rather, the gun, because it was a bottom-loading gun, was banned from being possessed or registered. If Heller, a certified law enforcement officer, could not obtain a permit, what chance would anyone else have? Heller decided that this was not a state of affairs he was willing to live with and began a fight to regain his Second Amendment rights.

Heller filed a lawsuit in 2003, along with five other residents of Washington, D.C., who were fed up with the local government's total infringement of their constitutional right.

The result of this lawsuit was the United States Supreme Court decision in *District of Columbia v. Heller*. A majority of the court dispelled the myth of the Second Amendment as a collective right and held that the right to bear arms is an individual and fundamental right. The court noted that the right is a fundamental (natural) right, stating that "[t]his is not a right granted by the Constitution. Neither is it in any manner dependent upon that instrument for its existence." Through this statement, the Court recognized the right to keep and bear arms as a natural and therefore fundamental right.

In its opinion, the Court analyzed each of the clauses in the Second Amendment separately and determined that "the right of the people" meant that the right belonged to the individual, like those enumerated in the First and Fourth Amendments. "To keep and bear arms" was held to mean "the carrying of the weapon . . . for the purpose of offensive or defensive action." The Court therefore determined that the D.C. handgun ban was an infringement of the natural, constitutionally protected right of self-defense, and struck down the requirement that a gun be disassembled and inoperable in one's own home.

One Giant Leap Back: A Fundamental Right *Can* Be Infringed

As much as the *Heller* decision has been celebrated for its long-sought-for conclusion that the right to keep and bear arms is an individual and fundamental right, there is also a huge gap in its protection. That gap is the fact that the Court, while giving pages of analysis on each separate clause of the Second Amendment, almost completely ignored the most crucial, the phrase "shall not be infringed." One would think that is because this phrase, above all the others, is the most self-explanatory. Rather than "should not" or other statements that would portend that the Founding Fathers wanted to give the federal government some leeway within this right, the words used are "shall not." "Shall not" does not mean "should not"; it means that the right *cannot*, for any reason, be infringed by any government without due process. The Court did not grant this phrase any analysis, noting only that "*of course* the right was not unlimited" (emphases added) and that the Second Amendment did not "protect the right of citizens to carry arms for any sort of confrontation." The statements made by the Court focused on the idea that certain types of weapons were not protected.

As well, the Court determined only the right to carry guns in the home, noting that the case did not "cast doubt on longstanding . . . laws forbidding the carrying of firearms in sensitive places such as schools or government buildings." But it also protects only certain weapons, not overruling *Miller* but modifying it to mean that "the Second Amendment does not protect those weapons not typically possessed by law abiding citizens for lawful purposes." *Miller* had held that the Second Amendment only protected the ownership and possession of weapons typically possessed by the military. But without an exhaustive analysis or an objective standard under which to judge whether or not a law infringes on the Second Amendment, the Court has left open the door for any government to continue its infringement. By not addressing the standard of review to be applied by courts to gun laws, the Court has left open the door for lower courts to decide each case as they feel, not as the Constitution requires.

At the moment, then, the state need only argue *at most* that the law passes strict scrutiny. The strict scrutiny standard essentially means that any law the government wants to pass that infringes on a constitutional right must affirmatively and effectively serve a compelling government interest by the least restrictive means. Anytime the court analyzes a law under strict scrutiny, there are three steps to ensuring that it passes constitutional muster: First, the law must be justified by a compelling government interest, which means that it is an interest that the government needs to maintain in order for it to deliver government services to people in its jurisdictions. For example, courts have held that maintaining a stable political system, protecting voters from confusion, undue influence and intimidation, and preventing vote-buying are all compelling state interests.

Second, the law must be narrowly tailored to achieve that interest, which means that it cannot be too broad, thereby affecting more people and rights than is required, or too narrow, meaning that it does not address all that the so-called compelling interest requires. The government has to prove to the court that the law actually advances the compelling interest, without being too broad or too narrow. It cannot restrict anything outside the purview of the interest or not restrict those areas that should be restricted in order to further the interest.

Third, the law must use the least restrictive means possible. It must be the least restrictive and least burdensome on those it affects. For example, the government cannot choose to pass a curfew law requiring all persons to be home by six o'clock because it wants to prevent the criminal activity of a few at night.

Given that public safety and therefore crime prevention are classified as a compelling state interest, and since the correlation between gun control and crime reduction has been *incorrectly* accepted as truth, then very few gun regulations will be overturned even when analyzed under the strict scrutiny standard; especially when the government can *lie* and argue that disarming the citizens will result in a lower violent crime rate. This is not the way that our most fundamental rights should be protected. The only way to ensure the protection of the *fundamental right to self-defense* is to require a higher standard, enunciated by the Supreme Court in some notable First Amendment cases, which prohibits the government from impairing such fundamental liberties absent "a need to further a state interest of *the highest order.*"[25]

Developed, though never precisely defined, in a series of opinions by Chief Justice Warren Burger and Justice Thurgood Marshall throughout the 1970s and 1980s, the use of this standard of review illustrated that the Court required that any impairment of the fundamental right to free speech by the government would have to be justified by only the highest of state interests and applied in the most narrowly possible fashion to the successful accomplishment of that interest. Generally, only the preservation of a free society was found by the Court to be of the highest state interest. Therefore, only those gun regulations that would be *vital* to uphold a free society would be upheld. Those would be the most highly rational laws, such as ensuring that violent felons do not possess weapons, which had factual bases, and for which regulations the government would not need to use deception to ensure their passage. But the idea of making it difficult for everyone to defend himself or requiring that the government know—via registration—who could defend himself, is the stuff of which tyrannies are made.

And, Don't Worry,
the State Can Still Take Away Your Rights

The *Heller* decision has another loophole that the Court avoided; that is whether or not the Second Amendment protections apply against only the federal or also against the state governments. While some lower state courts state that the Second Amendment protects the people of that state from both federal and state infringement, the majority of the courts hold that the Second Amendment protects the individual only from federal action and the states can do whatever they want. The problem is that, if the Second Amendment does not protect the people from state action, then in effect, the Second Amendment means nothing at all. There is a reason why almost all of the provisions of the Bill of Rights have been held to apply to the states.

Imagine if California decided to force Wicca on the people as the religion of choice, and all other religions would be banned. Would it really matter that this was not a federal regulation? This is why the majority of the amendments have been applied against the states by the Supreme Court. This is true of the First Amendment, even though it states that "*Congress* shall make no law . . ." Given that the Second Amendment simply says that "the right of the people shall not be infringed," containing no explicit mention of which government is prohibited from infringing, it should be an even stronger candidate for its application against state infringement. This is especially true since none of the *Heller* justices, not even those dissenting, endorsed the "states' rights" approach.

The Supreme Court in *Heller* noted that the right to keep and bear arms was not dependent upon the Constitution for its existence and therefore was a natural right that neither the state nor federal government has a right to infringe without due process. Natural Law teaches that there are certain rights and freedoms that are not granted to us by the government but rather come from human nature. Since these rights do not come from the government, the government cannot take them away. For example, the government cannot declare that all people must worship one god and that worshipping any other god is unlawful. The freedom of religion is a natural right and therefore no government can take that right away, absent due process.

If the government does try to take a natural right away, an independent judiciary can step in and protect the individual. It is therefore important to remember that if the government attempts to usurp a right that derives from nature—like the right of self-defense—we are protected from the government by the courts, which have the ability and the duty to prevent the government from such an attempt. The court must enforce the Natural Law and ensure that it is not taken away without procedural due process.

Like Natural Law, when the Constitution grants us certain rights and states that those rights cannot be infringed, this means that the government cannot take away those rights without due process of law. "Due process" is a term used in both the Fifth and Fourteenth Amendments. The Fifth states that "no person shall be . . . deprived of life, liberty or property, without due process of law." The Fourteenth Amendment states, "nor shall any *State* deprive any person of life, liberty, or property, without due process of law" (emphasis added).

In essence, both these amendments require that any deprivations of rights inherent in our humanity or directly protected by the Constitution cannot be taken away by any government without, at the least, a notice to the person of charges or proceedings, a hearing at which the person may speak and that is presided over by an impartial judge and a neutral jury; basically, a fair jury trial. It was the Fourteenth Amendment Due Process Clause that the Supreme Court used in order to incorporate most of the Bill of Rights against the states in a series of decisions.

Unfortunately, rather than incorporating the entire Bill of Rights in one round, the Supreme Court used a case-by-case basis to decree that each Amendment protects the people from state governments. This resulted in almost, but not all, of the first eight amendments being applied against the states. The Supreme Court never issued a decision that expressly incorporated the Second Amendment to the states, until *Heller*.

This loophole in *Heller* has garnered notice, and the Supreme Court recently agreed to hear an appeal of *NRA v. Chicago*, which is a case involving a local ban on handguns in the City of Chicago. The lower court held that the Second Amendment did not apply to the states unless it was directly incorporated by the Supreme Court. In a similar case, *Maloney v Cuomo*, the court held that *Heller*, and therefore the Second Amendment, was only applicable to the federal government and that therefore the states were allowed to infringe on the Constitutional right to keep and bear arms.[26] The *Maloney* court erroneously stated that "it is settled law . . . that the Second Amendment applies only to limitations the Federal government seeks to impose on this right."

To back up its phony settled-law argument, the *Maloney* court utilized *Presser v. Illinois*, which is Supreme Court precedent from 1886. This was a case decided far before the Supreme Court developed the incorporation doctrine, and therefore, as the *Heller* court noted, "did not engage in the sort of Fourteenth Amendment inquiry required by our later cases." The *Maloney* court, desperate to preserve its own political agenda, utilized a translucent shield to protect this agenda. Courts rarely use precedent that is over 120 years old, which has not been ratified in later decisions and laws. For example, a court would never think to use the analysis from one hundred years before *Miranda* to determine whether a confession was properly obtained. Or if it tried, the outcry would be deafening. This is what the *Maloney* court did. The Supreme Court will hear an appeal of *Maloney* as well.

Is this what the Founding Fathers imagined when they wrote the Bill of Rights, that the people's rights to defend themselves against a tyrannical government applied only as to the federal government, and the state could be as tyrannical as it wanted? To be fair, there is only one sensible reading of *Heller* on the question of whether the Second Amendment restrains only the federal government, or all governments. By writing that *the* right to keep and bear arms, like *the* freedom of speech, precedes the existence of the United States, by characterizing it as "ancient," and by describing its use against tyrants throughout history, the Supreme Court found and declared that the individual right to keep and bear arms is "fundamental" (meaning natural, not government created) and thus is immune from *all* government interference, absent a state interest of the highest order and due process.

Historical Ignorance Is Not Bliss

The philosopher Santayana once said that those who do not learn from history are doomed to repeat it. And it seems that we have not learned from history and we shall let the government lie to us once again. Currently there is a hue and cry about renewing the assault weapons ban that expired in 2004. In 2007, Rep. Carolyn McCarthy (D-NY), a strong supporter of renewing the Assault Weapons Ban, spoke of the mass murders at Virginia Tech and Columbine High School to justify the need for a ban on high-capacity assault rifles. The guns used in those tragic events were not assault weapons, but a legal variety of firearm. Yet, the government will lie and lie again to serve its own ends until the general public supinely believes it. One should consider what the result would have been if one student present at either of these massacres had firearms training and was able to carry a weapon to take down the killers. How many lives would have been saved?

President Obama has stated that he "has seen the impact of fully automatic weapons in the hand of criminals . . . [and] [t]hus supports making permanent the expired federal Assault Weapons Ban. These weapons such as AK-47s belong on foreign battlefields and not on our streets. These are also not weapons that are used by hunters and sportsmen." Such a short statement, yet so full of either mistaken beliefs or continuing government fraud.

As John Lott points out: First, the Assault Weapons Ban did not, as discussed, ban fully automatic weapons; second, the firing mechanisms banned are the exact same as those in the semiautomatic weapons used by hunters and sportsmen. Third and foremost, the percentage of deaths attributed to fully automatic weapons is so miniscule that no person could attribute them to the high murder rate of any city.[27] As should be clear, we do not know any better and we have not learned that governments, no matter from which party, are adept at deception.

Since, as noted earlier, there is no evidence that an assault weapons ban reduced crime in the United States, even when the research was compiled by bureaucrats in the Clinton administration who were assuredly searching hard, the federal government recently attempted to reinstate the assault weapons ban, this time claiming that it "will have a positive impact in Mexico, at a minimum."[28] In *Mexico*? Apparently, even though the expiration of the ban has not had an effect on overall violent crime rates in the United States, Attorney General Eric Holder feels that new laws in this country will help cure Mexico of its gun violence, even though we have not through our drug laws managed to cure it of its drug problems. And the basis of this lie is that more than 7,700 guns sold in the U.S. have been traced to Mexico.

What no one has determined is the number of those guns falling under the Assault Weapons Ban.[29] Yet the government throws the statistic out to the public, holding it to represent something that they do not know it does. But why question that; as long as we buy the lies and create scapegoats of American gun owners, does it really matter what the truth is? Apparently, not to the government.

Conclusion

Some would argue that registration and licensing weapons are not really infringements, but would anyone seriously argue that citizens must register with the police and obtain a license in order to exercise freely their political or religious beliefs? What would happen if the government attempted to force people to register or obtain a permit if they object to unreasonable searches and seizures? Once this dichotomy is noted, a rational person will never resort to such an argument again to justify disparate treatment of the right to bear arms.[30]

Noah Webster once said that "before a standing army can rule, the people must be disarmed as they are in almost every kingdom in

Europe. The supreme power in America cannot enforce unjust laws by the sword because the whole body of the people are armed." The gun bans and registration laws have in effect continued the transfer of power from the people, as envisioned by the Founding Fathers, to the government, progressively walking toward an end where the people will be helpless and the government all-powerful. Why would the government not take the opportunity to disarm us, while espousing the lies that it is not disarmament, that we continue to have a right to keep and bear arms, and that any regulations are only to ensure our safety?

If after reading this, you are too disturbed by the fact that the government can dictate whether or not you choose to protect yourself, then you may want to stop here. The lies the government tells you, about safety, security, liberty, and privacy are only going to get more unbelievable, including the fact that the government cannot only prevent you from receiving medical life-saving measures but also force you to ingest items you would otherwise refuse.

Lie #7

"Your Body Is Your Temple"

If we do not have control over our own bodies, we have control over little else. If anything belongs to us, reason would tell us that the thing we enter into and leave this world with—our body—belongs to *each of us*. Everything we do, our thoughts, our speech, our movements, and all physical action, come from our bodies. Therefore, having control over our bodies is one of the most fundamental rights we can possess.

In *The Libertarian Manifesto*, Professor Murray Rothbard argues:

> The case against outlawing narcotic and hallucinogenic drugs is far weaker than the case against Prohibition, an experiment which the grisly era of the 1920s has hopefully discredited for all time. For while narcotics are undoubtedly more harmful than is alcohol, the latter can also be harmful, and outlawing something because it may harm the user leads straight down the logical garden path to our totalitarian cage, where people are prohibited from eating candy and are forced to eat yogurt "for their own good."[1]

This totalitarian cage Rothbard described is already looming on the horizon. And some cages are already here.

The Oreo Police

In late 2006, New York City established laws banning trans fat, a type of unsaturated fat, from all city restaurants, as well as creating a requirement that fast-food restaurants post calorie counts alongside menus and other food offerings. Subsequently, several other governments have passed similar legislation, including the entire State of California, several Massachusetts cities, and some upstate counties in New York. Trans fat has been linked to heart disease and was commonly used to prepare fried and baked foods.

While many of us would agree that foods laden with trans fats are not a healthy option and should not be consumed in large quantities, shouldn't *we* be able to make that choice? Decisions about what we feed our children and ourselves are exceptionally personal and certainly should not be subject to government paternalism. These policies treat Americans as babies who cannot be trusted to make decisions regarding what goes into their own mouths and the mouths of their children. This government-knows-best attitude is nowhere grounded in the Constitution and is profoundly offensive to the Natural Law. So while it may seem that we are free to eat what we want, the government is duping us by taking many food choices off of shelves and menus or adversely influencing our choices. Like parents hiding Halloween candy from their child, the government is hiding choices from us. Except, we're not children and the government has no lawful authority to act as our parent.

Besides stripping us of our rights, do these health-police food policies even make us healthier? Learning to choose healthful foods amidst other choices is one of the ways people learn to take care of themselves. By eliminating variety, it may lead people to believe that they no longer need to be vigilant or even responsible in making decisions about what goes into their bodies. Why bother, when you can have the government do that instead? In taking away foods that contain trans fat, the government is not making the store shelves "safe" but it could create that mistaken impression in the minds of some consumers; there are still plenty of foods out there that could have a detrimental effect on a person's health. Indeed, countless food items and behaviors could have an injurious effect on your health if you never learn moderation.

The health police want to destroy your freedom of choice, and their tactics are not likely to improve health. Even the *New York Times* has a problem with all this. A December 2008 *Times* article argued that the "health halo" created by trans fat–free foods and other types of foods that claim to be more healthful are actually helping to keep us fat.[2] The theory goes that because we think that foods are made more healthful through these policies, we let our guard down and tend to eat more. Consequently, we don't actually become thinner or healthier as a result of these policies that cost taxpayers loads of money, deprive us of our rights, and make insulting assumptions about our decision-making abilities.

Health policies like the trans fat ban can work to put small mom-and-pop stores out of business. When the trans fat ban was first proposed, much of the opposition came from small business owners who would be required to do extra clerical work and spend money in the conversion process. Restaurants and bakeries also had to figure out how to re-create many of their recipes to make them taste good without the use of these fats. For instance, Stuart Zaro, president of Zaro's Bakery in New York, revealed that there was about a 20 percent increase in the cost of baking without trans fats. Additionally, bakeries are now forced to fill out sheets detailing the ingredients used in preparation of the food. As the economy worsens, we need to ask whether these policies causing many small local businesses and national chains to spend large amounts of money are really helping anyone.[3]

Also questionable is whether government interference was even needed to curb consumer use of trans fats since in recent years many companies and restaurants have been cutting down on or eliminating the use of trans fats due to consumer demand. It turns out that many Americans already knew to avoid trans fat–laden foods even before the government forced us to stop eating them.

The government's paternalistic nature toward its people is in no danger. The Obama administration appears to be moving full steam ahead in this government-knows-best direction. In May 2009, for instance, President Obama appointed Thomas Frieden, M.D., as director of the U.S. Centers for Disease Control and Prevention.[4] Dr. Frieden is the former New York City Health Commissioner, and held that post when New York City established the bans on trans fats and smoking in bars and restaurants.

On June 22nd 2009, President Obama signed the Family Smoking Prevention and Tobacco Control Act, which gives the Food and Drug Administration (FDA) the power to regulate the tobacco industry. The Act gives the FDA the power to regulate tobacco ingredients, cap nicotine levels, and control advertising.[5] In fact, regular cigarettes, cigars, and chewing tobacco are the only tobacco products off-limits to the FDA.[6] Unfortunately, we have learned over the years that when Congress grants virtually unlimited power to government agencies, they feel a pressing need to use it in the most foolish, yet ambitious ways possible.

On September 22nd 2009, the FDA exercised its authority under the Act and banned the sale of flavored cigarettes. The FDA argued that these products attract children and teenagers to smoking, and act as a gateway for young people to become habitual smokers.[7] Like the trans fat ban, this regulation removes individual choice and treats us like morons. In addition, it absolutely will not work to decrease teenage smoking or smoking-related deaths. The folks at the FDA *must* realize this fact; if they don't, they might be more dim-witted than we originally thought. Advertising is at the core of the tobacco industry's success. The industry revolves around recruiting new smokers. We're dealing with an industry that has succeeded despite the fact that its products slowly kill people! Banning flavored cigarettes doesn't put a dent in big tobacco's armor; rather, it's just another challenge. Should the government ban tobacco advertising? Ban tobacco? Or just stay out and let people make free choices?

Criminalizing Marijuana

Many of the Founding Fathers, including George Washington and Thomas Jefferson, cultivated hemp, the plant from which marijuana is derived.[8] In the late eighteenth century, many medical journals recommended the use of hemp seeds and roots for treating sexually transmitted diseases, inflamed skin, and incontinence.[9] Unfortunately, a change in our attitude toward drugs came in the nineteenth century, when a noticeable number of Americans became unknowingly addicted to morphine.

Although there was an attitude of concern about drug use, it took some time for the country to criminalize it. By 1937, marijuana was outlawed in twenty-three states, mostly in an effort to stop former morphine addicts from starting to use a new drug or as a backlash against newly arrived Mexican immigrants who sometimes brought the drug to the United States with them.[10] On October 1st 1937, under President Franklin Roosevelt, the Marijuana Tax Act went into effect, which imposed a prohibitive tax on the "evil" drug. Congress held just two hearings on the law, which was introduced by Rep. Robert L. Doughton of North Carolina. Harry Anslinger, arguing for the tax, stated to the House Ways and Means Committee that "traffic in marijuana is increasing to such an extent that it has come to be the cause for the greatest national concern. . . . This drug is entirely the monster Hyde, the harmful effect of which cannot be measured."

In addition, two veterinarians testified that dogs (not people, but *dogs*) do not respond well to marijuana. One of the vets stated, "Over a period of six months or a year (of exposure to marijuana) . . . the animal must be discarded because it is no longer serviceable." The testimony for the tax, as you may have concluded, was far from convincing. Furthermore, the committee rejected testimony from the American Medical Association, which pointed out the government's lack of evidence of harm to humans.

Just three months after Representative Doughton introduced the bill, in June 1937, the House passed it. One congressman commented on the bill, stating that it had "something to do with something that is called marijuana. I believe it is a narcotic of some kind."[11] In 1970, Congress passed the Controlled Substances Act, a comprehensive law regulating a myriad of controlled substances. It banned all marijuana outright.

In addition to prohibiting drugs for recreational use, the government has also criminalized the use of marijuana for medical use. In *Gonzales v. Raich* (2005), the Supreme Court decided that Angel Raich and Diane Monson could not use physician-prescribed medical marijuana to relieve their serious medical conditions. Raich and Monson had relied on cannabis treatments for many years. In fact, Raich's physician believed that ending such treatments "would certainly cause Raich excruciating pain and could very well prove fatal."[12] Nevertheless, federal agents entered Monson's house to take and destroy her six marijuana plants, despite the fact that both women were residents of California, which has authorized the use of medical marijuana since 1996. California law arguably conflicts with the Controlled Substances Act of 1970, the federal law that makes the "manufacture, distribution, and possession of marijuana" illegal, and makes no exception for medical use.

In a downright bizarre majority opinion, written by Justice John Paul Stevens, the Court held, 6 to 3, that the Commerce Clause (which was written to authorize Congress to keep commerce between the states regular, not to prohibit it) permits Congress to control marijuana, a substance that cannot legally enter the stream of commerce. In ruling for the government, the majority likened this case to the ridiculous case of *Wickard v. Filburn*, in which the Court concluded that the federal government could regulate the wheat a farmer grows for personal use. *Raich* does the seemingly impossible, as it *extends* the Court's decision in *Wickard* and wins the award for the most ludicrous adaptation of the Commerce Clause in American history. The Court stated that not only can the government regulate items harvested for personal use (the marijuana grown in *Raich* and the wheat grown in *Wickard*); it can regulate, through its power to control interstate commerce, something that can't even legally be bought or sold!

Unfortunately, the Commerce Clause has become the tool through which Congress wields virtually unlimited power. Based on Supreme Court precedent, the Court in *Raich* stated that the Commerce Clause permits Congress to regulate activities that "substantially affect interstate commerce." Furthermore, as the Court puts it, Congress need not "legislate with scientific exactitude,"[13] nor make any kind of particularized findings supporting its conclusions. The idea that it is not beyond the realm of possibility that Raich's medical marijuana would find itself in the stream of commerce was good enough for the Supreme Court to side with the government, as if women growing small amounts of marijuana in their own home for their own medical use ever have a chance of affecting commerce whatsoever.

Only Justice Clarence Thomas's dissent made sense. According to Justice Thomas:

> Diane Monson and Angel Raich use marijuana that has never been bought or sold, that has never crossed state lines, and that has no demonstrable effect on the national market for marijuana. If Congress can regulate this under the Commerce Clause, then it can regulate virtually anything—and the Federal Government is no longer one of limited and enumerated powers . . . *By holding that Congress may regulate activity that is neither interstate nor commerce under the [Interstate] Commerce Clause, the Court abandons any attempts to enforce the Constitution's limits on federal power.*[14] (emphases added)

Beyond Justice Thomas's eloquent defense of the Constitution, there is the Natural Law argument that if Diane Monson and Angel Raich thought using marijuana would help their chronic pain, who is the government to stop them? Even if there may be certain personal health risks involved in smoking marijuana, there are certain pain-relief benefits that Monson and Raich value over any possible risks. These are decisions for individuals and not the federal government to make. Just as the right to privacy lets a farmer grow as much wheat and bake and consume as much bread as he wishes, it also keeps the federal government out of the decision-making process for physicians and their patients.

Here is what the Court has done: It has prohibited the government from intruding upon the patient-physician relationship if the government wants to save the life of a baby in a mother's womb, but has permitted the government to intrude on the marital relationship between a farmer and wife and the patient-physician relationship if they are growing too much wheat or using any marijuana.

Moreover, the revived use of the Commerce Clause power for everything under the sun is a particularly scary exercise of government power because it seems the Clause can be stretched to cover basically any activity, commercial or noncommercial, interstate or intrastate.

The *Raich* case also unearths a battle between the states and the federal government regarding the use of medical marijuana. In 1996, voters in California voted for Proposition 215 (the Compassionate Use Act), which authorized use of medical marijuana. But, the high and mighty feds did not seem to take this vote into consideration. *Raich* proves that the *state's rights* don't matter, that the *people's rights* to make personal decisions don't matter; we all need to bow at the throne of federal authority, apparently. Here, the government's falsehood is once again, we can choose what to do with our own bodies. In truth, the government does not even allow individuals to make choices regarding their bodies when their home state and their physicians *expressly* permit them to make those choices.

The problematic nature of this clash between the state and federal governments is well illustrated by a June 2009 medical marijuana case. Charles Lynch operated a medical marijuana dispensary in Morro Bay, California, where people would bring medical marijuana prescriptions from California physicians. Lynch's business was run like any other pharmacy, not some type of covert drug operation. He held a grand opening in 2006, used signs to advertise, obtained a business license from the City of Morro Bay, and ran surveillance cameras for security. Yet, his business was raided by federal Drug Enforcement Administration agents eleven months after opening. Lynch was sentenced to a year and a day in prison by a federal judge, even though he could have been sentenced to up to twenty years in federal prison based on the large amount of marijuana involved.

Although the sentence was considered quite short in light of federal standards, it is a long time to spend in prison for doing something that was perfectly legal within his state. This state vs. federal government battle is bound to become more of an issue as several States are pushing for legislation similar to California's. In the meantime, the only thing going up in smoke is the fundamental right to control what goes into our own bodies.

The Right to Life

If you were diagnosed with a rare disease and had only a few months to live, would you try an experimental drug that may save your life? Would you like the choice to do so? Too bad; your government won't let you.

In addition to prohibiting people from easing their pain with medical marijuana and growing wheat for their own consumption, the federal government's red tape often makes it difficult for people who are dying to access potentially lifesaving drugs. The FDA's approval process is painfully long (the average time from lab to shelf is about twelve years),[15] and in the meantime people are dying.

Under the current system, a medication must pass three stages of clinical tests before it gets FDA approval. In each phase, the drug is taken by a limited number of people so as to ascertain its effects. Yet, it is often difficult for sick people to gain access to these trials, and only a restricted number of people are allowed to try the drugs. If the drug passes all three phases of testing, the pharmaceutical company marketing it must file an application formally asking for the FDA's approval to promote the drug. You can imagine how frustrating this process must be for those who have only a limited amount of time to live. One article asks, "If they are on the verge of dying, terminally [ill] patients argue, how is it ethical to deny them the only remaining chance they may have to recover or, at the very least, suffer less or live just a bit longer?"[16]

Although a limited number of people are able to use experimental drugs through clinical trials, it seems as though getting into these trials is a matter of luck more than anything else: "Many people with life-threatening diseases cannot find appropriate clinical trials, live far from research centers or do not meet eligibility criteria to participate in the trials. Additionally, doctors are 'lost in the bureaucratic mess of paperwork' when they attempt to access the FDA's programs designed to widen opportunities for the severely ill."[17] Clearly, this is another instance of government paternalism. As long as patients understand that there are risks involved in taking experimental treatments, they should be able to make their own life or death decisions.

John Gotschall, a municipal worker in Baltimore, Maryland, discovered he had brain cancer after suffering a seizure at the wheel of his car, which caused him to drive into a snowbank. At forty-four years old, after being diagnosed and told that he had only a few months to live, Gotschall qualified for a clinical treatment trial. The treatment worked, and his tumor vanished almost immediately. While this is a tremendously happy ending for Gotschall, the treatment was still not available to the public *ten years after it saved his life*. Many people have undoubtedly died, and will die, without ever being given this treatment option.[18]

There are many heart-wrenching stories about people who have lost not only their right to make decisions about their health, *but their lives*, as a result of the FDA's policies. David Baxter, a high school student from Woodland, California,[19] who was diagnosed with colon cancer, was prohibited from an experimental drug trial because, at age seventeen, he was too young to qualify. He never lived to see his eighteenth birthday.[20]

Alita Randazzo, another colon cancer patient, was told that her last hope for survival was the experimental drug Erbitux. When she tried to qualify for a trial of Erbitux, she was told the trial had closed. Randazzo died in 2002 without ever being able to take the drug.[21]

The Abigail Alliance for Better Access to Developmental Drugs is an organization founded in 2001, after twenty-one-year-old Abigail Burroughs's death. Burrough, a native of Fredericksburg, Virginia, died while trying to get access to experimental treatments for her cancer of the head and neck. Abigail's father, Frank Burroughs, has continued her fight through the Abigail Alliance. The group's goal is to change the FDA's rigid, anti-personal-choice system so that patients and their physicians have the right to choose between dying untreated and taking experimental drugs.

In 2006, in the case of *Abigail Alliance v. von Eschenbach*,[22] the U.S. Court of Appeals for the District of Columbia Circuit held that terminally ill patients had a due process right to experimental, but potentially lifesaving drugs. In the court's opinion, Judge Janice W. Rogers wrote, "A right of control over one's body has deep roots in the common law.[23] . . . The prerogative asserted by the FDA . . . impinges upon an individual liberty deeply rooted in our Nation's history and tradition of self-preservation."[24] The phrases "deep roots in the common law" and "tradition of self-preservation" mean that the right to control your own body preceded the existence of the United States; hence it is a fundamental—or natural—right.

The FDA, however, requested that the entire D.C. Circuit, rather than a three-judge panel, rehear the case. The Circuit complied, and ruled 8 to 2 against the Abigail Alliance. The Abigail Alliance appealed, but the U.S. Supreme Court declined to hear the case. The government deception, upheld through the Supreme Court's refusal to hear the case, displays the Court's sheer disrespect for fundamental rights that are protected by the Constitution and inherent in our humanity.

Here's an interesting tidbit: Three States—Montana, Oregon, and Washington—permit physicians to assist patients in ending their lives. The FDA, however, has made it nearly impossible for us to get experimental drugs when we want to *save* our lives. If the laws in some states let you *kill yourself*, how can the federal government not let you *cure yourself*?

Who's in Charge Here?

While one aspect of paternalism involves the government prohibiting individuals from putting certain foods and substances into their bodies, we are also infantilized when the government forces medical treatments upon us. This form of paternalism extends well beyond the important issue of being able to control your own body, as it often interferes with religious freedom as well.

In May 2009, FBI officials spent Memorial Day weekend frantically searching Southern California and New Mexico. Were they in search of a dangerous criminal? No. A terrorist? Guess again. They were trying to hunt down a thirteen-year-old boy diagnosed with Hodgkin's lymphoma, a type of cancer. The boy, Daniel Hauser, and his mother fled from their Minnesota town after a local judge ordered Daniel Hauser's parents to consent to chemotherapy treatment for Daniel. Eventually, Daniel and his parents obeyed the court order, and he underwent chemotherapy.

Daniel Hauser and his parents are part of a Native-American religion called Nemenhah, in which the belief in natural treatments and remedies is prevalent. Yet, the reasoning behind their refusal of the treatment is much less important than the issue surrounding it. Although Hodgkin's lymphoma is a highly treatable form of cancer, chemotherapy is also a very painful, sickening, and difficult treatment.[25] In fact, it is no treatment at all. It delays and arrests cancer. It does not and cannot cure the patient of cancer.

No matter the reasoning behind the refusal, the idea that the government could force us into a treatment is very scary. It is Daniel Hauser—not the government—who will be subjected to these treatments and who will suffer from all the nausea and other side effects that result from chemotherapy that he had freely chosen to reject. And it is not as though Hauser can use medical marijuana (which many physicians believe helps ease the side effects of chemotherapy), because, as we have seen, the government prohibits that, too.

Since beginning chemotherapy, it has been reported that Hauser's tumor has shrunk significantly. While she is still skeptical of chemo's effect on the body, Daniel's mother, Colleen, has commented that "something's working." Yet, Daniel is angry about being forced into the treatment and has said, "I get really sick when I do it . . . You get so dizzy and I get a headache right away."[26]

Hauser's story sounds remarkably similar to that of Billy Best, a sixteen-year-old from a small town twenty miles southwest of Boston, Massachusetts. Billy ran away from home to avoid cancer treatment. He returned only after his parents consented to the alternative treatments that Billy desired. In 1994, a court ruled in favor of Billy, allowing him to pursue alternative treatments. He eventually overcame his cancer without chemotherapy or radiation.

While chemotherapy is generally thought of as an effective treatment for Hodgkin's lymphoma, arguments against its use are not without merit. A report published in 2008 said that in addition to the immediate side effects, radiotherapy and chemotherapy have been associated with health problems that show up later in life, like infertility or cardiovascular damage.[27] The government has no authority from any source to force an adult to take any medicine, no matter the personal health risk. Through policies like this, the Natural Law is once again violated and we lose control over our physical selves.

As long as individuals know the relevant information regarding cancer treatment, it should be up to the sick person or his next of kin to decide whether he subjects himself to it. Technology is always changing—what is medically accepted one day may later be regarded as a bad treatment option. But one aspect of this never changes: the Natural Law. The Natural Law gives us control over our own bodies and keeps the government away. Given the fact that nothing is really conclusive in medical care, shouldn't we be able to weigh the options regarding health care for ourselves?

Why would the government even care about the choices we make regarding personal health? Radley Balko, a senior editor at *Reason* magazine, explains:

> [P]olicies governing how and when we give sick people access to the medication that could mitigate their pain, ameliorate the side effects of their treatment, or even save their lives, aren't based on compassion, individual rights, or even an honest assessment of science and risk. Instead, we have a patchwork of laws and enforcement policies driven by decades-old drug war hysteria, pharmaceutical paranoia, irrational aversion to risk, bureaucratic turf wars, and of course, politics.[28]

And all the while, the government-knows-best crowd is still telling us we have control over our own bodies.

As adults, our bodies belong to us. They don't belong to anyone else, let alone the government. The purpose of the federal government is to protect our constitutional and natural rights, not to restrict them. As children, our mothers and fathers know better than the government does how to raise us, and it is their job as parents to educate and groom us to make important decisions in life. Some of us will make conservative decisions, and others will make risky ones. Some of us will lead healthy lives, while others will pollute their bodies. Contrary to the government's belief, however, we have the right to make poor decisions and go against "mainstream" ideas. We're allowed to be individuals. We have the natural right to control our bodies. The government has no right to make decisions for us and thus infringe upon this sacred right.

Lie #8

"The Federal Reserve Shall Be Controlled by Congress"

On the foggy evening of November 22nd 1910, a train pulled out of the Lackawanna Railroad Station in Hoboken, New Jersey, and began its winding path to Jekyll Island, Georgia.[1] At the time, no one paid much attention to its departure, unaware that it carried some of the most powerful people in the United States on a course for the greatest fraud ever perpetrated on the American people. The train carried its passengers to a secret conference, where they would forge together the first draft of the Federal Reserve Act of 1913.[2] Amazingly enough, the Act essentially called for Congress to hand over its *constitutionally* granted power to issue and regulate money to a group of private bankers. It sounds unbelievable, as usually the federal government will fight tooth and nail to expand, not shrink, its constitutional powers; but the federal government voluntarily and *gladly* gave away this express power.

The years 1910 to 1913 were the height of the Progressive Era in American history. Congress, which would soon spearhead radical changes in the manner of the election of senators and federal taxation of personal income, authorized a privately held corporation to decide the monetary policy of the United States without oversight or accountability. And it justified its actions by two great lies: (1) the Federal Reserve will be controlled by Congress; and (2) it will bring about economic stability and prosperity for the American people.

The federal government not only claimed, with a straight face, that it could exert control over a private corporation in which it was not even to be a stockholder but also claimed that such an un-controlled private corporation would be working for the benefit of the American people rather than to enrich itself. It was to be the "lender of last resort" that would keep all Americans prosperous. As absurd as they sound, these myths continue to be believed and perpetuated even today.

From Gold to Toilet Paper

America's Founding Fathers recognized that the federal government would need to issue currency and regulate money, yet they also recognized a need for this currency to be backed by gold or silver or a stable commodity. Otherwise, they knew the government could simply print as much paper as it wanted, without thought to the consequences. Prior to the ratification of the Constitution, the Founding Fathers witnessed for themselves the disaster that awaits any currency not backed by gold or silver.

From the time of the Revolution to the time of the Civil War, a common phrase expressing worthlessness was "not worth a Continental"; but how many of us realize its derivation from the monetary system envisioned by the Constitution? At the time of the Revolutionary War, when this country was fighting for its independence from England, the Continental Congress was in dire need of money, and because it was low on gold (or hard money), it issued fiat money called the Continental. Fiat money is currency that the government has declared to be legal tender, thereby making it legally acceptable as payment for all debts, whether a creditor wants it or not, and whether it has inherent value or not. Unlike other forms of currency, fiat money is not representative, and therefore cannot be exchanged for a predetermined amount of an actual commodity, like gold or silver. In essence then, fiat money is just a piece of paper, worth only the amount that the economy will bear, no matter how much the government attempts to scam the people into believing it is worth.

Since the Continental currency was backed by neither silver nor gold, its value declined exponentially, and by the war's end, very few would accept it as payment. All fiat money is the same, and each time the government issues such currency, it lies to us all, both by pretending that the arbitrary amount at which it prices the paper is its actual worth and then by portraying that paper as a stable currency that the American people will be able to use in the future. "Not worth a Continental" is a phrase meaning "of no value."

With the lesson of the Continental in mind, the Founding Fathers summarily rejected the proposal to grant Congress the ability to "emit bills of credit." Rather, they drafted Article 1, Section 8, Clause 5 of the Constitution, which grants Congress the power "[to] *coin* money, regulate the Value thereof, and of Foreign coin, and fix the Standard of Weights and Measures" (emphasis added). Then, in Section 10, they prohibited the states from coining money and from "mak[ing] any Thing but gold and silver Coin a Tender in Payment of Debts." Thus, since Congress is prevented by the Tenth Amendment from assuming any powers not delegated to it, the printing of paper money, known as bills of credit, since there is no specific authorization, is prohibited by the Constitution.

When Congress printed Greenbacks during the Civil War, and they lost half their value within two years, the loss led to a series of historic decisions by the United States Supreme Court. In the 1869 case of *Hepburn v. Griswold*, Chief Justice Salmon P. Chase stated:

> [M]ost unquestionably there is no legal tender and there can be no legal tender in this country under the authority of this government of anything but gold and silver, either the coinage of our mints or foreign coins at rates regulated by Congress. This is a *constitutional principle* and of the *very highest importance* . . . Congress has *no power* to substitute paper or anything else for a coin as tender in payment of debts. (emphases added)

Consider that Chief Justice Chase had, in his prior position as Lincoln's Secretary of the Treasury, helped to formulate the Legal Tender Act of 1862, yet when asked to adjudge the Act's constitutionality, he admitted that it was not derived from any constitutional power, and he caused the Supreme Court to invalidate it. As a governmental official, he swore an oath to uphold the Constitution, yet he was able to draft a law that he himself would later admit to be unconstitutional.

Similarly, Rexford G. Tugwell, a member of FDR's "Brain Trust," who later became a Nuremberg prosecutor and ended his career as a Columbia Law School professor, stated, "To the extent that these [New Deal] policies developed, they were *the tortured interpretations of a document* [i.e., the Constitution] *intended to prevent them*"[3] (emphases added).

The same day that *Hepburn* was decided, two new justices were appointed to the Supreme Court. And only a year later, in the cases of *Knox v. Lee* and *Parker v. David*, the Supreme Court overruled the original legal tender decision. Straying from its *one-year-old* precedent, the Supreme Court in a 5 to 4 decision voted to reverse *Hepburn v. Griswold* and upheld the constitutionality of Congress's claimed power to print money during times of war. And the final nail in the coffin of real money, based on hard currency, came swiftly thereafter with the case of *Juilliard v. Greenman* (1884), which upheld the constitutionality of fiat money even in peacetime, noting that "making the notes of the United States a legal tender in payment of private debts" is "included in the power to borrow money and to provide a national currency."

Inexplicably, the Supreme Court went from the notion that Congress *not* having the power to make *anything* except coins legal tender was a constitutional principle of the very highest importance, to claiming to read into the Constitution the exact opposite principle, that Congress had the implicit right to emit bills of credit because it had the right to borrow money! Two opposite opinions by the same Court can only mean that someone lied or someone changed his mind on a matter of the highest importance, considering that the Constitution was not rewritten between 1869 and 1870.

In a telephone interview, Lawrence Parks, a noted expert on the legal tender cases, stated that a currently sitting justice on the Supreme Court has privately admitted to him that the 1870 Legal Tender Case was improperly decided and deeply flawed. Yet, the Supreme Court has done nothing to stop this sham from being perpetrated by our government. Supreme Court Justice Ruth Bader Ginsburg once claimed that "this is something best left to the politicians."[4]

Somehow, though, Congress allowed itself to read between the lines and find its power to emit bills of credit and then, even more astonishingly, to grant that right to a private corporation. In *A.L.A. Schechter Poultry Corp. v. United States* (1935), the United States Supreme Court held that Congress is not permitted by the Constitution to abdicate, or to transfer to others, the essential legislative functions with which it is vested. Considering that Congress has been given the right to regulate the value of money, and thereby the monetary policy of the United States, where did it get the power to delegate this enumerated power to a private entity like the Federal Reserve? Whatever Congress's reasons, since that delegation in 1913, the dollar's value *decreased* by 93 percent.[5] From 1789 to 1913, without a central bank with real power or lasting duration, the dollar's value *increased* by 13 percent.

The Birth of a Monster

The Federal Reserve scheme was not born in 1913, but rather has its roots with the proposals for a central bank dating to the earliest years of America. Alexander Hamilton, who wanted George Washington to be a king and thus serve for life, was a proponent of a large, centralized government and wanted to establish a central bank that would help finance the government. He was initially impeded from doing so by Thomas Jefferson, who argued that Congress did not have the authority to charter a bank, as it had only those powers granted to it under the Constitution. It was only in 1791, when George Washington offered his encouragement, that Hamilton's financial behemoth, the Bank of the United States, was formed. Fortunately for the country, the bank only had a twenty-year charter that expired, and was not renewed, during Madison's presidency.

This might have been the end of the Bank if not for the War of 1812 and the ensuing financial strain it placed on the federal government. President James Madison, previously a critic of the central bank, adopted the attitude of so many in his position, that in times of great stress, the Constitution be damned. In dire need of money, he signed legislation that authorized the creation of the Second Bank of the United States in 1816, interpreting the Necessary and

Proper Clause of the Constitution to allow for any laws to be passed which would be *helpful* in executing the federal government's delegated constitutional purposes.

The man credited as the Father of the Constitution, and its task of limiting the powers of the federal government, read into the document an idea that would in essence grant the federal government permission to do anything it chose—anything it found "helpful" rather than truly "necessary and proper." Did he lie to us when, in no need of currency, he said that the federal bank was unconstitutional; or is it more likely that he was lying to the American people when, in dire need of money, he claimed that the creation of such a federal bank was within the powers of the federal government? How can "helpful" mean the same as "necessary and proper"?

While branches of the federal bank sprang up around the country, the states began to balk at what they viewed as federal overreaching. They knew that the Constitution did not permit such a creation and that they could not sanction this sham by the federal government. Maryland made the first attempt to protect its sovereignty when its legislature imposed a tax on any bank not chartered by it. The only bank that fell under the statute was the Bank of the United States. Yet when it came time to pay the *legally* imposed tax, James McCulloch, head of the branch, refused to pay.

The result was *McCulloch v. Maryland*, where the United States Supreme Court held that the Necessary and Proper Clause of the Constitution grants to the federal government unstated, never-delegated, implied powers. So even though the Court admitted that the Constitution was silent on the creation of a bank, Chief Justice Marshall noted that the Constitution "had to be adapted to the various crises of human affairs."

In essence, Marshall read the Constitution to grant any and every power which was not expressly prohibited, as long as it was reasonably tied in to an express power. He stated that as long as the end was legitimate, then "all the means which are appropriate which are not prohibited . . . are constitutional." Therefore, though the entire document centers on enumerating the powers of the federal government so as to limit them, Chief Justice Marshall held that *this* clause is different, that it grants to the government broad, elastic, and unrestrained implied powers. By reading these broad powers, Marshall lied to all of us and deceived us about the spirit of the Constitution, for if "necessary" means "helpful," then the Constitution in essence allowed the federal government to do whatever it felt like, all under the guise of it being helpful to some other of its duties.

Of course, the Court also noted that the power is not limitless, and when it does go outside its boundaries, then the law would be nullified. But if the Necessary and Proper Clause can stretch the taxing and spending powers to encompass the charter of a federal bank, then what boundaries exist?

After *McCulloch*, the bank thrived until the presidency of Andrew Jackson. After an enormous struggle in the 1830s, he managed to bring it down and return to a system of free trade. Jackson was, coincidentally, the last president in American history to pay off the federal government's debt.[6]

Orchestrating Panic

The country unfortunately was destined to build up a great debt in the post-Jacksonian era. The Civil War resulted in the National Banking Acts of 1863, 1864, and 1865. The Acts resulted in the creation of newly chartered federal banks. Then, by prohibiting the state banks from issuing notes, Congress forced state banks to keep their deposits at the federal banks, thereby granting a monopoly to the new federal banks. As well, the Acts created a new lower minimum reserve requirement, which opened the banking world to expanded lending possibilities due to decreased amounts of reserves required for each loan. Finally, the Acts created a hierarchal structure to these banks, ensuring in essence that the banks would not have to stand on their own and take responsibility for their own debts. The Banking Acts paved the way for a central bank, for unimaginable public debt, and for ruinous inflation.

Still, many bankers voiced complaints that the system was not centralized enough, that there was not a large financial body which could serve as a "lender of last resort" to bail them out when they expanded beyond their capabilities. They complained of monetary "inelasticity," shorthand speak for their inability to expand credit without any barriers and without worry about the consequences. The bankers were complaining that they could not create inflationary booms through massive credit expansion. The reserve requirements, which required that the banks have only *15 percent* reserves, were still too high for them.

Would you want your bank to be able to cover *less* than 15 percent of its obligations to its depositors? The bankers wanted to be truly insured against any chance of collapse, to ensure that there would always be more money to print and someone there to pick up after their mess. They envisioned one giant central bank creating regulations, ensuring maximum profits, and insulating them from the consequences of their own negligence and their own excess. Sounds familiar.

But in order to create their behemoth, the bankers needed to derail the opposition: politicians who opposed a central bank and wanted to retain the decentralized system. The first step was the creation of committees in Indianapolis and New York, in 1897 and 1898, respectively, which would be composed of disinterested experts, many from the heartland of the country. The chief goal was to ensure a grassroots-type movement without the outward involvement of the bankers, as people would assume that any plan extolled by bankers would be bad for everyone but the bankers. The committees' neutral evaluators included representatives of the Rockefellers and the Morgans who sent out questionnaires to financial executives and traveled to Europe to interview heads of European central banks. No one consulted those who would be most affected by the creation of a central bank, the persons who would be paying for it. At the end of their time, both committees predictably called for the establishment of a central bank.

Less than a year after the committees decided that a central bank was the only way to ensure economic stability and prosperity for all, the inflationary tendencies of the secretary of treasury caught up with America. Some noted that J. P. Morgan, returning from a European vacation with the Rothschilds, was the originator of rumors that the Knickerbocker Bank could not afford to pay its debts. This was the same Rothschild family whose patriarch once stated, "Permit me to issue and control the money of a nation, and I care not who makes its laws."[7]

Once a run began at the Knickerbocker, panic quickly spread, and the inflationary spending habits of the country had a predictable result: The Panic of 1907.[8] Soon after, politicians and the media called for federal regulations of the banks, claiming that those in charge could not be trusted with even local finances if they could adversely affect national liquidity. In essence, one well-placed rumor, stating only the truth that no bank could survive a run on its money, collapsed all relevant opposition to a central bank as the American people forgot their history and forgot their Constitution in the panic of the fear of losing their life savings. The American financial system was ripe for the taking.

Legally Sanctioned Cartels

This brings us back to the fateful train ride in 1910, and the secret passengers making their way from Hoboken to Jekyll Island, a privately owned island off the coast of Georgia. On that day, six men boarded that train, in furtive secrecy and deception. Only first names, and in some cases nicknames, were used to ensure secrecy. If one man saw another on the platform, he was instructed to feign ignorance of the other's identity. No one was to know that they were traveling together or even where they were traveling. And if questions were asked, all men answered that they were to go on a hunting trip. One man even carried a shotgun with him, to ensure the deception appeared genuine; the shotgun was borrowed from one of his friends, and an autobiography would later note that the man had never in his life fired a gun.

The question is, why such deception? Why did it matter that no one knew that the men were together? The associations of these men, and not their names, speak to this question. As one of the men later stated, if it was known that these men had drafted the banking bill, Congress would never have passed it, given that the stated purpose of the bill was to ensure that the grip of the few large banks controlling the banking industry was broken, yet it was they who were writing it.

The list of passengers on that train reads like a Who's Who of banking: Senator Nelson Aldrich, father-in-law of John D. Rockefeller; Frank Vanderlip, vice president of Rockefeller's National City Bank of New York, the largest bank in America; Charles Norton, president of Morgan's First National Bank of New York, America's second-largest bank; Henry Davison, senior partner of J. P. Morgan Company; Benjamin Strong, head of J. P. Morgan's Banker's Trust Company; Paul Warburg, representative of the Rothschilds; and of course Abraham Andrew, the Assistant Secretary of the Treasury, ensuring that the federal government would have some say.

These men represented approximately one-quarter of the wealth of the entire world. Yet they were willing to create the Federal Reserve, an entity whose stated purpose was to wrest away *from them* the control of America's money. These men were not the types who would willingly part with the power they had thus far attained. And, given that the names of Morgan, Rockefeller, and Rothschild are recognizable to this day, it is apparent that they did not.

Purportedly each other's biggest competitors, having spent their lives fighting for dominance in banking and the financial markets, the men were able to come together for a week and agree on a draft of what was to become the Federal Reserve System. Their only debate was whether to choose partial or full centralization. With the knowledge that Congress would not approve an entirely banker-controlled central bank, they chose the politically astute partial centralization, realizing correctly that once legally passed, the Act could easily be revised in the future as people adapted to the idea.

They were not, as stated, preparing banking reform that was to ensure prosperity for the American people. Rather, they were able to come together so as to form a partnership that would secure their positions in the market and enhance their bottom lines. In other words, these bankers that day formed a cartel, a cartel that would ensure their continued dominance and survival: a cartel with legitimacy granted by the federal government and sold by deception.

In order to ensure acceptance by the people, a fund of about $5 million was donated by the bankers to academics and scholars and created the National Citizen's League for the Promotion of a Sound Banking System, whose sole task was expounding the importance of creating a Federal Reserve Bank.[9] The league was tasked with issuing statements by expert economists stressing that Wall Street's "control would be tempered by the influence of the Federal Government . . . which will be great."[10] One of the most outspoken supporters paid by the League was Professor J. Laurence Laughlin, from the University of Chicago, which had been endowed with nearly $50 million by Rockefeller.[11] The public was easily swayed by "neutral" scholars, giving credence to what John Adams said 125 years earlier, "[a]ll the perplexities, confusion and distress in America arise, not from defects in the Constitution, not from want of honor or virtue, so much as from downright ignorance of the nature of coin, credit and circulation."

There was a final hindrance to their plan, the upcoming presidential elections. The bill had been written and would quickly pass the House and Senate, but the final step was the need for a President who would not veto the bill. President William Howard Taft, who had previously stated that he did not support the bill and would veto it the first chance he got, was running for reelection. At the time, his reelection was almost certain, as the Republicans were the popular party and Taft was not facing any campaign problems. But the bankers, in order to pass their bill through, needed their Democratic candidate, Woodrow Wilson, to take the presidency. This was the same man who had stated during the 1907 Panic that "[a]ll this trouble could be averted if we appointed a committee of six or seven public-spirited men like J. P. Morgan to handle the affairs of the country."[12] Wilson could not be a more perfect candidate.

It was soon apparent that Wilson would not be able to garner enough votes to overcome Taft. It was at this point that ex-president Theodore Roosevelt, a Republican, entered the race as an independent. The bankers had found a way to divide Republican votes and therefore ensure the election of their Democratic candidate. Naturally, the majority of Teddy Roosevelt's campaign was funded by close allies of J. P. Morgan himself. Wilson won the election, though with only 45 percent of the popular vote. In a two-man race, without the Republican split, Taft was likely to have won, and the Federal Reserve Act would have lost. Instead, less than a year after his election, Wilson signed the Federal Reserve Act into law.

The Non-Federal, Non-Reserve, Federal Reserve

When signing it into law, President Wilson claimed that the Federal Reserve Act would "supplant the dictatorship of the private banking institutions" and "stabilize the inflexibility of the national bank note supplies." As advertised, the Federal Reserve was to be a politically independent private entity, yet it was also to be controlled by Congress. It was to ensure economic stability and prevent future crises. Originally, the Act was only given a life of twenty years, but that time ran out when FDR was president.

The Federal Reserve is composed of three parts. The first is the Board of Governors, which is responsible for determining monetary policy. Seven people are appointed by the President and confirmed by the Senate for a term of fourteen years, and they decide how much money they will print, what the interest rate will be, and essentially control every aspect of our monetary system.

Then there are the Regional Reserve Banks, which hold the cash reserves of the system, supply currency to member banks, and act as the fiscal agents of the government; each is run by a regional president and regional bank boards elected by member banks.

Finally, there is the Open Market Committee, which implements the monetary policy provided by the Board of Governors. It does this through the manipulation of the money supply via the purchase or sale of government securities. In essence, when the Fed buys government securities, money is made and interest rates fall; when it sells government securities, the money supply is reduced and interest rates rise. The committee is made up of the board as well as five of the regional directors. Bond dealers who earn large commissions on every transaction handle the purchases and sales of the securities.

The most common claim about the Federal Reserve is that it is accountable to the federal government because it is required to report to Congress twice a year regarding its activities. But what the chairman reports and what actually occurs are very different. Because the government has no power over the Federal Reserve, under current law the Federal Reserve cannot be audited. As well, its decisions do not require ratification by anyone in the executive or legislative branches of the government. Each time Congress has requested that the Federal Reserve submit to a voluntary audit, only refusals have been received. The Chairman of the Fed is therefore free to say anything he wants to Congress, and there is no way to verify the truth of his statements.

The monetary policy decisions made by the Fed are made at secret meetings, and Congress, as well as the public, are only made privy to brief reports released weeks later. Any transcripts made of the deliberations are destroyed. Every other government agency, even the CIA and NSA, are required by law to maintain all documents and transcripts of their activities.[13] Since the Federal Reserve is not a government agency, these laws do not apply.

I have said this many times on air and elsewhere, and even the Fed's supporters agree with me on this: The job of the CIA is to steal and to keep secrets; yet, we know far more about the CIA than we do about the Federal Reserve.

The Federal Reserve is a misnomer. As an initial matter, there is nothing "federal" about it. The government does not own a single share of stock in the Federal Reserve. A Chairman of the House Banking Committee (now known as the House Financial Services Committee) even once noted that whether the Federal Reserve worked with the government's fiscal policy or chose another direction was based mainly on the Federal Reserve Chairman's mood. Considering that the United States dollar is the currency of the world and the Federal Reserve controls the dollar, one could argue that the Chairman of the Federal Reserve is more powerful than the President. Money is power, and economic and political events around the world can be manipulated through U.S. monetary policy.

Not only is the word *Federal* in "Federal Reserve" a government lie, but so is the word *Reserve*. A reserve implies, and many people assume, that money is being stored away to use in a crisis, and that gold and other hard money are stored in order to ensure that all debts can be paid. This is not the case. Though original notes issued by the Federal Reserve stated, "This note is legal tender for all debts public and private, and is redeemable in lawful money at the United States treasury or at any Federal Reserve Bank," this was changed by a 1963 amendment. At that time the Fed began to issue its first series of notes without the redemption promise, while taking notes with the redemption promise out of circulation.

The notes now read, "This note is legal tender for all debts public and private." By removing the promise, ". . . and is redeemable in lawful money . . ." the Federal Reserve, with the support of the federal government, eliminated a constitutional monetary system and replaced it with paper and public debt.

Then, when some financial institutions attempted to privatize, the Monetary Control Act of 1980 granted to the Federal Reserve control of all national depository institutions, so that all financial institutions that offered deposits against which checks could be written were now under its control, whether or not they had ever been a part of the Federal Reserve System.[14] Now the monopoly was also granted the ability to force cartelization on those who wanted to remain private.

The public debt continues to grow exponentially with no end in sight. While the cost to the Federal Reserve for printing a note of any denomination is four cents and the Federal Reserve prints money from air, it charges the federal government interest for the monetary loans. As well, the Federal Reserve earns interest on the government securities in its ownership. Therefore, the Federal Reserve makes money each time it prints money, and thus it is encouraged to print more money, no matter whether it has any gold to back it up.

The term "reserve" is highly fallacious. The Fed does not want to reserve or save; it wants to spend, because the more it spends, the more interest it makes. The only president to issue an Executive Order beginning the process of abolishing the Fed was President John F. Kennedy, and he was dead three weeks later. His Executive Order Number 11110 returned to the Treasury Department its constitutional authority "to issue silver certificates against any silver bullion, silver, or standard silver dollars in the Treasury."[15]

Essentially, the President intended to give back to the federal government the ability to introduce currency backed by silver, without any need for a Federal Reserve. Each ounce of silver, at that time totaling about $4 billion in the government's possession, could back the new currency. The effect on the Federal Reserve would have been that the new silver-backed money would become preferred to Federal Reserve Notes, which were not backed by anything, and therefore the new currency would eventually end the need for the Federal Reserve and its monopoly money.[16]

As to the justification for the creation of such a financial behemoth that has come to control every aspect of our monetary policy, where is the economic stability and prosperity promised to us? Since the creation of the Federal Reserve, we have experienced the Great Depression, a recession in the early 1980s, the market crash of 1987, and finally, the economic crisis we find ourselves in today. And during all these events, there has also been the constant depreciation of the dollar. These are the result of the inflationary habits of the Federal Reserve, inflationary habits that no one can control or prevent, not without the abolition of the Fed. Rather than dethroning the moneyed elite, the Federal Reserve was their vehicle for a further power grab.

As F. A. Hayek, a noted Austrian economist, once said, "[t]o put it [money] in the hands of an institution which is protected against competition, which can force us to accept the money, which is subject to incessant political pressure, such an authority will never give us good money."[17] *The American dollar today is worth just 7 percent of what it was worth in 1913, when the Fed was established to **stabilize** it.*

Money *Does* Grow on Trees

Those who argued for the Federal Reserve Act focused on the fact that we needed to ensure that our currency was "flexible." They argued that this flexibility was crucial to ensuring that the federal government and the country did not run out of money. Where they criticized the gold standard for not being able to sustain the economy and allow for growth, they argued that this protection would ensure that we never ran out of money. In essence, the Federal Reserve Act brought into law the idea that money could come from nowhere. Not many people realize how the system works, or where our money comes from.

What supporters of the Federal Reserve Act further argued is that if state banks did not have someone to look out for them, they would in essence overissue their notes and reduce the amount of money they kept in reserve because of their need to make a profit. This action would lead to inflation and economic instability. One would think that if bankers were decentralized and could not depend on each other, then they would sink or swim on their own. In order to continue in prosperity, the bank would likely check itself and make sure that it was safe.

It is actually only when banks are able to cartelize, that is, form their own regulating partnerships so that they can protect themselves from the problem of a bust if they overextend, that they look to the Fed to "protect" them. In a cartel, they can make an agreement to warn each other when reserves are low and therefore not cash the checks from the deposits of banks whose reserves are low. In essence, this is central banking, and this is the Federal Reserve, federal sponsored cartelization, resulting in all of the same worries that purportedly brought the Federal Reserve as an option in the first place.

Private independent banks were not able on their own to do what they could with the Federal Reserve behind them. As Professor Murray Rothbard stated, private "banks . . . would never be able to expand credit in concert were it not for the intervention and encouragement of the government. For if banks were truly competitive, any expansion of credit by one bank would quickly pile up the debts of that bank in its competitors, and its competitors would quickly call upon the expanding bank to redeem in cash."[18]

In essence, a bank could not expand too quickly and therefore cause inflation, without risking its own crash. But when the banks get together and work from one central place, no one needs to worry about crashing because it cannot pay back its debts, since it and its competition are all backed by a "lender of last resort." It's like a teenager with an unlimited credit card, who knows that no matter how much money she spends, her parents will always pay the bill. And then imagine that the parents were able to force their neighbors to contribute to payments for that bill. Well, we are those neighbors, paying the bankers' bills through the constant fall of the value of our dollar.

The Federal Reserve does something similar to fractional reserve banking, except that it has no reserves at all. Let's say Congress is having a bad year by spending more than it takes in (that would be every single year since the end of the presidency of Andrew Jackson) and some of the bills from social programs have come in, but there is no money in the Treasury. That's okay, they say, and head over to their favorite banker: The Federal Reserve Bank.

Now, their banker knows that the government already owes him a lot of money, but it's all right because the interest payments are making the banker very rich. So the banker (the Fed) takes out his checkbook and writes Congress a nice check, with a lot of zeroes at the end of it. The check is signed, and Congress walks away happy. The Federal Reserve does too, even though it should actually be very worried considering that the check should bounce because there is no money in the Federal Reserve account, at least not technically, but that is not a problem. It is called "monetizing the debt," and if you or I tried to do it, we'd be going straight to jail. But this is one of the functions of the Federal Reserve, and the government is glad to accept it. Not only accept it, but now the Federal Reserve can charge interest on money that it created out of thin air.[19]

Now the best part is that the government cashes that check and starts spending the money. Those who get the money from the government put it in their bank accounts. And here is where things might get a little complicated. The local bank gets this money; let's say it is a deposit of one hundred dollars. The local bank is very happy because that one-hundred-dollar deposit will allow it to lend out nine hundred dollars.

Surprising? Not at all, as banks are only required to have 10 percent of their debts on deposit at any given time. This is called "fractional reserve banking" and is practiced in order to hide the fact that banks spend their clients' money; they don't actually "save" it for them. So the bank is happy as well. Even though this "money" came from nowhere and did not exist until the moment that the Federal Reserve issued a check, it is still valid and legal money that can be spent. This is all valid and legal, but illusory, and in direct contravention to the Constitution.

Finally the Perfect Tax: Infinite *and* Invisible

It was a very hot Las Vegas day in May 2003, and Robert Kahre had the air-conditioning on full blast when the door to his office swung open and he was confronted with a gun pointed directly at his head. Before he had time to question, he and more than twenty of his workers were handcuffed and held in the sweltering sun without water, while IRS agents swarmed inside, paving a path of disarray. To anyone observing, the situation looked as though Mr. Kahre and his workers had committed multiple felonies. But no, all Mr. Kahre had done was pay his workers, and they chose to accept his payment.

What the IRS was unhappy about was that the form of payment was U.S. government-minted gold coins. The coins had a face value of 50 dollars but the gold in them was actually worth 806 Federal Reserve dollars. Because there were no tax code regulations that distinguished between coin and paper money, Kahre and his workers paid taxes on the face value of the coins. So in essence, if a worker earns one gold coin a week, his annual salary is only 2,600 dollars, and therefore he is not required to pay taxes. And everyone knows that the federal government is never happy when it does not get taxes, especially from someone like Mr. Kahre. The government charged Kahre with 109 counts of tax-related crimes, including tax evasion, willful failure to file, and conspiracy to evade taxes.[20] The government brought fifty-two total charges against the other defendants combined.[21]

Fortunately for Kahre and his employees, the jury did not agree with the government, and all those charged were either acquitted or released after a hung jury.[22] The government has not yet decided whether it will retry him,[23] but considering the results already obtained, one can hope that the Constitution will prevail this time around, and the government will stop scamming us by pretending that any crime was committed.

Kahre's story illustrates the worst part of the Federal Reserve— that it is in essence imposing a secret tax on each and every one of us, a tax that most will not complain about because we do not realize it exists. Most of us do not know how the system works, so we do not complain and live in not-so-blissful ignorance, not entirely blissful because we are still paying for the inflationary money tricks that the Federal Reserve is allowed to play. This is why a family in the 1950s was easily able to survive happily on one income, whereas now it takes two working people to retain that same standard of living. Even if we attempt to save for our retirement, the more we save, the higher this invisible tax will be on us. But the worst effects are usually on the poorest of us, those living on a fixed income, such as the retired or disabled, who are receiving a specific monthly amount. When the value of the dollar falls, then the price of goods adjusts to that, and the buying power of those on a fixed income dwindles. The secret tax is called inflation, and it is the Fed's most lethal weapon.

But why would the government constantly expound private banking and allow the Federal Reserve to grow to its size without any regulatory control? If there was no advantage for the government, why would it not only allow the fraud to continue but also support it at every step? To understand the answer, we must understand the concept of inflation and deflation. We need to know how the concept affects the value of money, and therefore the value of our labor.

The idea of a central bank in Western culture, to control the banking and finance structure of a country, harkens back to 1694 and the creation of the Bank of England by King William III. The

King wanted a perpetual money machine for the monarchy so as to assure that the King's treasury would never run out of money and to circumvent the uprisings that would ensue with increased taxes. With the power of banking, the King could print more money on the sly, so it would not be directly linked to him, and therefore fund his armies and treasury without stealing by assessing taxes. Then, when the money flooded the market, the purchasing power of money bottomed out. And the King, having spent the money before this time, profited, while the people lost out on payments of their labor. Yet, the people, not being knowledgeable about inflation, did not blame the King and no uprisings happened. The monarchy continued this tradition, and it migrated to America as soon as there was profit to be had.

In essence, Congress struck a deal with the private bankers who would run the Federal Reserve, granting them absolute power over the control of America's money (a power delegated *to Congress* in the Constitution) in exchange for infinitely deep pockets. Whenever Congress needs money, the Federal Reserve prints it. And the more money printed by the Federal Reserve, the more inflation, and the less worth is attached to each day's labor. And the best part, for Congress, is that this tax is not only invisible and infinite, but Congress also does not have to attempt to raise the money, either through taxation or transfer of funds from expenditures; it can just get it without any direct, immediate consequences. Rather, the consequences land on the American people, who are forced to work harder and longer hours in order to get the same buying power that they used to get with a shorter day's work.

Essentially, the Federal Reserve, through its inflationary policies, has found a neater way to do what used to be done by monarchs when they ordered their Treasury officials to shave off or clip coins as they passed through the Treasury. If a private person did that, or if the king's treasury officials did that and helped themselves to what-ever they could shave or clip, and got caught, that would be instantly recognized as theft and fraud; yet when the Federal Reserve does the exact same thing to paper money that the King did to coins, no one says a word, because Congress has legalized the theft. And the only person who pays is you, when you attempt to take out your 401(k) and notice that the money you put in for the past twenty years is really only going to buy you less than the amount you put in, less than had you accumulated the cash in a shoe box. The Federal Reserve has in essence diluted the value of the 1914 dollar to seven cents. But don't worry; at least the same banks of today will always be doing business, having been bailed out by the Fed many a time before.

What we have to understand is that nothing in life is free, every-thing has a price, and right now the invisible tax is having a large impact on the middle class, lowering standards of living and causing job losses, while the economic elite gain the benefit of being the first to spend any issue of money before it is deflated in worth. A one-time Chairman of the Fed, Alan Greenspan, even admitted that if the top-secret monetary policies sometimes leaked prior to the Fed's actions,[24] those to whom it leaked could make a fortune.

For anyone who would question the impact on the value of the dollar without the backing by gold, and for whom the example of the Continental does not suffice, compare what you could buy with an ounce of gold only forty-five years ago as compared to today. In 1964, an ounce of gold was worth thirty-five U.S. dollars, which could buy a gentleman a very nice business suit; in 1979, the same suit could be bought for three hundred U.S. dollars, coincidentally, the price of an ounce of gold at the time;[25] today, a nice suit can still be bought for three hundred U.S. dollars, yet the price of gold is now around twelve hundred dollars an ounce. And if that were not enough, the prices of oil, milk, and eggs have not actually risen;

that is, they are worth the same if priced in 1908 twenty-dollar gold pieces; rather, the only thing that has changed is that the dollar of today has the same buying power as the nickel of a hundred years ago.[26] These are just some illustrations of how unstable the purchasing power of fiat money is compared to gold, of which the same amount can buy today what it could buy forty-five years ago.

Requiem for a Dollar

Economist Jeffrey Sachs of Columbia University recently noted that "the US crisis was actually made by the Fed. Monetary expansion generally makes it easier to borrow, and lowers the cost of doing so, throughout the economy . . . The Fed, under Greenspan's leadership, stood by as the credit boom gathered steam, barreling toward a subsequent crash."[27] This is shocking candor and a damning admission from a Big Government guy.

It looks as if we haven't learned from our mistakes, as recently a new proposed bill would grant the Federal Reserve sweeping new powers. Even the *Washington Times* sometimes forgets that the Federal Reserve is a privately run corporation, as it claimed the Fed is ". . . already arguably the most powerful agency in the U.S. government."[28] When even the conservative media reports the Fed to be a government agency, you know that the deception spawned by the government has been so pervasive that no one thinks to question the myth. Until we realize that our monetary situation is run by a private banking cartel, we cannot gain stability in the economy and the dollar will continue to plummet.

In the same article, the *Washington Times* quotes Treasury Secretary Timothy Geithner, attempting to justify the new, broad powers being granted to the Fed, stating that we need to prevent future crises, and in order to do that, in order to make our system stronger, we have to give one entity "clear accountability, responsibility and authority for preventing future crises." This sounds like a recycled Wilson speech right before enactment of the Federal Reserve Act. It also sounds like someone utterly ignorant of history or willfully deceptive about it.

Once again, an expansion of the Federal Reserve Act is being called for in the guise of a need for economic stability. Proponents claim that granting expanded powers to a central regulatory authority is the only way to ensure that stability occurs. Will we keep ignoring the lessons of history and allow the government to continue to delude us into believing that it is running the Fed and we need the Fed to keep our economy stable? How can one say with a straight face that because we worry that private bankers will go off the deep end and cause an inflation, we should therefore ensure that a group of bankers working together will ensure that this does not happen? They never have in the past and won't do so now. And the government now appears to believe its own lies, as President Obama is expounding the Fed's role as supercop of the markets and is expounding that he will not let the country forget history.

The President might not let us forget the federal government's version of history, but maybe he should take a look a little bit further back and note that the economy has become more and more unstable the more that power has been given to the Fed. As Senator Christopher J. Dodd, Chair of the Senate Banking Committee, once made clear, giving the Federal Reserve more power is like awarding your son a bigger, faster car right after he crashes the family sedan. Maybe this time we should listen. Thomas Jefferson foresaw this two hundred years ago, when he said: "If the American people ever allow private banks to control the issue of their money, first by inflation and then by deflation, the banks and corporations that will grow up around them will deprive the people of their property until their children wake up homeless on the continent their fathers conquered."

Lie #9

"It's Only a Temporary Government Program"

Milton Friedman, the esteemed Nobel prize–winning free market economist, famously noted, "Nothing is so permanent as a temporary government program,"[1] and, "The government solution to a problem is usually as bad as the problem."[2] Examples of temporary government programs that have become permanent fixtures include income tax withholding, rent control, and social security.

Another example is the National Defense Act, which was created in 1916 during World War I and was also used in World War II. It is known to be the most comprehensive piece of military legislation ever passed by Congress. The Act permitted the President to make obligatory orders in times of war that take precedence over any market forces or lawful private contracts. The government is then allowed to seize operations of private companies for the purpose of wartime efforts at whatever price it has deemed appropriate, and any resistance would result in a felony. By setting prices below market value, the federal government was able to conceal the true costs of both World Wars. The Act was a violation of private property rights, and the Supreme Court has since eliminated executive wartime power to seize private property unless that power is expressly given by Congress. So, therefore, in the realm of "temporarily" seizing private property, it requires two branches of the federal government to make an unconstitutional act constitutional!

Although the National Defense Act has been phased out, several similar programs that were passed in times of crisis as a "temporary fix" still linger today. It seems the American government has never refrained from using the "opportunity" presented in a crisis as an excuse to expand the government and indulge in the money of tax-paying Americans.

America was founded on basic principles of limited government. Then, throughout American history when situations such as war or economic downturn became apparent, these principles were often abandoned and the federal government expanded. These expansions, which run counter to fundamental American values, were often permitted because they happened in times of emergency. Yet, instead of going away once the emergency situations subside, these programs have lingered and eroded the way our government functions. Over and over, these "temporary" government programs have proved to be nothing but permanent.

"Temporary" Government Program #1: Taxation

At the root of government expansion lie taxes. The government funds its wars, its welfare system, and its programs through the taxes it places on citizens. Sadly, Benjamin Franklin's old adage, "In this world nothing can be certain, except death and taxes," has proven to be an immutable truth.

Big government and high taxes were far from what the Founding Fathers had in mind. Paradoxically, taxes acted as a catalyst to America's revolt from Britain. In his book about America's tax system, Timothy J. Gillis explained:

The rebel colonists remembered why they and their forefathers had come to the New World. The colonists were people, or offspring of people, who fled environments where royal favor and grants were common and success could depend much less on what a person did than on whom he knew. They remembered that government taxation and fiscal policy were primary means of subjugating liberty and imposing tyranny, both petty and great. This influenced the colonists to construct limited and frugal government.[3]

In America's youth, the possibility of freedom from taxes was alive and well for its citizens. So, what has happened over the years to make no taxes seem like an impossible dream?

As the United States grew, so did the federal government. The idea of limited government was pushed aside in favor of collecting funds for various crises. The first big expansion of the federal government's budget, and in turn the people's taxes, came in 1861 with the start of the Civil War. The federal income tax laws that were passed in the 1860s by the Union and Confederacy were unpopular, unconstitutional, and immoral, and they were repealed by Congress in 1871. After the federal income tax was repealed, the government paid off the rest of the Civil War debt in twenty-four years with money from excise taxes and customs duties. There were excise taxes on items such as playing cards, gunpowder, feathers, telegrams, iron, leather, pianos, yachts, billiard tables, drugs, patent medicines, and whiskey. Many legal documents were also taxed, and federal license fees were collected for almost all professions and trades.[4]

In 1893, the income tax returned. This time, however, the country was not at war, and many citizens viewed the tax as unjustifiable. In 1895, a lawsuit claiming that the federal income tax was unconstitutional was brought and eventually reached the Supreme Court. The Court held that since the income tax was based on income from real estate, it was unconstitutional because the Constitution requires that direct taxes imposed by the federal government on the states be proportional based on population.[5]

A little over a decade after this ruling, President William Howard Taft proposed a law which circumvented many of the Constitution's impediments to the 1893 income tax. Get this: A president who swore an oath to uphold, preserve, protect, and defend the Constitution proposed a way to avoid and evade it, a way that would purport to allow the federal government to steal cash from groups of individuals with impunity. This law would allow the federal government to tax corporations (as opposed to individuals), and was passed by Congress with near unanimity. Later, in 1913, the United States ratified the Sixteenth Amendment, which permits the federal government to tax the income of individuals.

The government did not waste any time before taking advantage of its new power. Just eight months after the Sixteenth Amendment was ratified, President Woodrow Wilson signed a law that levied a 1 percent tax on net personal incomes over $3,000.[6] The law also provided for a 6 percent surtax on incomes exceeding $500,000.[7] These taxes were aimed at the wealthiest Americans, however, and did not reach the vast majority of the people.[8] In 1918, only 5 percent of Americans paid income tax, and the income tax remained a "class tax" until World War II.[9]

During World War II, however, the federal government expanded its assaults on personal income. The government passed the Revenue Act of 1942, declaring that it was just a war measure. It significantly increased the marginal tax rates, and added a 5 percent "Victory Tax" on annual income exceeding $624.[10] Under this Act, the income tax rolls increased *from 13 million persons to 50 million persons* in just one year.[11] The government also implemented a system requiring that employers withhold federal income taxes from employee wages and salaries.[12] Finding it unrealistic to arrest all tax evaders, the government saw income tax withholding as a device to extract income automatically from the taxpayers.[13] It also helped folks "save" money for the government, as it guaranteed the government a steady revenue stream during the costly war.

Milton Friedman, who worked at the Treasury Department during World War II, was involved in the development of the withholding tax.[14] Recently, Friedman stated that the tax was developed because the government needed to raise massive amounts of money quickly and temper the growth of inflation.[15] Friedman explained, "I wasn't as sophisticated about how to do it then as I would be now, but there's no doubt that one of the ways to avoid inflation was to finance as large a fraction of current spending with tax money as possible."[16]

In his memoir, *Two Lucky People*, which he coauthored with his wife, Rose, Friedman conceded that during World War II, he "was helping to develop machinery that would make possible a government that I would come to criticize severely as too large, too intrusive, too destructive of freedom."[17] According to Friedman, "I really wish we hadn't found it necessary and I wish there were some way of abolishing withholding now."[18] The author of the truism about the permanence of temporary government programs was himself the regretful author of the most pernicious and permanent of temporary government programs whereby the federal government steals money from each of our paychecks, every time we receive one.

Through income taxes, the government taxes our personal production, only to redistribute our hard-earned cash to others (often wastefully). This is an oppressive infringement on personal liberty and one that we should not passively accept. The idea of abolishing income taxes is hardly radical. The Founding Fathers did not support them, and they are a relatively new custom in America. Nevertheless, the only politicians who had the backbone to suggest such a policy in the 2008 presidential election were Ron Paul and Bob Barr.

Congressman Ron Paul's plan to abolish the income tax and, consequently, eliminate wasteful federal programs like the wars in Iraq and Afghanistan, foreign aid, agricultural subsidies, and the United States Department of Education, is absolutely consistent with the intent of the Framers.[19] Under Paul's plan, much more responsibility would be taken on by the States, within which funds would be handled by local politicians who can better gauge the needs of their citizens than the federal government can.

When explaining his stance on taxes, former Congressman Bob Barr stated, "It is not enough to eliminate the income tax. We also must also repeal the 16th amendment, which authorizes Congress to levy an income tax. Without doing so, there would be an ever-present danger that a future Congress would attempt to bring back the income tax on top of the Fair Tax or any other alternative to the income tax."[20] These ideas are in step with the Framers' intent, but until Americans wake up and realize that they do not *need* to accept an oppressive income tax, these plans will remain far from mainstream.

Frank Chodorov argued, in "Taxation Is Robbery," that the government immorally pilfers our money from us through any and all forms of taxation. He wrote, "Those who hold to the primacy of the individual, whose very existence is his claim to inalienable rights, lean to the position that in the compulsory collection of dues and charges the State is merely exercising power, without regard to morals."[21]

When the government takes from us, it is just as immoral as any other type of burglar. Because humans have an indisputable right to life, it follows that we have the same right to enjoy the products of our life's labor. Yet, when the government taxes us, the right to our own existence is qualified. Do you know anyone—*anyone*—who comes home with his paycheck and check stub and after examining what he earned and what the government took from him says: "I don't think I gave the government enough money this week"?

In addition to taxation itself, there is a whole host of government programs funded by our tax dollars that were originally proposed as "temporary," but then stuck around for the long haul.

"Temporary" Government Program #2:
Rent Control

During World War I, the federal government introduced rent controls, which are ordinances or laws that place a ceiling on the amount a landlord can charge for rent, but stopped them in the late 1920s.[22] Rent controls were implemented again during World War II, via the Emergency Price Control Act (EPCA) of 1942. They were brought back strictly as a *temporary* "emergency measure," mainly in order to help the wives and children of soldiers who were serving in the war, and were to be dismantled after the war.[23] The EPCA allowed the federal government to regulate the maximum price of residential rents in an effort to counteract inflationary prices and housing charges. It helped tenants, but it severely harmed the landlords who owned the apartments the tenants leased. Nevertheless, in a few American cities, like New York City, rent control is far from temporary.

Today, proponents of rent control justify it as a device to ensure that people who have lived in their apartments for a long time will not be removed due to rising rents in their area. Yet, the rationale behind rent control today is far from sound: It deprives landlords of the right to control the amount they charge to tenants, it acts as a disincentive to invest in real estate, it arbitrarily favors certain groups of people over others, and it allows government—rather than people's free-market choices—to dictate what people pay for a good in a given neighborhood. It also constitutes a taking since it consists of the government prohibiting owners of private property from putting the property to its highest and best use.

A proponent of abolishing rent control, pop social scientist Malcolm Gladwell, argued that in New York (where rent control is prevalent), rent control is behind the problem of tax-delinquent landlords. He wrote:

> Right now thousands of buildings in the city are in receivership—either abandoned by landlords or under the tenuous control of the city because their owners couldn't pay their taxes. Tax-delinquent buildings tend, almost exclusively, to be older buildings, because older buildings tend to have much higher upkeep costs and also tend to have many more tenants with artificially low rents . . . they are the buildings now getting burned down, or run down, or boarded up because rent regulation makes it impossible for landlords to take care of them.[24]

Rent control discourages anyone from even going through the grief of being a landlord since the government precludes it from being profitable.

The government regulation has also had an effect on the interpersonal relationship between landlords and tenants. As a result of these artificially low rents, landlords and tenants will naturally harbor some animosity toward each other. One article describes: "No wonder landlords resent the legalized thieves masquerading as tenants; in turn, the parasites hate their host because he isn't giving them even more. A couple of landlords have actually killed rent-controlled tenants to end their decades of sponging."[25]

Landlords have also been taken advantage of by wealthy politicians. For example, it was uncovered in 2008 that New York Congressman and rent regulation advocate Charlie Rangel rented several rent-controlled Harlem apartments and combined them into an opulent home. Rangel defended his grand residence on the cheap by claiming that one of his apartments was really his congressional office. The building's landlord would surely have raised objections to this arrangement if Rangel had not been a powerful politician who could put him out of business.[26]

The wisdom gained from this infuriating story is that it is not difficult to make rent control laws (which are supposedly in place to help the poorer members of society keep a roof over their head) advantage the wealthy. One article comments, "Ah, the ironies of rent-control: politicians with a millionaire's net-worth and second homes in the Dominican Republic collect rent-controlled apartments like stamps while the handicapped squat beneath bridges."[27] While rent control was originally meant only to help wives and children while husbands and fathers were fighting in World War II, it has become an enduring and harmful legacy in some of America's cities.

"Temporary" Government Program #3: Social Security

The Social Security program was enacted through the Social Security Act of 1935. Its stated intention was to be a temporary program that would provide financial assistance after retirement. Money was taken from the payrolls of current workers and then redistributed to retirees. Based on this fact alone, it becomes apparent that from the start Social Security was *not* a temporary program. How could a *temporary* program take money from you *now*, and promise to give it back to you *later*?

The Social Security system is a hapless cycle and a Ponzi scheme. It is a program rife with poor planning, as FDR and the drafters of it did not predict that the average life span would increase in the future and failed to plan for population surges, like the "baby boom" which occurred shortly after WWII. Today, FDR's program has left a terrible burden on the federal government's budget and continues to take money out of the hands of those who earned it. The program has also infantilized America's seniors by making retirement into an expected social norm, therefore leaving little genuine choice for the aging population.

Upon its creation, Social Security excluded many women and minorities from receiving its benefits. Typically, only practitioners of certain professions (jobs that were commonly held by white males) were eligible to get financial benefits from Social Security. People in many jobs—such as teachers, nurses, hospital employees, social workers, librarians, domestic servants, railroad workers, farm employees, and government employees—were not required to pay into or able to collect from Social Security. Consequently, the Social Security system tended to discriminate against those classes of people who made lower wages and were not easily able to save for retirement.

In subsequent years, the types of professions that were included in the financial benefits grew, but unfortunately so did the costs to taxpayers. Only by excluding large groups of blacks from Social Security—a government decision based on race—could FDR get this infantile socialism supported by Southern Democrats in Congress. Nevertheless, Social Security still failed miserably at being even an efficient or equitable socialist program, if there is such a thing. The problem with socialism, according to former British Prime Minister Margaret Thatcher, is that sooner or later the government runs out of other people's money. Indeed ours has. Because of its immoral, unlawful, unconstitutional structure, almost since its inception, Social Security has needed billions in taxpayer bailouts.

Milton Friedman criticized Social Security for redistributing wealth from the poor to the wealthy. The system winds up making people with large salaries pay a lower percentage of their total income than those making less money. Additionally, richer people tend to have longer life expectancies than poor people because wealthy people can often afford better quality health care and healthier lifestyles. Because the Social Security system pays until death, the wealthy often collect benefits for a longer period of time than do the poor.

The truth is that the Social Security system is a Ponzi scheme so elaborate and well funded it could make Bernie Madoff blush. Yet, while Madoff spends the rest of his life behind bars, the government is allowed to get away with its nearly identical scheme. Because who is going to put a stop to the government's theft when the government fails to regulate itself?

Through Social Security, the government takes your money, and then gives you an IOU in return. Economist Thomas Sowell exposes Social Security as a pyramid scheme and describes the many problems associated with it:

> Social Security has been a pyramid scheme from the beginning. Those who paid in first received money from those who paid in second—and so on, generation after generation. This was great so long as the small generation when Social Security began was being supported by larger generations resulting from the baby boom. But, like all pyramid schemes, the whole thing is in big trouble once the pyramid stops growing. When the baby boomers retire, that will be the moment of truth—or more artful lies.[28]

So, just as in every Ponzi scheme, some people are going to get swindled out of their money. We see this today, as the government is running out of funds while trying to dole out money to the large number of retiring baby boomers. The baby boomers are a generation who paid a great deal of money into the Social Security system, and money was plentiful while they were in the workforce because that generation was so much larger than the one it was supporting. Yet, now, who is going to support the baby boomers? There is no money left to support this large generation of retiring people who contributed to the system in large sums of money. The government keeps pushing their retirement age up, so that it can spread out the relatively small amount of money it has to the vast amount of recent retirees. Social security is supposed to be a rainy day fund for retirees, but now that the rain is pouring, the government is finding the fund is running dry.

If only the large population of recently retired citizens were the only problem with Social Security today, but this is one of many problems. Money that comes in through Social Security taxes has often been spent by politicians on endeavors other than funding for the Social Security system.

> What has happened is that the Social Security taxes that were supposed to go into a trust fund have in fact been spent by the politicians. The government bonds turned over to the Social Security system in exchange for this money changes absolutely nothing. These bonds are just claims on future general tax revenues . . . The only purpose served by the bonds is to make numbers look good when the reality is very different . . . Debts are hidden, rather than paid.[29]

So, in essence, the government takes our money and uses it not for the purpose it purported, and we will probably never gain that money back. It does not take a criminal mastermind to detect the inherent deception and thievery involved in this situation. The so-called "lockbox" for Social Security that we hear politicians pontificate about has never existed. Instead the government treats Social

Security as its slush fund, with insincere promises to pay back more than it stole.

This is thievery at the highest possible level. In terms of dollars paid, the American Social Security system is the single largest government program in the world. The United States wastes more of our money on Social Security than it does on extremely expensive programs such as national defense or medical programs such as Medicare and Medicaid.[30] So, while politicians lie by pretending that our money is safe and that we will someday redeem the IOU, they have quietly orchestrated the biggest swindle of all time.

FDR'S Legacy of Lies

While present-day politicians are certainly to blame for trying to sweep the problems of Social Security under the rug while still collecting our money, they are not to blame entirely. There is no easy or fair way out of Social Security, because ending it today means stealing the money of those who paid yesterday. Also, the system has caused the elderly and retired to become a class of dependents, in that they plan their retirements with the expectation that they will be receiving a pension from the government.

Today's politicians have been left between a rock and a hard place by the mess bequeathed on them by the Ponzi scheme's chief founder and principal swindler: Franklin D. Roosevelt. FDR was only able to get Social Security to pass because of the unique political climate during his presidency. Between the lagging economy he made worse, and later the war he manipulated the U.S. into, FDR was able to enact many "New Deal" measures that took (and continue to take) away our property and our freedoms, are unconstitutional, violate basic laws of economics, and are plain damaging to America.

Social Security is unconstitutional in that it violates the Due

Process Clause of the Fifth Amendment, which prohibits the government from taking the property of citizens without due process, meaning, a trial. A scheme in which the government taxes the money we earn, takes it, and gives it to others leaves Americans with no choice in the matter but to surrender their money (property). This is a violation of both our Fifth Amendment rights and our Natural Law rights.

From a more personal perspective, Social Security has had a profound impact (for the worst) on American culture. Part of growing old in America now involves settling down, retiring, and living off of government money. The government has managed to turn what is for many a healthy, vibrant, and mature stage of life into a reversion where the elderly beg for an allowance from the paternalistic figure of government.

Before "retirement" was institutionalized by Social Security, there was no such thing as a stage of life where people were left to grow old in the lonely isolation of their living rooms or in Florida. It used to be that the living standards of older people were upheld through a variety of sources: employment income, savings, and help from children.[31]

One article by Mises Institute writer Dale Steinreich describes the harms that came with the invention of retirement:

> Retirement is among the most economically wasteful and socially destructive institutions created by government. The most experienced and knowledgeable workers are bumped from productive employment to the world of golf courses, bingo parlors, and TV watching. . . . Retirement punted older people out of the active community of enterprise, where they are most needed for both their skills and their positive cultural influence. They have also been marginalized in society at large, so that young people tend not to interact with them on a daily basis.[32]

Indeed, the elderly community has become the butt of many cruel and demeaning jokes in our society, and much of this has to do with FDR's harmful legacy of lunacy.

All of the programs highlighted in this chapter stemmed from the federal government's attempts to gain more power so that it could exert more control over the people. These supposedly "temporary" government programs have also left lasting effects on the American economy, American people, and our ability to be free. The role of the federal government, however, is to stay *out* of our lives, not to set up programs to dominate us, correct every wrong, address every social need, and lie about it.

Lie #10

"I'm from the Government, and I'm Here to Help."

In a 1988 speech, President Ronald Reagan declared, "There seems to be an increasing awareness of something we Americans have known for some time: that the ten most dangerous words in the English language are, 'Hi, I'm from the Government, and I'm here to help.'"[1] That day, there was laughter when a convivial Reagan uttered the words to the Representatives of the Future Farmers of America. As is usually the case, there's a morsel of truth within humor. Or, in this case, a big chunk of truth.

President Reagan followed up by explaining, ". . . we need to look to a future where there's less, not more, government in our daily lives. It's that philosophy that brought us the prosperity and growth that we see today." In that speech, Reagan put forth his best effort to debunk the monstrous myth that the government is here to help us. The federal government has trumpeted its ability to intervene during disasters and in times of emergency but, more often than not, the result is an explosion of federal power, wasted resources, frustrating red tape, and not much else.

Washington's fondness for creating new bureaucratic departments in response to perceived domestic problems often makes those problems much worse. If it was not such a humanitarian disaster, the federal government's response to Hurricane Katrina in Louisiana and Mississippi in the summer and fall of 2005 would provide an almost comic example of conflicting orders, crippling bureaucracy, and inept political appointees that led to a major American city being transformed into a third-world scene of death, squalor, and chaos. From natural disasters to recalls of food and drugs once touted as safe and tested by the FDA, to staging phony press conferences, it seems the feds never defuse problems, and only spread fear and confusion. And when people are afraid and confused, they often let the government get away with telling them what to do because they don't know what else to do.[2] Perhaps the federal government is so bad at doing these things because it is institutionally incapable and constitutionally barred from these functions.

FEMA: Federal Emergency Mismanagement Agency

In 1979, President Jimmy Carter merged several disconnected aid groups into one large agency, thereby creating the Federal Emergency Management Agency (FEMA). Yet, the new system proved to be disorganized and chaotic from the beginning. In 1985, after facing fraud allegations, FEMA Director Louis Giuffrida resigned. In 1989, after the agency's poor handling of Hurricane Hugo in South Carolina, Senator Fritz Hollings (D-SC) commented that FEMA was the "sorriest bunch of bureaucratic jackasses I've ever known."[3]

Conceptually, FEMA makes no sense. Why should the federal government oversee rescues from natural disasters? Wouldn't it be more appropriate to leave these matters up to state and local governments who better understand the needs of their own people and land? As I said in my article, "Franklin Delano Bush":

If a state government is not prudent, and a natural disaster strikes, why should American taxpayers bail it out? That would provide no incentive for prudence in the future. Why should American taxpayers cover for the blatant failure of Louisiana politicians to be prudent with tax dollars? The federal government's debt is exponentially larger than Louisiana's.[4]

There is no lawful basis for FEMA. And as is demonstrated throughout this chapter, FEMA is a disaster in and of itself, and repeatedly fails in its mission to help out the victims of natural disasters.

Several occasions arose over the years where FEMA was caught unprepared and lacking an appropriate response to disaster. Under the Clinton Administration, FEMA expanded and became a pit for taxpayer dollars. After 9/11, President Bush brought FEMA under the Department of Homeland Security, switching its focus from rescue to preventing terrorism. Yet, this change in the agency's concentration left the country vulnerable to *imminent* natural disaster against the possibility that there could be another terrorist attack. This shift in gears, the incompetent leadership, and the inefficient bureaucratic red tape primed FEMA for the mess it caused after Hurricane Katrina.

When Hurricane Katrina hit the Gulf Coast in late August 2005, the storm was one of the most powerful to hit American soil. It would reveal failures—at the federal, state, parish, and city levels—to plan appropriately and to act quickly for this disaster. Yet, the magnitude of the storm is absolutely no reason to dismiss FEMA from all responsibility. Immediately after the storm hit and for long after, the streets of New Orleans were a chaotic, unrecognizable mess. Sure, the federal government was *there*, but it certainly was not helping. Drinking water and ice could not be found, evacuations were not efficient, and there was no plan as to how to evacuate sick or elderly people who could not necessarily transport themselves. The existence of FEMA caused many people to think they would not need to create their own evacuation plans because they thought the government would have it under control. Sadly, they were wrong. FEMA let New Orleans go to hell.

According to the Disaster Accountability Project (a nonpartisan, nonprofit organization that collects data about disaster preparedness and acts as a watchdog over government agencies such as FEMA), several parishes (counties) in the New Orleans region had no evacuation plans drawn up at the time Katrina hit. And of the parishes that did, many had not updated their plans in years. Maybe the Louisiana parishes were under the impression that the federal government was there to help. Tragically, many lives were lost due to this huge lie the government told us.

It is not as though FEMA merely failed to act; it prevented people from taking action themselves. FEMA turned away private donors who wanted to deliver vitally needed goods to victims. One FEMA official turned away a Wal-Mart truck full of supplies. It was as though self-righteous FEMA was saying, "Hey, we have this under control. We don't need your help." Anyone who has seen pictures, videos, or stories about Katrina would tell you that the government needed all the help it could get. But instead of admitting its incompetence, FEMA's administration acted like stubborn children. FEMA claims that it did not let the supply trucks in because they posed some sort of safety hazard, but it really just didn't want anyone to steal its thunder. Economics Professor William L. Anderson wrote about the issue:

> Now, it did not matter to FEMA officials that a large number of people needed the provisions that the Wal-Mart truck was carrying. While I am sure that any member of FEMA would employ rhetoric

to the contrary, but I stand by my point. It does FEMA no good at all for Wal-Mart to do something for which FEMA receives no credit. Furthermore, this "securing the area" business is nonsense, and the people at FEMA know it. Yes, there are risks that people take going into areas just after something devastating like a hurricane or earthquake has occurred, but the vast majority of people who put themselves into such situations know beforehand about the nature of the dangers they are facing.[5]

Even after the storm had passed, FEMA was not out of the hot water to which it subjected itself. The agency did a wonderful job of proving itself to be as wasteful and bungling as ever. In an effort to provide a source of temporary housing for Katrina victims, tens of thousands of residential trailers were issued by FEMA. But, in its ineptitude, FEMA handed out trailers from a supplier who used a high concentration of formaldehyde in building the structures. Almost immediately after the trailers were doled out, hundreds of displaced families called FEMA to complain of health issues such as rashes, bloody noses, breathing difficulties, and illness probably due to the concentrated level of formaldehyde used to manufacture the trailers. Additionally, there were allegations that exposure to high levels of formaldehyde could be linked to serious long-term health issues, like cancer or miscarriages. There is also some speculation that FEMA tried to sweep the connection between formaldehyde exposure and cancer under the rug.

In May 2006, FEMA asked the National Center for Environmental Health / Agency for Toxic Substances and Disease Registry (ATSDR) to do a "health consultation" on the trailers. ATSDR's chief of toxicology, Christopher De Rosa, M.D., told FEMA that cancer risks and other possible health problems would need to be included in the report. In an effort to save face, FEMA cut out Dr. De Rosa and forced some of his staff to prepare a consultation that would omit information on the risk of cancer and other key health information. De Rosa wrote to FEMA:

> I am concerned that this health consultation is incomplete and perhaps misleading . . . Formaldehyde is classified as "reasonably anticipated to be a human carcinogen." As such, there is no recognized "safe level" of exposure. Thus, any level of exposure to formaldehyde may pose a cancer risk, regardless of duration. Failure to communicate this issue is possibly misleading, and a threat to public health.[6]

In June 2009, *USA Today* reported that there are still thousands of families living in the temporary trailers, but that FEMA and HUD announced programs giving trailer residents $50 million (of taxpayers' money) in housing vouchers in an effort to make some amends for their formaldehyde catastrophe.[7] So, in the spirit of Reagan's words, the government was here to "help," and it was terrifying, corrupt, and quite expensive. The American people wound up paying the price for the government's deception, both in their health and in their taxes.

FEMA's disingenuous and blatantly corrupt practices did not end with the trailer fiasco. In fact, this incident was just the beginning. Serious misconduct, such as racial discrimination, sexual harassment, and cronyism, are among the allegations made about the FEMA office in downtown New Orleans.[8] Even more disturbing, that type of "toxic" office culture has greatly hampered the Katrina recovery. In one year's time, more than thirty employment-related complaints were filed against Doug Whitmer, the chief of staff at the New Orleans FEMA branch.

Amidst these allegations, the head of FEMA, Nancy Ward, did

not even fire the chief of the New Orleans office. Instead, Ward opted to reassign him to a FEMA office in Texas (with the twisted logic that he can cause further damage somewhere else?). After the corruption, poor management, and wasteful use of government funding was exposed, FEMA announced in April 2009 that the New Orleans Recovery Office was being shut down.[9] So much for helping people in need.

In September 2008, Hurricane Ike hit the Gulf Coast area. Did FEMA learn from the myriad mistakes it made in Katrina by 2008? No, it seems that FEMA made nearly all the same blunders with Ike. The Disaster Accountability Project had a hotline in September 2008 whereby Ike victims could provide information regarding their experiences with FEMA and problems with hurricane preparedness. Some of the common complaints were: People had no ice to cool insulin, baby formula, or other medications, and FEMA never publicized the location of shelters and places to get necessary supplies like food and water. Others said that when they had been trying to call FEMA, they received a recording saying that it was not a valid number. Another caller said that once she did get through to the FEMA hotline, she was instructed to go on the Internet for more information, even though simple logic would tell you that most hurricane victims did not have Internet access because electric power was lost for weeks.[10]

Carey Giudici, a guest blogger on the Disaster Accountability Project's blog, said it best, "Most agreed that the storm itself was much less of a problem than what has come afterwards."[11] Much of the reason why the storm wasn't the worst of things was because FEMA failed on many counts. She and other people quoted discussed communication problems between hurricane victims and relief services, because many did not know where to go to get supplies.

In the aftermath of Katrina, much debate occurred about

rebuilding New Orleans. Should the government pay to rebuild a city on the Gulf Coast that is mostly below sea level? One commentator on economics and environmental issues wrote, "To me, though, it doesn't seem to be a triumph of the human spirit to rebuild a city with a population of a half-million with most of the residences under sea level. These seem like the worst sort of government subsidies."[12]

Should enormous amounts of taxpayers' dollars really be given to a rebuilding effort, just so the same thing can likely happen all over again? This situation simply does not make good sense, but neither do most of the policies FEMA proposes. From one perspective, a below-sea-level city is almost definitely not safe, and we should not be encouraging people to move there. From another viewpoint, should American taxpayers have to pay to recover and rebuild a nearly infinite number of times? This is an especially frustrating cycle when FEMA squanders or uses most of that money so inefficiently.

The statistics prove FEMA's ineptitude. The Greater New Orleans Community Data Center report on the rebuilding process in New Orleans shows that while the city has bounced back somewhat, it seems like growth has stagnated.[13] For example, households actively receiving mail in Orleans Parish plummeted from 198,232 before Katrina to 133,966 two years after Katrina.[14] Households receiving mail have increased, but gradually. In 2009, only 152,904 households were receiving mail in Orleans Parish, a far cry from the nearly 200,000 households pre-Katrina.[15] Before Katrina, there were 275 child care centers in Orleans Parish, 98 two years after Katrina, yet only 142 in 2009.[16] The average daily transit riders in New Orleans fell drastically from 71,543 before Katrina, to 19,744 two years after Katrina.[17] Today, the New Orleans transit authority, on average, sees 31,007 transit riders per day.[18] Finally, the fair-market rent for two-bedroom apartments in the New Orleans area was merely $676 per month before Hurricane Katrina.[19] Over the last two years, rents have hovered near $1,000 per month.[20] It doesn't take a rocket scientist to recognize FEMA's failures in New Orleans. Plenty of work is left before New Orleans experiences real growth again.

FEMA'S Public Relations Team Wins a "Prize"

Not only does FEMA lie to us, it doesn't even do a spectacular job at covering it up. In 2007, Fineman Public Relations, a crisis communications firm, issued its list of Top 10 PR Blunders. First place was won by FEMA based on a fake press conference it held earlier that year during the Southern California wildfires. In October 2007, FEMA arranged to have its own employees role-play as independent reporters and ask soft questions to FEMA's deputy director, Harvey E. Johnson. FEMA gave real reporters only about fifteen minutes notice about the press conference, and consequently not many came.

This boldfaced lie to the American people is inexcusable, and the public relations firm that bestowed this "prize" on FEMA's staff commented, "Already troubled by continued claims of inadequate disaster response and wasteful use of funds, the Federal Emergency Management Agency (FEMA) truly fumbled when it held what the *Washington Post* described as a 'phony press conference' in response to Southern California wildfires."[21]

Moreover, one of the FEMA staffers involved in this debacle was actually *promoted* to deputy director of public affairs after the phony conference. So, yet again, FEMA was not even able to learn from its past blunders.

Through making us pay for FEMA's faulty work, the federal government has created a contract between itself and American taxpayers. Yet, this is unconstitutional because it's a contract we never agreed to or have any way of escaping. There is no constitutional argument to be made for the feds taking tax dollars and giving them to private persons, even if they are disaster victims. It is one's personal choice to give money to a charity, not something that can be required by our federal government. Think about it: It is impossible to be charitable with someone else's money.

Nothing in the Constitution authorizes the federal government to engage in wealth distribution, yet no one in Washington stopped Congress from dumping $200 billion of the taxpayers' money into New Orleans. Nothing in the Constitution authorizes the federal government to bail out politicians who felt it unnecessary to maintain the levees that broke when Katrina struck, but Congress said to Louisiana politicians after Katrina, "Don't worry. We'll just steal from the American people." So, keep working and earning money, America! Your money is going below sea level.

FDA

Medicine is prescribed primarily to make us healthy. And often it has that effect. But, sometimes prescribed or even over-the-counter drugs can go terribly wrong. Years after people have been taking them, the government goes ahead and says, "Oops!" Often, by the time it says, "Oops," it is too late, and the American people have already paid the price.

Until the twentieth century, the federal government rarely regulated the content or sale of food and drugs. The Food and Drug Administration (FDA) was created in the 1920s under a climate of fear created by muckraking journalists like Upton Sinclair, who exposed the disgusting and unsafe conditions inside the meatpacking industry. By the 1950s, FDA bureaucrats had begun expanding their premarket approval process, meaning that they were enlarging the part of the agency that checks drugs "for safety" before they reach consumers.

Yet, only a nation of sheep would think that the government alone can keep us safe and healthy. The Framers obviously omitted from Congress's powers all that FEMA and the FDA have done and tried to do. Despite the apparent congressional intent of reducing to zero the risk of using pharmaceuticals, unsurprisingly, the FDA has failed to do so. Instead, the FDA began the process of dictating standards for clinical drug trials and tests and conducting a lengthy approval process that a manufacturer needed to pass before bringing a new or modified drug to market."[22] So, instead of bringing the risk of using drugs to zero, the FDA has created a nation of people, many of whom believe the lie that the risk of using drugs has been brought to zero. This is an extremely dangerous situation.

It seems as though the FDA's supposed purpose is to help Americans so drugs that would hurt us never make it to the shelves. This all *sounds* well and good, but the problem is that harmful drugs *do* make it to the shelves and often stay on them for quite some time. The FDA is not helping us at all; it is giving us a false sense of security. The government lies when it presents the FDA as an organization that will keep us safe. But, we can't push all the blame off on the FDA.

Often, there are more FDA recalls than there are days of the week; these recalls are usually reported in the media. So, we lie to ourselves when we say, "Okay" and pop any pill on which the government places its stamp of approval. We lie to ourselves when we forgo looking at labels or doing our own research about the safety of something because we trust that the government did our homework for us. The federal government can't deliver the mail or manage Medicare or run Amtrak on time; can it really be expected to keep pharmaceuticals safe?

There is a long list of drugs that the FDA has approved and then later said were unsafe. In the summer of 2009, it was reported that pain medications Vicodin and Percocet, which combine acetamino-phen (the ingredient used in Tylenol) and other painkillers, would likely be taken off the market due to the risk of liver damage. The same FDA panel also voted to limit the maximum single doses of over-the-counter acetaminophen to eight pills of a medication like Extra Strength Tylenol. A safety panel voted on these matters, and though the FDA is not required to follow the advice of its panels, it usually does.

Around the same time, in July 2009, the FDA decided to require Chantix and Zyban (two drugs to help people quit smoking) to issue the FDA's strongest suicide and depression warning. The drugs come with a possibility of side effects like depression, change in behavior, or suicidal thoughts. These are serious potential side effects, and drugs like these are widely used. Chantix was only approved in 2006, and annual sales had already reached $846 million at the time of the recall.[23]

Jim Grichar argues that the FDA not only does an exceedingly poor job at fulfilling its purpose, but that it does not even have a purpose and should be abandoned because the free market will do a better job at regulating drugs than the FDA has ever done. "In the absence of the FDA," Grichar said, "and with trial lawyers looking for multi-billion dollar settlements in lawsuits, pharmaceutical manufacturers and medical equipment manufacturers have every incentive to be cautious in bringing out new drugs and new medical devices. To this end, they would avail themselves of independent private reviews of the results of clinical trials and tests."[24]

This proposed system makes a great deal of sense in that it gives the burden of being held accountable back to the pharmaceutical companies that produce these drugs. With all that liability on their hands, companies are bound to be more careful. And if they are not careful, they will cease to exist.

The free market and our own judgment are really the only legitimate entities that can keep us safe. When the government lies and tells us that it can foolproof pharmaceuticals for use, we rely on it and put ourselves and our families in danger. The government knows that it cannot handle the massive undertaking of keeping us safe, but it wants us to think it can. Private companies are far better, faster, and more accurate at rating goods and products and communicating to us, and then we can be free to choose. When a company like Underwriters Laboratories (UL) acts as our informant, we have choices. Instead, when the government prohibits, we have fewer choices. This "nanny state" that the government has created automatically leaves us with less choice, and less choice means a departure from true freedom.

You Are What You Eat

Not only drugs, but the government also deceives us into thinking that our food is safe from bacteria or disease, because federal agencies oversee and check our food for us. In recent years a vast universe of food has been recalled as unsafe by the FDA: our beef, spinach, peanut butter, eggs, tomatoes, and many more items (even dog food) have been deemed unsafe over and over again. Clearly many FDA employees are asleep at the wheel, while taxpayer money goes down the drain.

In addition to failing to keep our food from making us physically sick, the FDA has also wreaked a great deal of havoc and hysteria through its food recalls. During the spring and summer of 2008, the FDA went on a wild goose chase in search of bacteria-laden tomatoes. While the FDA spent weeks of its employees' time and millions in taxpayers' dollars trying to figure out the source of the bad tomatoes, the tomato industry and consumers suffered as major companies like McDonald's refused to use tomatoes in any of their food. In July, eleven weeks into the recall, the FDA decided that maybe people were not getting sick from tomatoes after all. Its scientists began to think that maybe the sickness was coming from peppers or cilantro that is often mixed with tomatoes in foods like salsa or guacamole.[25]

They were correct; correct, after terrifying the public; correct, after wasting millions in tax dollars; correct, after causing *over one hundred million dollars in losses* to the perfectly safe and utterly innocent tomato industry;[26] correct, after exercising power that the Constitution does not grant to the federal government. That's your government at work.

If you have a failing organization that already wastes tons of money, what is the best solution? Unsurprisingly, the federal government thinks that expanding it so more of our money can be wasted is the answer. The *Wall Street Journal* reported in July 2009 that the Obama administration is planning to toughen safety standards to try to prevent contamination of foods and ensure food industry compliance with federal standards. Generally, "tougher" means more expensive. So, the likely outcome is that government will get bigger, taxes will go up, and our food will be just as unsafe this year as it was last year.

Lie #11

"We Are Winning the War on Drugs"

The "war on drugs" is a deceptive name for what has really become a war on the American people through the government's assault on human freedom, the prison system, and all taxpayers. Despite nearly four decades of battling against the use and selling of drugs, the government's so-called "war on drugs," both at home and abroad, has largely been a failure. The tide of drugs imported into this country has not slowed, despite astronomical spending by the government and the imprisonment of record numbers of Americans, often for the possession of insignificant amounts of recreational drugs. Legislators, police, and prosecutors have encouraged judges to lock up more and more Americans, causing prisons to be bursting at the seams and ruining countless lives, a great many of them among racial minorities.

This government lie is hardly new; in fact, the "war on drugs" is in effect a reincarnation of prohibition. The sale of all alcoholic beverages was outlawed in 1920, with the passage of the Eighteenth Amendment. Closing the legal market on something that consumers desire simply opened a black market, and in the 1920s, there was a great deal of corruption and violence caused by the government's ban. It actually created the lawlessness that characterized the era. Consequently, gangs and organized crime flourished. By 1921, the murder rate in America jumped.[1] After seemingly recognizing the harm that Prohibition had caused, the United States enacted the Twenty-First Amendment in 1933 to allow people to drink as they pleased.[2] After Prohibition was repealed, the homicide rate began to fall.[3] This is not a coincidence.

After the alcohol ban was repealed, much of the organized crime that was facilitated by Prohibition simply switched businesses and entered into the illegal drug market. Today (several decades after the "war on drugs" commenced), the black market for drugs is thriving. The parallels between today's prohibition and yesterday's prohibition are glaringly obvious and point to the government's severe case of amnesia and its Victorian attitude about our bodies; except that this time, the stakes are higher. In our twenty-first-century global economy, the violence is not confined to the U.S.; it is worldwide. Ironically, in its metaphoric war on the use of drugs, the government has facilitated actual wars, actual violence, and actual death. It's about time that the government put its weapons (and our cash) down and began to use some common sense.

The War on Taxpayers

Ethan Nadelmann has written extensively about the futile war on drugs. He is a former Princeton University professor and is the founder and executive director of the Drug Policy Alliance, an organization that promotes alternatives to the drug war. In one 2003 speech he stated:

> We're a wealthy nation. If we want to lock up millions of our fel-
> low citizens, we can afford to do that. . . . On the other hand, our

economy is not what it once was. In the 1990s, incarcerating millions of people was something we could afford—10, 20, 30 billion
dollars: a drop in the bucket of the national economy. But now . . .
we can no longer afford this failed war on drugs.[4]

If America could not afford a war on drugs in 2003 when Nadelmann
wrote this, we *certainly* can't afford a war on drugs now with our ailing
economy paired with ever-increasing government expenditures. Yet,
is the question really "Can we afford it?" Wouldn't "Why *should* we
pay for it?" be a more appropriate question?

American taxpayers are once again forced to foot the bill. And a
mammoth bill it is, as the United States spends at least $40 billion
a year on costs directly related to the drug war, and then several
billion more in indirect costs.[5] The costs—of spraying Colombian
crops, of hiring numerous DEA and other government employees,
of locking up more people on drug charges than all of Western
Europe locks up on all charges combined[6]—are astronomical. And
these are only the direct costs. What about the welfare dependence
that comes from creating a class of people who have drug-related
crimes on their records and often cannot obtain employment?

The drug war is indeed perpetuating a harrowing cycle for people
with drug use or drug sales in their past. For example, let's say you
were charged with sales and then were forced to spend some time in
jail. Once you served your time and were released from prison, you
decide to apply for some jobs. When you fill out employment applications, you are asked whether you have had a criminal record. If
you check the "yes" box, chances are that you won't be the employer's first choice. If you check the "no" box, you are lying and could
get into further trouble if the employer does a background check or
finds out that you lied. There are no great options here.

Then, because you cannot find a legitimate job, it is difficult to make a living. This makes turning to the sale of drugs an easy and almost sensible option, even if that is not the choice you wanted to make. The point is that when the government locks ordinary people away for committing nonviolent, nonvictim, harmless drug crimes, it sets people up for repeat offenses.

It also makes welfare a very plausible option. Either way, taxpayer money goes to the huge cost of filling prisons or the huge cost of supporting people and their families when the breadwinner is imprisoned or unemployable. And the cycle generally does not end with one person. Children who grow up in houses where their parents are drug dealers, in housing projects, and on welfare generally are not primed to have the brightest futures. They grow up around these things, and this lifestyle becomes normalized and passed on. Whole generations of families grow up around this, and it is unhealthy, dangerous, and expensive. This cycle is detrimental, and the government's holier-than-thou values have been unable to stop it.

Why We Fight

Yet, the drug war keeps going, and going, and going. Regardless of who is in power, Republican, Democrat, liberal, or conservative, the war on drugs has been happening for four decades. Why? Is the government so arrogant and stubborn that it can't look at the statistical information and see that these policies simply do not work? Do politicians just like squandering our money? These questions are still open, but it seems likely that the government *knows* these policies do not work. It must. Yet, politicians lie to us and wax poetic about eliminating the use of drugs because it sounds like a good thing to say from a stump. Well, it's about time they come back down to earth.

Politicians like to speak about the war on drugs because combating drugs sounds moral. The people from good families, with good morals, and good character that we want to represent us in the government feel the need to propagate this squeaky-clean image. Advocating for a drug-free society generally helps this image and is something the public wants to hear. Politicians are afraid to veer away from it. The mainstream public is afraid to disagree. Basically, we all waste $40 billion a year to keep up a useless, ineffective appearance.

Who's fooled by this charade? Anyone who picks up a newspaper, tabloid, watches TV, or goes on the Internet could tell you that politicians are far from angels. They have affairs, they steal money, they gamble, they drink to excess. Many have even used drugs that they themselves have voted to make illegal. And the truth is, many ordinary American people have used drugs as well; for this is the reason that the drug war is such a large enterprise.

At its heart, the war on drugs is about false morality and personal freedom. People do risky things every day. Sure, some people are more averse to risk than others and would never climb a mountain or go bungee jumping. Yet, some people love doing these death-defying stunts, and their quality of life would be damaged without doing them. Drugs are not much different. Once you take the government's sense of morality out of the equation, and simply look at drugs as dangerous and addictive substances, drugs are really not much different than other risks. So, instead of spouting on and on about the morality of this issue, couldn't politicians take on the cause of freedom?

This gets back to the heart of what this book argues: The government lies to us when it tells us the drug war is for our own good or when it tells us that the war on drugs is working. The government lies to us by covering up what the drug war is actually about—image, power, and usurping the rights of Americans.

Anthony Gregory, senior researcher at the Independent Institute, a free-market think tank in Oakland, California, eloquently wrote:

The ideology of the war on drugs is the ideology of totalitarianism, of communism, of fascism and of slavery. In practice, it has made an utter mockery of the rule of law and the often-spouted idea that America is the freest country on earth. The United States has one of the highest per capita prison populations in the world, second only to Rwanda, thanks largely to the drug war, all while its federal government imposes its drug policies on other countries by methods ranging from mere diplomatic bullying to spraying foreign crops with lethal poison, from bribing foreign heads of state to bankrolling and whitewashing acts of mass murder conducted by despots in the name of fighting drugs.[7]

Reported incidents reveal a gross abuse of police power during drug raids. In Philadelphia, a group of narcotics squad members entered Jose Duran's tobacco shop with guns drawn and then smashed some of the store's surveillance cameras with a metal rod before arresting the owners for selling tiny, *empty* ziplock bags which the officers claimed were drug paraphernalia. After breaking the remaining surveillance cameras, the police stole money from the cash register and handfuls of Zippo lighters.

Similar stories about abuse of police power were reported by seven other small shops in the Philadelphia area. All of these jack-booted raids were apparently led by narcotics officer Jeffrey Cujdik.[8] At least three people who formerly acted as informants for Cujdik claimed that the officer would give them cartons of cigarettes that he stole from the stores he raided. In one raided store, officers opened up the refrigerators to drink and take the juice and energy drinks kept inside.

No matter who performs actions like this, they are against the law. But, people's rights are often trampled, with the war on drugs used as a justification. These Philadelphia raids are just a few examples of the government-engineered assaults on our rights through the war on drugs. Several federal civil rights lawsuits were filed against Cujdik and his brother Richard, who is also an officer, other drug squad members, and the City of Philadelphia.[9] As of this writing, the outcomes of the cases have yet to be determined.

The government uses the drug war to justify taking away our rights guaranteed by the Fourth Amendment of the United States Constitution, which prohibits "unreasonable searches and seizures" and bars search warrants on anything but those based upon "probable cause" of criminal activity and issued by judges. Since the war on drugs began almost four decades ago, most searches and seizures reaching the United States Supreme Court have been approved. According to Yale Law School Professor Steven Duke, the Court has held that a search based on an invalid warrant does not require any remedy so long as the police acted in "good faith."

So people can be stopped in their cars or in airports, trains, or buses, and then submitted to questioning or held to be sniffed by dogs. Police may search an open field without warrant or cause, even if trespassing on it would otherwise be a criminal offense. Police may use helicopters to look into our homes and backyards, private property they could not lawfully or constitutionally enter without a search warrant. They can search our garbage cans without giving a reason. And if they have "reasonable suspicion," the police may search our bodies.[10]

The erosion of our Fourth Amendment rights caused by the war on drugs has not been confined to cases involving drugs, either. Duke explains:

> The pressure to uphold police activities in drug cases generates new "principles" that thereafter apply to everyone, whether or not drugs are involved. If the police are authorized to search for drugs

on suspicion, they can also search for evidence of tax evasion, gambling, mail fraud, pornography, bribery and any other offense. The putative object of a police search does not limit what can be confiscated. If police conduct is a lawful search, they can take and use any evidence they see, however unrelated it may be to what got them into the home—or the body—in the first place.[11]

So, even people who have never touched a drug in their lives are subject to the loss of Fourth Amendment rights brought about by the war on drugs, because a supine judiciary, cowed by the need to appear antidrugs, has lowered the bar for what police conduct is lawful and constitutional.

There are many examples of "wrong door" raids where the police bust into the homes of individuals only to find that they entered the wrong house and found no drugs. For example, New York City police accidentally entered into the wrong house during a predawn raid. They handcuffed Mini Matos, a deaf, asthmatic Coney Island woman, while her children cried. Ms. Matos begged the police to permit her to use her asthma pump, but she was ignored until the officers realized they had entered the wrong apartment.[12]

In 2003, the NYPD mistakenly raided the home of a fifty-seven-year-old woman. The violent manner in which they entered the apartment literally scared her to death and she died of a heart attack on the scene.[13] And it is far from surprising that one of these raids could scare someone to death. These types of raids are "typically carried out by masked, heavily armed SWAT teams using paramilitary tactics more appropriate for the battlefield than the living room. In fact, the rise in no-knock warrants over the last twenty-five years neatly corresponds with the rise in the number and frequency of use of SWAT teams."[14]

One very tragic story involved state law-enforcement agents who raided the home of Cheye Calvo (the mayor of Berwyn Heights, Maryland) after the agents had tracked a package containing marijuana that was left on the front porch of Calvo's house. Calvo brought the package into his house, and the drug agents "burst into the house without warning, shot and killed Calvo's two dogs, and bound Calvo and his mother-in-law."[15] Sadly, this was all a mistake made by the agents. Neither Calvo nor anyone in his home had anything to do with the drugs.

In November 2006, a ninety-two-year-old woman was shot and killed in her Atlanta home when three officers raided it on a drug bust. Katherine Johnston, the elderly woman who was killed, did not have any drugs. The police had the wrong house. The officers had obtained a search warrant after an undercover officer had allegedly purchased drugs at Johnston's home earlier on the day in question. The warrant was also a "no knock" warrant, meaning that they could come into the home without asking the occupant to let them in.

The officers announced themselves as police, and broke down the front door. Out of fear, Johnston used a gun her niece bought her for protection and shot at the officers, wounding them. In retaliation, they shot back and murdered her. Johnston had lived in her home on 933 Neal Street in northwest Atlanta for seventeen years. Johnston's distraught niece, Sarah Dozier, was "mad as hell," and stated that the police had "shot her down like a dog."[16] By the end of 2008, all three officers had pled guilty to various felonies in connection with the massacre. They began serving substantial prison sentences in early 2009.

Drug Money Supports Terror

The Office of National Drug Control Policy has begun running ads that say, "Drug money supports terror." The ads ask, "Where do terrorists get their money? . . . If you buy drugs, some of it might come from you." This is another lie. Here is a kernel of truth the government fails to comprehend: It is not the demand for drugs that is responsible for nurturing and harboring terrorists, it is the prohibition of the drugs that wreaks the most global havoc. Drugs are profitable because there is a ban on them. And items found on the black market generally are not cheap.[17] So while the government goes and blames *terrorism* on people who buy drugs, it is *the government itself* that is actually perpetuating terrorism through its nonsensical drug policies. Apart from that, plenty of your tax money was used to fund these fruitless ads.

In fact, the war on drugs is responsible for a great deal of violence around the world. Recently there have been many brutal killings and much horrific violence related to drug cartels in Mexico, who have been warring with Mexican and U.S. officials. All of this was in the name of the drug war. Drug lords are engaging in a violent competition to export illegal drugs into the U.S. and reap the great rewards of the black market. As a result of these gang "drug wars" caused by the government "war on drugs," many innocent people have lost their lives.

Since January 2007, there have been an estimated 9,903 drug-war-related deaths in Mexico, more than the U.S. fatalities thus far in the Iraq War.[18] Many children have also been exposed to the brutal war. In Tijuana, schoolchildren have seen bodies hung from overpasses and stuffed into refrigerators.[19] Furthermore, twelve corpses, with their tongues cut out, were dumped into a vacant lot across from an elementary school.[20] The stories are downright tragic.

The War on Big Government

The war on drugs has been a disaster for America. Using drugs, killing babies in our wombs, and taking our own lives are all actions committed against our bodies. Yet, while the government permits us to have abortions and commit suicide, and lets us get high on one chemical, alcohol, it prohibits us from getting high on other chemicals, which it calls "drugs." Does that make any sense? Everyone should have the right to make choices about his or her own body, period.

While on a larger scale the war on drugs is about wasteful government expenditure and an infringement on our Fourth Amendment rights, on a more personal level it is about the choices individuals make concerning their own bodies. We should be allowed to control what enters our bodies. If someone very badly wants to ingest a chemical substance into his body, he should be able to do so regardless of any government law; and thousands do so, every day. According to Professor Murray Rothbard:

> Propagandize against cigarettes as much as you want, but leave the *individual free to run his own life*. Otherwise, we may as well outlaw all sorts of possible carcinogenic agents—including tight shoes, improperly fitting false teeth, excessive exposure to the sun, as well as excessive intake of ice cream, eggs, and butter which might lead to heart disease. And, if such prohibitions prove unenforceable, again the logic is to place people in cages so that they will receive the proper amount of sun, the correct diet, properly fitting shoes, and so on.[21] (emphases added)

Furthermore, we know from the utter ineffectiveness of Prohibition that drug laws will never serve as a deterrent to drug use. Will Rogers opined that "[i]nstead of giving money to found colleges to promote learning, why don't they pass a constitutional amendment prohibiting anybody from learning anything? If it works as good as the Prohibition one did, why, in five years we would have the smartest race of people on earth!"[22] Rogers was being facetious, but he certainly has a point.

Generally, someone who seeks to disobey laws that punish victimless crimes does not look up the jail sentence for the crime he is about to commit, so why criminalize drug use, and give drug users and sellers long stints in prison? Do these laws really change people's mind-sets? Hardly. There is no logic here, and billions of dollars per year are wasted because of this lack of foresight. On this issue, Milton Friedman wrote, "Every friend of freedom . . . must be as revolted as I am by the prospect of turning the United States into an armed camp, by the vision of jails filled with casual drug users and of an army of enforcers empowered to invade the liberty [and property] of citizens on slight evidence."[23]

Finally, America's children have also often fallen victim to the drug war. Getting in trouble with the law at a young age follows many youngsters into adulthood. These children are plagued with emotional baggage and possibly a criminal record, simply for trying to satisfy their curiosities. If we really want to raise healthy, happy children, it is up to families, peer groups, and communities to restrict harmful behavior—not the government. Close-knit relationships and good examples reach much further than the government ever could, and they do not cost taxpayers a dime.

We must stop this foolish war, and stop letting the government talk us into it year after year, election after election. As we have learned throughout this book, the government does two things very well: it scares us to death, and it spends our money. The war on drugs is no different than any other government scam employed to steal our money. When will there be a "War on Big Government," in which the taxpayers get money from Washington to keep the federal government from spiraling further out of control?

Lie #12

"Everyone Is Innocent Until Proven Guilty"

One beautiful day in Washington, D.C., a twelve-year-old girl named Ansche Hedgepeth was arrested by an undercover transit officer on her way home from school. She was handcuffed, taken to a juvenile processing center, fingerprinted, photographed, and detained for three hours. Ansche was not arrested for murder, or assault, or theft; rather, she had the audacity to eat a French fry on the subway. And the United States Court of Appeals for the D.C. Circuit sanctioned her three-hour incarceration.[1] (This case, which would have normally been brought in a District of Columbia city court, was filed in federal court in Washington because the girl's mother claimed that the Washington transit authority had violated her daughter's right to equal protection under the law.)

If children on the subway are subjected to such unconstitutional conduct, imagine what adults face when police officers have the right to lock them up and treat them as guilty before even the semblance of a trial is held. And then imagine a court system that denies the presumption of innocence until the jury is impaneled. And then imagine judges who permit it; and a government that denies it.

Probably the least questioned and most believed government lie is also the most famous maxim of the American judicial system: that all persons are presumed "innocent until proven guilty" beyond a reasonable doubt. This presumption of innocence is a standard taught to the youngest of school children and which the government hails as a founding principle of justice because it presumes that, like the oft-repeated Lord Justice William Blackstone ratio, "Better that ten guilty persons escape than that one innocent suffer."[2]

Of course, "innocent until proven guilty" has been at the core of Western judicial systems since biblical times.[3] We are indoctrinated so thoroughly that the average person rarely considers whether the phrase is true or not. Yet when we carefully examine the system, we find that it does not function as the government would like us to believe. Beneath the surface of various platitudes, the falsity of the presumption of innocence becomes readily apparent.

Presuming the Presumption

The presumption was first recognized by the United States Supreme Court in *Coffin v. United States* (1895), in which it stated that "the principle that there is a presumption of innocence in favor of the accused is the *undoubted law*, axiomatic and elementary, and its enforcement *lies at the foundation* of the administration of our criminal [law] system"[4] (emphases added). Somehow though, this undoubted law of presumed innocence has been tossed to the wayside in the courts, though the government continues to teach it in its classrooms. But what was once elementary is now a complicated and convoluted field of the law.

In 1951, in the case of *Stack v. Boyle*, the Supreme Court held that "the traditional right to freedom before conviction permits the unhampered preparation of a defense, and serves to prevent the infliction of punishment prior to conviction . . . Unless this right to bail before trial is preserved, the presumption of innocence, secured only after centuries of struggle, would lose its meaning."[5] Yet less than twenty years later, President Nixon signed a bill into law that allowed judges to consider the factor of "danger to the community" in noncapital bail cases, with the Department of Justice "arguing that the presumption of innocence was *merely a rule of evidence with no application to pretrial proceedings*"[6] (emphases added). Apparently, even though one is "innocent until *proven* guilty," what the government hides is that this principle applies only *during* the trial, and that the government believes that defendants are "guilty until trial," if convenient for the government, under the auspices of community safety.

Does that make any sense? Before you've even had a chance to go to trial, pretrial proceedings, which contain much lower protections of the innocent than those of a trial, can drop what is often cited as the most elementary principle of the justice system. Astoundingly, what the Supreme Court had just reaffirmed in *Stack v. Boyle* as a traditional freedom that secured the presumption of innocence was now being legislatively eroded on the claim that such grand principles do not apply between an arrest and the beginning of the trial, a period of time that is almost always much longer than the trial itself.

Even if we were to accept that people the government deems "dangerous" should be kept separate from the community, they do not deserve to be treated like convicted criminals. Yet even though the government has often claimed that they are not, this is not the reality. Once in jail, there is no distinction made between the "innocent" and the guilty. Instead, the indicted-but-not-convicted prisoners are mixed in with those convicted "in overcrowded jails . . . regularly subjected to degradations and restrictions amounting to punishment."[7]

Imagine that, punishment beginning before you have even had

a chance to prove your innocence (even though the government should actually be proving your guilt). Is that consistent with the presumption of innocence? The U.S. Court of Appeals for the Second Circuit, in *Wolfish v. Levi* (1978), certainly did not think so. It held, in this class action suit brought by all persons detained at New York's Metropolitan Correction Center, that the "restrictions" imposed on innocent defendants were unjustified and violated "their right to be treated as innocent until proven guilty."[8]

Unfortunately, the Supreme Court of the United States chose to approve the actions of the government, while attempting to maintain the myth that one is innocent until proven guilty. On appeal, then-Justice Rehnquist wrote that the presumption of innocence did not have any application before trial.[9] The result of this, noted by Justice Thurgood Marshall, was effectively the same as if the Court had chosen to decree that the "presumption did not exist at all."[10]

These cases, which assume that once you are arrested you will be considered guilty until your trial starts, began the resulting erosion of the presumption of innocence. And while schoolchildren are still taught that this maxim is true (at least in government-owned schools), the government continues its lie, claiming that it has not abridged this right and justifying itself with the constant "for the public safety" argument. These "supposedly innocent" people cannot be judged as such because they may present a danger to society. And whether or not the argument has justification, its outcome still results in people—like little Ansche Hedgepeth—who should be considered innocent under our system being adjudged as guilty and punished before they have the chance to defend themselves. In essence, these people are considered "guilty" until they have a chance to prove their innocence at trial.

If our courts can lose sight of such a presumption of innocence and continue to authorize the police to arrest you at any time for even the most minute crimes, like not *wearing a seat belt while parked*, or *juggling cigar boxes* on a sidewalk in Times Square in New York City without a license, or being *quietly drunk in a bar* in the State of Texas recently, then our rights extend only as far as the police subjectively allow.

Guilty Until Proven Insane

While pretrial presumptions of innocence are allowed to be thrown out the window, the government reminds us that *during* trial, one is still "innocent until proven guilty." Strangely enough, this, too, is also not always true. In certain states, when a defendant in a criminal case asserts the insanity defense, the burden of proof as to his insanity rests with the defendant.[11] Given that insanity means that you are legally, if not factually, innocent—because you could not have the mental capacity required by the law to commit the crime—then forcing the defendant to prove his own insanity (and thereby his innocence) is a direct violation of the presumption of innocence, which is supposed to permeate our entire justice system. While the Supreme Court in 1895 stated that in a federal prosecution the burden would be on the prosecution to prove that the defendant belongs "to a class capable of committing crime,"[12] some courts still allow the presumption of sanity, and therefore guilt, to stand unless the defendant affirmatively proves his insanity and therefore his innocence.

Such conduct was upheld by the Supreme Court in 1952, in the case of *Leland v. Oregon*. The Court held that an Oregon law requiring that the defendant prove his insanity *beyond a reasonable doubt* was not a violation of the Fourteenth Amendment, even though it essentially required him to prove his innocence.[13] This is especially shocking considering that, unlike other states that only required the defendant to prove this by a preponderance of the evidence,

Oregon required proof beyond a reasonable doubt. This is the same burden, the same obligation of coming forward with evidence, the same level and quality of proof as the government must meet in its case-in-chief in order to obtain a conviction. This is also an utter rejection of the presumption of innocence.

What is most shocking about such a requirement is that it shifts the burden of proof from the prosecution to the defense. In every criminal trial, the prosecution has the burden of proving every element of the charged crime—every component of guilt—beyond a reasonable doubt. The defendant does not have to examine any witnesses or present any evidence. The defendant does not have any burden; he is not required to prove anything at all. This is the meaning of "innocent until proven guilty," that the defendant is presumed innocent and the prosecution must prove to the jury that he is guilty *beyond a reasonable doubt*.

Therefore, when the courts enforce a requirement that the defendant prove his insanity, this means that they are presuming him sane, thereby also presuming an element of guilt. If the jury takes as a given *any* element of guilt, and the defendant needs to prove to the jury that that element is not so, that is a perversion of our system of justice. The courts should never sanction such a requirement. Yet some do, and the Supreme Court has allowed them that discretion. And still we believe that the presumption of innocence is holding strong?

Discarding Actual Innocence

Sadly, the Supreme Court has also held that once an innocent man is found guilty by a jury, he cannot appeal on the basis that he has proof of his *actual innocence*. The court held that the Due Process Clause did not require that "every conceivable step is taken, at whatever cost, to eliminate the possibility of convicting an innocent person."[14] So while the basic premise of our system is preached to be that no innocent man be jailed, no matter how many guilty go free, apparently this does not apply when the cost of ensuring this gets too high.

The idea of a cost-benefit analysis applied to innocents in the justice system is not the most heartwarming of thoughts. Leonel Torres Herrera, who was convicted of killing a police officer and once convicted of that death, pled guilty to the death of another, is the example of where such a path will lead. After being sentenced to death, Herrera appealed based on "actual innocence." In effect, he provided proof that he had not committed the crime, including the affidavits of a lawyer, a former classmate, and a former cellmate of his brother's, all three of whom swore that Herrera's brother had confessed to them of committing the crime. He also had a statement from his nephew attesting that he had witnessed his own father kill the police officers. This was the evidence that Herrera presented in order to argue that he should not be executed. None of the five people had reason to lie. Yet the Supreme Court decided that this was not important and that "actual innocence" was not a matter for appeal, since the defendant could instead work to get a pardon.

Imagine being jailed, about to be executed for a crime you did not commit, and having to depend on an elected official to take mercy on you, even when this will ensure that he is portrayed as "soft on crime." This is what happened to Herrera. Though he appealed to the governor, he was denied and the heartless, lawless future President who denied an innocent man his life was then-Governor George W. Bush of Texas. Only four months after the Supreme Court ruled that actual innocence does not matter, Leonel Torres Herrera was executed. His last statement was, "I am innocent, innocent, innocent. Make no mistake about this; I owe society nothing. Continue the struggle for human rights, helping those who are innocent . . . I am an innocent man, and something very wrong is taking place tonight. May God bless you all. I am ready."

How can we say that the idea that "it is better for guilty men to go free than for one innocent man to be punished" is still a mantra of our justice system, if a man who has definite proof of his innocence cannot be saved by the highest court in the land? The justices of the Supreme Court did not seem to have much of a problem permitting the execution of a man, even when confronted with proof of his actual innocence, justifying their actions by stating that the courts would be too busy if they were forced to review every case. But this is not every case: Herrera brought forward more than doubt about his guilt; he brought actual evidence of innocence. And if that is the case, how can anyone tell him that he deserves to die? Of course the court also noted that *assuming* that "in a capital case, a truly persuasive demonstration of actual innocence made after trial would render the execution of the defendant unconstitutional . . . the threshold showing for such an assumed right would necessarily be extraordinarily high."[15]

First the court held that killing an innocent man is not unconstitutional, then it declares that even if it was, the man must prove his innocence under the most extraordinary of standards of proof to be able to invoke the natural right to live.

Government Lies About Guilt

The *Herrera v. Collins* decision is especially frightening when considered in the light of the falsely convicted persons who have been proven innocent through DNA analysis. It only shows how indisputably false is the idea that our system protects the innocent. And while the government can continue to preach what it wants us to believe, it is widely apparent that the innocent, especially after they have had their day in court, no longer matter, even when they have incontrovertible evidence of their innocence.

The Innocence Project, a nonprofit organization created by Barry Scheck and Peter Neufeld, strives, through DNA analysis, to free the innocent who have been wrongly convicted and incarcerated. Unsurprisingly, one of its discoveries was that governmental misconduct was a factor in 50 percent of their first seventy-four DNA exonerations. The majority included suppression of exculpatory evidence by the police and prosecution, knowing use of false testimony, coercing witnesses, and fabricating evidence.[16] These are the actions of the same governments whose schools so strongly claim to believe in "innocent until guilt is proven."

The prosecutors and police officers, who are supposed to enforce the law, are actually ensuring that the innocent are proven guilty, all the while claiming that their suspects are presumed innocent. The question is though, if they believed their lies, why would they suppress and fabricate evidence? Why would they feel the need to coerce witnesses? Either they want the innocent to be jailed or they actually do not believe in the presumption, and feel that those whom they suspect are "guilty" are indeed guilty, no matter what the law says and no matter what evidence contradicts their beliefs.

The examples of this type of conduct are wide-ranging; but one extreme example lies in the case of Jeffrey R. MacDonald, M.D. Dr. MacDonald was a twenty-six-year-old Army captain living on base with his wife and two young daughters and leading a very fulfilling life. Having accomplished the goals he had set for himself, Jeffrey was a successful and happy man. But that happiness was shattered on February 17th 1970. Intruders broke into his home, brutally murdered his wife and two daughters, and attempted to murder Jeff himself. Resuscitated by the military police, he was rushed to the hospital, where he remained in the Intensive Care Unit for over a week for treatment of his multiple stab wounds, as well as a collapsed lung. While on the way to the hospital, Jeff described the intruders as a woman with long, blond hair covered by a floppy hat, and two other males, one white and the other black. With these descriptions he provided to police, he hoped that justice would be served and those responsible for the killings would be held responsible. Yet, rather than follow up, the government focused on Jeff as its prime suspect from the beginning of the case, even when the Army had investigated and cleared him and had given him an honorable discharge.

It took them nine years, until one of the Army lawyers assigned to the case, Brian Murtagh, was transferred to the Department of Justice and realized that the case had not yet been closed. As there were no suspects, Murtagh decided to refocus attention on Jeff. And his witch hunt led to what amounted to a story backed by only the most minute of circumstantial evidence. Unfortunately for Jeff, the one witness who could have helped, Helena Stoeckley, who had testified for the prosecution so many times in many other cases and had herself confessed to the crime, was determined to be an "unreliable witness," and therefore those persons to whom she had confessed were not permitted to relate that testimony to Jeff's jury. During her testimony, Helena admitted to owning a blond wig and floppy hat but had destroyed them, because they connected her to the murders. Still, the jury convicted Jeff, and he was sentenced to three life terms. His conviction was originally overturned by the U.S. Court of Appeals for the Fourth Circuit, and he had a taste of freedom, until in 1982, when the Supreme Court reinstated his conviction and returned him to prison.

Of course, Jeff filed multiple appeals, but the trial judge denied them all. Helena Stoeckley continued to confess to various individuals her role in the murder. Jeff also found out that the prosecution had hidden exculpatory evidence and lied to the jury, claiming that no signs of intruders were found even though Jeff found case file notes stating that long, blond wig fibers had been found, as well as black wool fibers not linked to the house. He also learned that a crime lab tech had falsely testified that the synthetic blond hair found at the scene did not come from a wig. This same crime lab tech would later be fired from the lab when evidence was found of multiple deceptions in various cases.

One of the prosecutors on the case, James Blackburn, was later disbarred and charged with twelve counts of dishonesty, including embezzlement and changing court documents. A former U.S. Marshal came forward twenty-six years later (How could he live with himself—waiting so long before coming forward—while Jeff was in a federal prison?), avowing and passing a polygraph stating that he had witnessed a conversation between Helena Stoeckley and the prosecutor, wherein she confessed to committing the murders, and the prosecutor threatened to indict her for murder if she testified to that.

Even when DNA results were finally available in 2006, eight-and-a-half years after they had been ordered, and multiple hairs were found at the scene that did not match Jeff or the rest of his family, one of which was grasped in two-year-old Kristen's hand as if torn from her attacker's head, the federal judge who replaced the original trial judge refused to grant a new trial.

Finally, in 2007, after Helena had died, Jeff heard from Helena's mother, who stated that Helena had confessed to her and explained that she could not tell the truth on the stand because she was afraid of the prosecutor, and the mother had not come forward earlier because she, too, was afraid. Even with all this evidence, the trial judge held that since Helena was dead, even if all the testimony about and from her was true, there was no way anyone could know how her fear of the prosecutor affected her testimony, and therefore the appeal was denied. Jeff's actual innocence was of no import to the government. All that mattered was that he was not denied any constitutional protections at his trial. Doesn't the Constitution protect against wrongful imprisonment?

After thirty years of fighting for his innocence, Jeff, with the help of the Innocence Project, has filed another appeal with the Fourth Circuit. He might be able to make it out of jail for his sixty-sixth birthday and be given the freedom that innocent people have as a natural birthright.

Civil Commitment: Presumption of Innocence Need Not Apply

Even though the Supreme Court had in its early days stressed that the presumption of innocence was undoubted law, it failed to apply its own precedent when deciding a case of civil commitment. Apparently, when it is a case of civil commitment, then the people who were wrongfully committed to mental hospitals would be comforted there by friends and family. Sounds ridiculous, right? Well, that is what the Supreme Court reasoned in 1979 in *Addington v. Texas*. The case involved Frank Addington, a Texan who had been charged with misdemeanor assault. His mother filed a petition to have him involuntarily and indefinitely committed to a state psychiatric hospital. The Supreme Court held that the burden for involuntary civil commitment did not have to reach "beyond a reasonable doubt," rather, only proof by "clear and convincing evidence" that such a commitment was necessary.

The Court distinguished between incarceration in criminal cases and civil commitment, finding that there was a large difference between the two and that the second did not require a "beyond a reasonable doubt" standard. Considering that civil commitment is for an indefinite period, rather than a set period as is the case for criminal sentencing, the fact that the Supreme Court could find that it required a lower threshold of proof, and therefore in essence discard the standard required when one is "innocent until proven guilty," we may have approached the old Soviet system in which nonconformists were institutionalized—a system we supposedly waged a forty-five-year-long cold war in order to upend.

In the majority opinion, Chief Justice Burger noted:

> [I]t is not true that the release of a genuinely mentally ill person is no worse for the individual than the failure to convict the guilty. One who is suffering from a debilitating mental illness and in need of treatment is neither wholly at liberty nor free of stigma . . . It cannot be said, therefore, that it is much better for a mentally ill person to "go free" than for a mentally normal person to be committed.[17]

Apparently, the Chief Justice felt that since the mentally ill are never really at liberty, then it was okay to commit the innocent. Such convoluted reasonings have no place in our law. Sometimes we must tolerate the mental instability of a few to preserve the freedom of us all.

Money Can Buy You Guilt

Anastasio Prieto was driving his truck toward home along US Route 54, just north of El Paso, Texas, on a late summer night in August 2007. While enjoying the beautiful countryside passing him by, he noticed a weigh station and pulled over to have his truck inspected. A state trooper approached him and asked whether he could search Anastasio's truck for contraband. Not protective of his own privacy,

Anastasio said, "Of course," knowing that no contraband would be found. During his conversation, Anastasio did mention that he happened to be carrying $23,700, his life savings, used to pay bills and maintain the truck, which he carried with him because he did not trust banks. What he did not realize was that his opinion of banks would be his undoing.

The money was confiscated, and Anastasio was detained, photographed, and fingerprinted while canine dogs sniffed his truck. The state police, who believed that Anastasio must be guilty of *something*, turned the cash they seized from him over to the federal Drug Enforcement Administration. Though no evidence of illegal substances was found, the DEA explained to Anastasio that they would be keeping the money, and that in thirty days he would receive notice of federal proceedings to forfeit the money permanently to the government. Anastasio was told that if he wanted to get the money back, he would have to petition a court and *prove* that the money was legally obtained by him and not the product of criminal conduct.

That's right; even though not a single shred of evidence of any illegal activity was found in his truck, Anastasio was considered guilty and would have to *prove* his innocence. Thankfully, the ACLU stepped in and sued the DEA on behalf of Anastasio. With the lawsuit looming, and fearing a more public revelation of its Gestapo tactics at a trial, the DEA returned the money months later.[18]

Sadly, the case of Anastasio Prieto is not an isolated incident. As much as the government continues to stress the myth that people are innocent until proven guilty, forfeiture laws debunk this myth. And, unlike in Anastasio's case, courts often sanction such actions. In a similar case, Emiliano Gomez Gonzolez and his friends had pooled their savings together, for a sum total of $124,700, in order to purchase a truck. They found the truck they wanted and agreed with a used car dealer in Chicago to purchase it for cash. Unfortunately, when Emiliano arrived in Chicago, the truck had been sold. Rather than spend the money flying back, and not having a credit card of his own, Emiliano requested that a friend rent a car for him. He packed the money in his trunk and headed home to return the money to all those in the partnership.

Unfortunately, he was pulled over by a Nebraska state trooper somewhere on Interstate 80. The officer searched his car and found the money. Of course, the money was automatically seized because a canine sniffed drug residue in the trunk *of a rental car*. The Eighth Circuit Court of Appeals held that "possession of a large sum of cash is 'strong evidence' of a connection to drug activity." Even though the money had never been tied to any drug purchases; even though, as the dissent noted, Emiliano had never been convicted of a drug-related crime; even though no actual drugs or drug paraphernalia were ever found in the car; and even though the only connection was some drug residue in a rental car that was "no doubt driven by dozens . . . of patrons during the course of a given year."[19]

Because the courts do not take seriously the presumption of innocence, because they will permit government theft based on suppositions, because they essentially reject the natural right to use and possess one's property unmolested by the government, because they do not accept the right to be left alone, they permit the government to perpetuate these horrendous injustices. Think about it. You and I could not have lawfully stolen Mr. Gonzolez's cash and had a court let us keep it because he could not prove it was his. So, if the government "derive[s]" its "just Powers from the Consent of the Governed," as Jefferson wrote in the Declaration of Independence, then how can the government do *anything* that we as individuals cannot? Even though Emiliano Gonzolez was never convicted of a crime, the life savings of the individuals involved as well as his own were forfeited to the government that stole it.

The government often justifies these takings as a way to take the profit out of crime. Yet when the agents of the state become accustomed to seizing property and not having to return it, they will often then take that property for their personal use. Such was a case that I was confronted with while on the Superior Court bench in New Jersey in 1990. A young man had been arrested for allegedly transporting women across the George Washington Bridge for certain illicit purposes. After the police arrested and charged him, they seized the car that he had supposedly used for such purposes.

Lucky for the police, the car was a beautiful $85,000 Mercedes Benz coup. (The present-day version of this car sells for $160,000.) Even luckier for the chief prosecutor of the county, the police proceeded to gift the car to him, and he proceeded to use it as his own *personal* car. Imagine the outrage of being presumed innocent, having your car seized, and then, walking down the street, observing the men who had *stolen* it, driving it. Imagine then that you had no legal recourse, that the law that was meant to protect you instead validated the theft.

Unfortunately for the prosecutor, the defendant who was driving the car did not own the Mercedes; his father did. Needless to say, when the young man and his father petitioned me to have the car returned, I did just that. A few years later, I was accosted by the former prosecutor's wife as the judge who had taken *her husband's car* away. The former prosecutor who used the car has since been convicted of unrelated crimes, incarcerated, disbarred, and presently works as a night security guard at a hotel.

These stories are just a few about the forfeiture laws in the United States, but they so aptly debunk the myth that one is innocent until proven guilty. Once your money or property is seized, which can be done for no apparent reason, it is *your* burden to prove *your* innocence and *your* ownership of *your* asset. The reason that we have laws stating that one is innocent until proven guilty is because it is so very hard to prove a negative. Just imagine trying to prove that the twenty dollars in your wallet right now are yours legally, that you did not steal them, especially if there is no specific accusation as to whom you stole the money from, when you stole, it, or how. Instead, like sheep we permit the government to say, "I am going to assume that this is stolen, and if you want it back, prove to me that it is not." Now imagine that the money was your entire life savings.

Guilty by Presumed Association

In 2000, the U.S. Department of State Country Reports on Human Rights Practices, reporting on the Egyptian custom of trying those accused of terrorism in front of military tribunals, noted that "military courts do not ensure civilian defendants due process before an independent tribunal." Yet only a few years later, the federal government apparently felt that this statement did not apply to it and enacted a law allowing any noncitizen suspected of being a terrorist to be tried by a military commission.

The last time the government used a military tribunal in this country to try foreigners who violated the rules of war involved Nazi saboteurs during World War II. They came ashore in Amagansett, New York, and Ponte Vedra Beach, Florida, and donned civilian clothes, with plans to blow up strategic U.S. targets. They were tried before a military tribunal, and President Franklin D. Roosevelt based his order to do so on the existence of a formal congressional declaration of war against Germany.

In the uproar caused by Attorney General Eric H. Holder Jr.'s 2009 announcement that the alleged planners of the 9/11 attacks are to be tried in U.S. District Court in New York City—and the suspects in the attack on the U.S. destroyer *Cole* will go on trial before military tribunals at Guantanamo Bay, Cuba—the public discourse has lost sight of the fundamental principles that guide the government when it makes such decisions. Unfortunately, the government has lost sight of the principles as well.

When President George W. Bush spoke to Congress shortly after 9/11, he did not ask for a declaration of war. Instead, Republican leaders offered and Congress enacted an Authorization for the Use of Military Force. The authorization was open-ended as to its targets and its conclusion, and basically told the president and his successors that they could pursue whomever they wanted, wherever their pursuits took them, so long as they believed that the people they pursued had engaged in acts of terrorism against the United States. Thus was born the "war" on terror.

Tellingly, and perhaps because we did not know at the time precisely who had planned the 9/11 attacks, Congress did not declare war. But the use of the word *war* persisted nonetheless. Even after he learned what countries had sponsored terrorism against us and our allies with governmental assistance, Bush did not seek a declaration of war against them. Since 9/11, American agents have captured and seized nearly eight hundred people from all over the globe in connection with the attacks, and now five have been charged with planning them.

Virtually all of those seized who survived interrogation have been held at Guantanamo Bay. Bush initially ordered that no law or treaty applied to these detainees and that no judge could hear their cases, and thus he could detain whoever he decided was too risky to release and whoever he was satisfied had participated in terrorist attacks against the U.S. He made these extraconstitutional claims based, he said, on the inherent powers of the commander in chief in wartime. But in the Supreme Court, he lost all five substantive challenges to his authority brought by detainees. As a result, some detainees had to be freed, and he and Congress eventually settled for trying some before military tribunals under the Uniform Code of Military Justice and subsequent legislation.

The casual use of the word *war* has led to a mentality among the public and even in the government that the rules of war could apply to those held at Guantanamo. But the rules of war apply only to those involved in a lawfully *declared* war, and not to something that the government merely *calls* a war. Only Congress can declare war—and thus trigger the panoply of the government's military powers that come with that declaration. Among those powers is the ability to use military tribunals to try those who have caused us harm by violating the rules of war.

The recent decision to try some of the Guantanamo detainees in federal District Court and some in military courts in Cuba is without a legal or constitutional bright line. All those still detained since 9/11 should be tried in federal courts because without a declaration of war, the Constitution demands no less.

That the target of the *Cole* attackers was military property manned by the navy offers no constitutional reason for a military trial. In the 1960s, when Army draft offices and college ROTC facilities were attacked and bombed, those charged were quite properly tried in federal courts. And when Timothy McVeigh blew up a federal courthouse in Oklahoma City; and Omar Abdel Rahman attempted in 1993 to blow up the World Trade Center, which housed many federal offices; and when Zacarias Moussaoui was accused in the 9/11 attacks, all were tried in federal courts. The "American Taliban," John Walker Lindh, and the notorious would-be shoe bomber, Richard Reid, were tried in federal courts. Even the "Ft. Dix Six," five of whom were convicted in a plot to invade a

U.S. Army post in New Jersey, were tried in federal court. And the sun still rose on the mornings after their convictions.

The Framers of the Constitution feared letting the president alone decide with whom we are at war, and thus permitting him to trigger for his own purposes the military tools reserved for wartime. They also feared allowing the government to take life, liberty, or property from any person without the intercession of a civilian jury to check the government's appetite and to compel transparency and fairness by forcing the government to prove its case to twelve ordinary citizens. Thus, the Fifth Amendment to the Constitution, which requires due process, includes the essential component of a jury trial. And the Sixth Amendment requires that when the government pursues any person in court, it must do so in the venue where the person is alleged to have caused harm.

Numerous Supreme Court cases have ruled that any person in conflict with the government can invoke due process—be that person a citizen or an immigrant, someone born here, legally here, illegally here, or whose suspect behavior did not even occur here.

Think about it: If the president could declare war on any person or entity or group simply by calling his pursuit of them a "war," there would be no limit to the government's ability to use the tools of war to achieve its ends. We have a "war" on drugs; can drug dealers be tried before military tribunals? We have a "war" on the Mafia; can mobsters be sent to Gitmo and tried there? The Obama administration has arguably declared "war" on Fox News. Are my Fox colleagues and I in danger of losing our constitutional rights to a government hostile to our opinions?

I trust not. And my trust is based on the oath that everyone who works in the government takes to uphold the Constitution. But I am not naïve. Only unflinching public fidelity to the Constitution will preserve the freedoms of us all.[20]

Guilty Solely Through Existence

If you find that the standard of "innocent until proven guilty" has been categorically breached by the government time and time again, with no regard for due process and with continuing deception, then I can only imagine your outrage when you learn about a Federal law that in essence ensures you are guilty no matter what your intentions may be. This is the Sherman Antitrust Act of 1890. This one-hundred-twenty-year-old piece of legislation was the beginning of the ambiguous "Progressive" antitrust laws in the United States. It was hailed as ensuring that consumers would now be safe from the big, bad corporations who were going to get together and make everything unbelievably expensive.

After the Sherman Act became law, the business folks had a lot of trouble: If their prices were too high, that meant they were intending to monopolize; if they charged lower prices than the competitors, then they were charged with unfair competition; and if they charged prices similar to everyone else, then they could all be charged with conspiracy.[21] Because the law is unclear, and its interpretation is constantly shifting and changing, a businessperson cannot know whether she or he is doing something legal or illegal. The president of United States Steel Corporation noted in a speech in 1950, which he entitled "Guilty Before Trial," that if the antitrust laws persisted and were to be enforced "impartially against all offenders, virtually every business in America, big or small, is going to have to be run from Atlanta, Alcatraz, Sing Sing, Leavenworth or Attica."[22]

Unlike the "supposed" presumption of innocence for individuals in the justice system, the business folks under attack from antitrust laws are in essence guilty until proven innocent, and there is no standard on how to prove their innocence. Supreme Court Justice Robert Jackson, when he was head of the Antitrust Division of the

Department of Justice, noted that it "is impossible for a lawyer to determine [in advance] what business conduct will be pronounced lawful by the Courts,"[23] and that this was an embarrassing situation for everyone involved. Basically, anytime anyone goes into business, he can be automatically guilty of one violation of the Sherman Act or another, solely through the setting of prices for his product.

The government always claims to have good reasons for antitrust laws. Its original reasoning was that "trusts [an ancient word for commercial agreements] tended to restrict output and drive prices up." Of course, there was no evidence in support of this theory at the time that the Sherman Act was passed. Rather, there is actually evidence that the trusts reduced prices, and Congressman William E. Mason (R-IL) stated, on June 20th 1890, that "trusts have made products cheaper, have reduced prices" but then also claimed that this was irrelevant, because by making prices lower, the trusts had effectively "destroyed legitimate competition and driven honest men from legitimate business enterprise."[24]

The basic rationale behind antitrust legislation is, as usual, the public safety; specifically economic safety. The feds claim they can prevent companies from restricting the market and therefore raising prices and preventing technological advancement. The government assumes that without its protection, the people will be gouged by corporations who would form monopolies or cartels, or "trusts," and engage in "predatory practices."

These are the government terms that strike fear into the average person. All of us, even those who have not studied economics in any way, have learned the dangers of these actions. We hear the word *monopoly* and think that it means the end of competition in the market, and the beginning of one giant corporation taking every little cent of our money. Yet, when one actually considers the monopoly in a free market, it should be simple to see that the only monopoly that could survive was one that offered the best products at the best prices.

Any corporation needs customers who are willing to buy from it. If it is monopolistic and does not offer the best products, other entrepreneurs will start their own business, and customers will leave the monopoly and move to the competition. And if it does offer the best product for the best price, then why is that movement a bad thing? Do we honestly mind paying less for a better product because it is produced by a company that sells more than 50 percent of those products in a given market? In reality, the only monopolies existing currently are those run by the government, like the post office and utility companies, which are *immune* from the antitrust laws. *Sadly, as we know, the government does not practice what it preaches.*

But if the whole purpose of the Sherman Act, as stated by the government, has been to ensure competition, was not part of competition the idea that some lose while others win? Even the government could not keep its sham reasoning straight. And the reason for this was explicitly stated by the *New York Times*, on September 29th 1890, which concluded "[t]hat so-called Anti-Trust law was passed to deceive the people and to clear the way for the enactment of this . . . law relating to the tariff."[25] Tariff laws were, of course, very beneficial to the government collecting the tariffs, so there is no question why it would want to ensure that the public was kept from those truths because the Sherman Act falsely proved to everybody that the government was protecting them.

What the government hid was that it was protecting the people not from rising prices, but from reduced prices. This can be seen from the cases of *U.S. v. Standard Oil of New Jersey* and *U.S. v. American Can*. These are the seminal antitrust cases that influenced all those that were to follow. In the 1911 case of *U.S. v. Standard Oil of New Jersey*, among the charges laid was raised prices to consumers. Yet petroleum prices had decreased during the alleged monopolization, declining from thirty cents per gallon in 1869 to six cents per gallon at the beginning of the antitrust trial.[26] The company was in the end broken apart by the United States Supreme Court because it had allegedly *"intended* to monopolize."

The same result occurred with *U.S. v. American Can*, a 1949 case where a judge found that the company had "coerced its customers into signing long-term leases."[27] As pointed out by D. T. Armentano, this so-called coercion was effected largely by attractive terms and generous price discounts for large orders. It was freely offered and freely bargained for. The company had violated antitrust laws because it gave bulk-order discounts! What is most egregious is that the judge ordered the company to *raise* its prices, reasoning that this would help the more expensive and less efficient companies compete in the market.[28]

Ayn Rand once aptly stated that *"free* competition *enforced* by law is a grotesque contradiction in terms." The result of this deceptive contradiction of enforced free competition is illustrated most effectively in the case of the Aluminum Company of America (Alcoa), which was charged with 150 violations of antitrust law and which the federal government pursued for over thirteen years in court, even though at the end of this terrible odyssey, the trial judge in 1939 dismissed all the charges. Unfortunately for Alcoa, the United States Court of Appeals for the Second Circuit essentially faulted Alcoa for being too successful, deeming that it was anticompetitive not because it attempted to drive out competitors through immoral tactics, but rather because it was too efficient and charged prices that were "too low."[29]

Yet, if these are the "monopolies" that the government is protecting us from, the lowest-price monopolies, is the government even performing anything remotely beneficial to the public? Why is the government spending massive amounts of its time and our money prosecuting corporations for charging low prices? If we agree that low prices are good for consumers, the only reasoning behind the government's actions stems from the settlements that are often the result of these antitrust suits. Corporations are paying out millions of dollars in fines for their purportedly harmful activities. And while prices go up for the consumer, at least the government has been able to make a quick buck, all in the guise of the "public interest" myth.

When people argue that the laws protect competition and efficiency, they should be reminded of these decisions. In essence, the antitrust laws are like pulling over drivers driving at the speed limit and staying within their lanes because careful conduct could be evidence that they are drunk drivers who are trying not to appear drunk, and when finding they are not guilty of being drunk, finding them too sober to drive.

Like traffic tickets for the state and local police, modern antitrust cases are just quick cash cows for the federal government. That is the modern law of antitrust: assuming guilt by status; fitting the circumstances to whatever crime may be needed; and using "crime" to fill government coffers.

The Presumption of Deception

We have merely touched upon the multitude of ways in which the government seizes our bodies, steals our property, and crushes our liberty with one side of its mouth, while proclaiming the presumption of innocence with the other. This presumption is the most fundamental jurisprudential value that "keeps the government off our backs," to quote Justice Douglas. If the government can destroy this, however slowly, what will be next? What will remain of our freedom?

Lie #13

"The Constitution Applies in Good Times and in Bad Times"

On April 16th 2007, Seung-Hui Cho, a student at Virginia Tech University in Blacksburg, Virginia, came to school and killed thirty-two of his classmates with a gun before taking his own life. By January 2008, President George W. Bush had signed into law a measure that aimed to keep firearms from people with mental illnesses.[1] The law provided up to $1.3 billion in federal grants to states, so that they could improve their tracking of mentally ill people who should not be permitted to purchase guns.[2] A law like this was proposed in the mid-1990s, but the mental health lobbies argued that it stigmatized the mentally ill.[3] After the tragedy at Virginia Tech, however, fear smothered freedom. Not one member of Congress voted against the law.[4]

When disastrous situations like the Virginia Tech shooting or 9/11 or Pearl Harbor occur, it is a tragedy for those affected. Yet, oftentimes the federal government utilizes the panic surrounding these situations to grab more power for itself. The government lies by telling us that it *must* infringe upon our rights in order to keep us safe. But if the steps taken by the government are truly necessary evils, why doesn't the government tailor the scope of its power as narrowly as possible? Instead, the government enacts laws quickly amid the hysteria, thereby using people's emotions and irrational fears to gag and blindfold them while their rights are swindled away. Many of these laws are then interpreted broadly as a mechanism for the government to seize more power, acquire more resources, and waste more taxpayer money.

Typically under these climates of hysteria an "anything goes" attitude prevails in Congress and, like patriotic lemmings, many politicians follow the leader and succumb to wishes of the political party to which they belong. Because they constrain their speech in an effort to be politically correct, justice is lost, and unconstitutional laws are passed.

Often the people don't speak up either, because they, too, are afraid and tend to trust government to protect them in times of crisis. We are socialized not to rebel, not to question authority or to resist going along, because it is not polite to speak up, to state the obvious, to rein in government power. Those who object to government over-reaches are often put on the defensive and asked: What do you have to hide? Yet, we need to amend this thinking because in many of these hysteria-laden situations, we lose our rights and our identity as a free people. Thus, long after the crisis has settled, Americans still must endure the legacy of laws passed during the hysterical climate.

Guns

In recent history, liberal and even conservative politicians have developed an obsession with stricter gun control laws, a policy that they believe will decrease violent crime in America. Some of them honestly believe that fewer guns will lead to fewer crimes. Some are just afraid of guns. And some want a disarmed public. Sadly, they are all wrong. Every European despot in the past two hundred years has attempted to disarm the public so as to make and keep it docile. American politicians, most of whom have never been near a gun for self-defense, will not address this. In their effort to pass gun control laws, politicians have used national tragedies to exploit our fears.

President Bill Clinton, who had been a staunch supporter of gun control throughout his presidency, used the tragedy at Columbine High School in Littleton, Colorado, to bolster his argument for more stringent gun laws. On April 20th 1999, two deranged Columbine students, Eric Harris and Dylan Klebold, shot and killed twelve students and a teacher. They injured twenty-one students, three of whom were trying to escape from the building. Immediately after the massacre, Harris and Klebold shot and killed themselves.

President Clinton, most Democrats, and many Republicans saw this tragedy as an opportunity to resume the gun control debate in America. In 1999, the United States Senate consisted of fifty-five Republicans and forty-five Democrats. The Columbine tragedy, however, caused the Republicans, a party that typically supports gun rights, to let their guard down,[5] or show their true colors. Less than a month after Columbine, with Vice President Al Gore serving as the tie-breaking vote, the Senate voted in favor of a bill requiring background checks for firearms purchasers at gun shows and pawn-shops.[6] (Luckily, this bill never passed the House of Representatives, and thus was never enacted into law.) In light of Columbine, Clinton also launched a national campaign advocating less violence in music, movies, and video games.[7] In fact, Clinton signed an executive order mandating a study of how the entertainment industry markets music, movies, and video games.

It seems following each tragedy involving guns, the government attacks the guns and not the sick individuals who abuse them. The government paints guns as evil, and conjures up the notion that we will be safer only if criminals have less access to guns. This is completely false. Lance Kirklin, a student wounded in the Columbine shooting, put it best when he said, "You don't see guns jumping off the table and shooting people."[8] The problem is not easy access to weapons. The problem lies in the nature of the killers who commit these horrific crimes. No law restricting individual rights will stop them from carrying out their objectives.

The government, however, continues to succumb to hysteria over guns, as well as violence in movies, video games, and music. It ignores the real source of the problem because it cannot regulate what people think. On the other hand, it can throw money around restricting the use of everything under the sun, and pretend that it is solving problems that no law can prevent.

The government should not interfere with individuals' rights to protect themselves against murderers like the Columbine and Virginia Tech students. Brave citizens used their right to bear arms to suppress a shooting at the University of Texas, Austin, on August 1st 1966. On that date, Charles Joseph Whitman, a twenty-five-year-old Florida native and former UT engineering student, opened fire from the twenty-eighth-floor observation deck of the school's landmark 307-foot tower.[9] Whitman killed sixteen people and wounded thirty-one before he was killed by police.[10] Until the Virginia Tech massacre, the Texas shooting was the country's deadliest.[11]

Whitman's shooting could have been much worse, though. Brave Texans used their guns to fight back and prevent Whitman from doing even more damage. One English professor, who stored his deer rifle and boxes of ammunition in his office, shot at Whitman from his office window.[12] A man by the name of Bill Helmer, a witness to the shooting, stated that Whitman was leaning over the edge of the observation deck to shoot at people, but did not have this luxury once people started shooting *at him*.[13] According to Helmer, the Texans' exercise of self-defense forced Whitman "to shoot through those drain spots, or he had to pop up real fast and then dive down again. That's why he did most of his damage in the first 20 minutes."[14] Unfortunately, the Virginia Tech campus was a gun-free zone.[15] Texas Representative Joe Driver, remembering the UT shooting, stated that "[i]f Virginia Tech had not kept the campus a gun-free zone, people could have been saved."

The government's approach to gun control is clearly wrong and terribly misguided. We must not allow the hysteria of a post-tragedy environment to bolster the government's ability to restrict our rights and prevent us from defending ourselves against killers. The right to defend yourself, your property, your freedom, or any known innocent is a natural right. Your right to use available technology to effectuate that defense is a natural right as well. The Supreme Court of the United States, as we have seen in previous pages, has characterized the right as fundamental. I'll be blunt: A major reason we have these tragedies like the University of Texas, Columbine, and Virginia Tech is because there are too few of us who carry guns, not too many.

Our Rights Were Necessarily Infringed After Pearl Harbor

In the past, attacks on our soil have also led to dangerous and unconstitutional government behavior. After the attack on Pearl Harbor, the federal government hastily installed a system of rationing based on its claim that suddenly certain commodities were scarce and the fear that others would become scarce.[16] The first items to be rationed were automobile and truck tires, in January 1942.[17] During 1942 and 1943, the government also rationed cars, bicycles, typewriters, gasoline, fuel oil, kerosene, coal, stoves, rubber footwear, shoes, sugar, coffee, processed foods, meats, canned fish, and milk products.[18]

Rationing severely restricted Americans' freedom to purchase the type and amount of goods they desired, and also resulted in a black market for rationed goods.[19] It also reinforced the federal government's power over individuals. It was utterly unnecessary. All the rationed goods could be bought for three or four times the government-set price on the black market. Without rationing, market forces would have established the prices at far less than what the black market did. Needless to say, rationing did not apply to the federal government. FDR and Congress had all the typewriters, sugar, coffee, milk, and vehicles they wanted. Americans accepted this like sheep.

The government also saw fit to strip ethnic Japanese of their liberty after the Pearl Harbor attacks. On February 19th 1942, President Franklin Delano Roosevelt signed Executive Order 9066, which authorized the removal of people of Japanese descent from the West Coast of the United States.[20] Congress later passed a law imposing criminal penalties on people who violated the order or the regulations issued pursuant to it.[21] Through its new, self-created authority, the government systematically took away the freedom of Japanese-Americans, just as it did in the previous century to African-Americans.

Initially, curfews were imposed.[22] Then, Japanese-Americans were required to report to relocation centers.[23] Finally, they were physically moved to concentration camps.[24] Gordon Hirabayashi of Washington State was a Japanese-American who, in May 1942, violated curfew and two days later failed to report to register for evacuation.[25] Hirabayashi was prosecuted and convicted in federal court for violating the government's curfew and evacuation order.[26]

In *Hirabayashi v. United States*,[27] the first significant case involving Executive Order 9066, Chief Justice Harlan F. Stone wrote the opinion of the court. In order to limit the Court's task, Stone decided that the Court need only rule on the curfew requirement and could omit discussing the requirement that Hirabayashi report to a relocation center.[28] Stone was able to do this because Hirabayashi was to serve his sentences for each offense concurrently; he was to serve only three months in prison, even though he was sentenced to two, three-month sentences.[29] The Court ruled 6 to 3 that curfews were permissible because the nation was at war with the Japanese.[30] According to Stone, "Distinctions between citizens solely because of their ancestry are . . . odious to a free people whose institutions are founded upon the doctrine of equality. . . ."[31] Nevertheless, Stone ruled that discrimination was justified in this case, because "the danger of espionage and sabotage, in time of war and of threatened invasion, calls upon the military authorities to scrutinize every relevant fact bearing on the loyalty of populations in the danger areas. . . ."[32]

The Supreme Court had another chance to dismantle the "hysteria" law that was Executive Order 9066, but instead, it validated government regulations that were even more destructive to freedom. In *Korematsu v. United States*, the Supreme Court held that the government could ship Japanese-*Americans* off to desert internment camps under the guise that it was a valid security measure. The tremendous racism, xenophobia, and unconstitutional acts that permeated this decision were ignored at the time, because of fear.

Sensationalism accompanied the fear people had about the risk of Japanese-Americans acting as spies for the Japanese government. At the time, nearly all Americans who were not of Japanese ancestry seemed to support the mass jailing of about 120,000 men, women, elderly, and young children. This was in spite of the fact that about two-thirds of the Japanese people brought to the camps were native-born United States citizens.[33]

Justice William Francis ("Frank") Murphy, an FDR appointee to the Court and one of two justices dissenting in *Korematsu*, believed that there were limits to military discretion, and he would not submit to what he saw as a clear instance of government abuse. He declared that incarcerating people because of membership in a group that is an immutable attribute of birth "goes over 'the very brink of constitutional power,' and falls into the ugly abyss of racism." Justice Murphy warned that "[r]acial discrimination in any form and in any degree has no justifiable part whatever in our democratic way of life."

He believed that by reasoning that all Japanese people are potentially disloyal to the United States based on the disloyalty of some Japanese individuals, the federal government had adopted "one of the cruelest of the rationales used by our enemies to destroy the dignity of the individual and to encourage and open the door to discriminatory actions against other minority groups in the passions of tomorrow." His words resonate powerfully today, when similar xenophobic sentiments motivate some to doubt the lawful behavior of Muslim-Americans due to the hysteria after 9/11.

Although many, like Justice Murphy, eventually recognized the internment camps as an atrocity and trampling of rights guaranteed by the Fifth Amendment, the decision in *Korematsu* was *never overruled*; which means that it still stands as the precedent for cases involving the incarceration of Americans in the name of national security. Moreover, in the post-9/11 environment, it seems, at least superficially, that most Americans are reluctant to continue the legacy left by the *Korematsu* case. One commentary about racial profiling after September 11th 2001, argues:

The tension between national security and civil liberties is taken for granted. Yet the national security side of the equation is speculative and rests on the familiar warning that if this war is lost there will be no rights or liberties for anybody at all. Even those who embraced color blindness, primarily in attacks on racial remedies, have given up their beliefs. Whatever the pros and cons of racial profiling, color blindness and racial profiling are inherently incompatible.[34]

In climates of hysteria, it seems that none of our liberties is off limits to the government. Even more vitally, individuals need to be vigilant, recognize, and react when the government is taking away rights—especially those of minority groups, be they racial, ethnic, or religious—that have absolutely nothing to do with security and everything to do with government abuse of power.

Bioterrorism and a Slew of Scary-Sounding Influenzas

After 9/11 and the anthrax letter scare, the U.S. Department of Health and Human Services announced that it wanted some model legislation regarding how states should react to bioterrorism attacks or other "pandemic" situations. The Model State Emergency Health Powers Act was drafted for the Centers for Disease Control (CDC) by academics at the Center for Law and the Public's Health at Georgetown and Johns Hopkins Universities and released on October 23rd 2001.[35] The recommended legislation gives the government a great amount of power in "emergency" situations. It can quarantine a town and the people inside of it, and take their property (including civilian-owned guns).[36]

The so-called model is yet another device to usurp the civil liberties of Americans. In a Heritage Foundation lecture, Sue Blevins, President of the Institute for Health Freedom, an advocacy group for letting the free market regulate the delivery of health care, critiqued the model act:

> Although this model legislation was recommended as a means to help states protect citizens against bioterrorist attacks and deal with national defense issues, the draft bill goes much, much further. It calls for giving state public health officials broad, new police

powers—all in the name of controlling epidemics of infectious diseases during public health emergencies.[37]

This expansion of the police power could mean almost any amount of power could be allocated to state governments if the state adopts the act, even the power to empower a militia in the name of health regulation, so fundamental constitutional rights are definitely at risk.

In a statement issued by the Association of American Physicians and Surgeons, the group stated that the model act "turns governors into dictators."[38] After many criticisms were levied, a new model code was written a few months later. This new version contained a few provisions that caused the act to impinge less on civil rights, yet mostly it just removed the inflammatory language of the original draft while keeping most of the substance. The model provisions still allowed for the government to destroy the property of citizens without compensation as long as the government "reasonably suspects" that the items may endanger public health.[39] It also still stated that the public health authority can be enforced at gunpoint by "organized militia."[40]

According to the group that drafted the Model State Emergency Health Powers Act (MSEHPA), "44 states and the District of Columbia have introduced a total of 171 bills or resolutions that include provisions from or closely related to MSEHPA" as of July 2006.[41] So, the government's infringement on our constitutional rights is a very real threat. This is an especially real risk given the number of "pandemics" that have appeared recently. My guess is that you have never even heard of these infringements.

In 2003, when the SARS (Severe Acute Respiratory Syndrome) virus was making headlines and scaring people all over the world, the Centers for Disease Control recommended the quarantine of people who fell ill of the disease.[42] The CDC's Web site also states that if ship or airline passengers who *possibly* have SARS refuse to be isolated, "many levels of government (federal, state, and local) have the authority to compel the isolation of sick persons. . . ."[43] SARS also prompted places like Buffalo, New York City, and the State of Minnesota to come up with plans to quarantine victims of an outbreak or bioterrorist attack. They even set the ground rules for a legal appeals process for those who did not want to be quarantined.[44]

In his book, *How Patriotic Is the Patriot Act?* the philosopher Amitai Etzioni discussed the relationship between bioterrorism and civil liberties: "There is a danger that without such public persuasion and a reframing of the debate—if the adjustment of law and policy will continue to take place under panic, especially following a major attack—public authorities will overcorrect as we have seen in other areas."[45] Since Anthrax in 2001 and SARS in 2003, there have been Bird Flu and most recently Swine Flu. The government has blown these viruses out of proportion, releasing dire warnings, recommendations, and cancelling classes at public schools. The media then take a cue from the government and sensationalize the coverage of these issues with fear-inducing language. Some of the coverage has been so over-the-top you would think the world is coming to an end, when really, the swine flu's effect seems quite similar to the normal strains of influenza that people commonly get in the winter months, and Bird Flu never materialized as a major pandemic.

Americans need to learn how to deal with the fears that the government and media are constantly trying to monger, allegedly for our own protection. Otherwise, we allow vital rights to get swept under the rug. Americans need to calm their hysterical tendencies and do it quickly. In late June 2009, Congressman Ron Paul (R-TX), a physician, warned that nearly $8 billion of taxpayers' money will be spent to fight Swine Flu. He also noted that the government's interference with the Swine Flu "could result in mandatory vaccinations for no discernable reason other than to enrich the pharmaceutical companies that make the vaccine,"[46] and to give the impression that the government is protecting us. The scary thing is that the predictions of this foreboding statement are entirely feasible because of the Model State Emergency Health Powers Act.

The RICO Laws Are Meant to Keep Us Safe from Mobsters

We've all seen depictions of mobsters: *The Godfather, The Sopranos*, we see them on television and read about them in newspapers. There's always an air of mystery and intrigue surrounding the mob, and people always fear the unknown. The federal RICO (Racketeer Influenced and Corrupt Organizations) statute was created and passed with the intention to combat organized crime, something that has always been sensationalized by the public. Yet, although RICO was meant to remedy mob crimes, government prosecutors and other lawyers later began to realize that the general language used in RICO could be used to prosecute almost anything. RICO is an especially powerful set of statutes since it has both civil and criminal penalties. Of course, states have salivated at the prospect of seizing such powers as well, and many have passed their own state RICO laws.

By the mid-1980s, the ABA determined that over 90 percent of the private, civil RICO lawsuits were against legitimate businesses, labor unions, spouses in divorce proceedings, and heirs to wills.[47] Near my farm in New Jersey, one politician has actually brought a RICO lawsuit against the local political leaders who dumped him from the party's campaign ticket and forced him into a primary election. On the criminal side, RICO was being used mostly to bring federal charges against alleged white-collar criminals for things such as inside trading of stocks.[48] RICO laws were not meant to be used in any of the aforementioned contexts, but the government has lied repeatedly through its blatant misuse of the RICO statutes.

When the federal RICO statutes were enacted in 1970, the laws were meant solely to target organized crime groups. Organized crime in America really became a problem after Prohibition-era bootlegging, so the creation of the RICO laws represented a long-awaited federal tool for prosecutors to fight mobs that often spanned many cities and states.[49] In *The RICO Racket*, a 1989 book consisting of a collection of essays written about the misuse of the RICO statutes, then-Judge Samuel A. Alito, Jr. wrote:

> The legislative history of RICO has fueled a vigorous debate about RICO's intended scope, for while the plain meaning of the statutory language is broad, the great bulk of the discussion in the congressional committee reports and floor debates focused narrowly on the Mafia and, specifically, Mafia infiltration of legitimate business.[50]

The language of RICO is unnecessarily broad; but the fact that preliminary discussion of RICO centered exclusively on the Mafia demonstrates that the government has abused these laws.

The mishandling of RICO becomes particularly troubling given the potentially heavy penalties that accompany a RICO violation, which include long prison sentences, large fines, and the forfeiture of property. Many of the contract or tort claims that get brought under RICO would not have penalties nearly as severe if RICO was not invoked. In this way, the broad use of RICO fills our prisons and wastes money prosecuting things that generally would be punished with less severity under the proper state law.

Furthermore, the threat of harsh federal penalties creates further inequities in terms of the power differential between prosecutors and defendants. One *Reason.com* article states:

> Many critics have pointed out that disparate punishment by state and federal jurisdictions for the same crime invites abuse of prosecutorial discretion at both state and federal levels. State prosecutors may use the threat of a federal prosecution as a bargaining tool to wrangle a guilty plea. Federal prosecutors may decide to prosecute only those defendants whose convictions will bring political rewards. Federal prosecutors are free to cherry-pick high-profile or politically expedient cases, knowing that the cases they reject probably will be prosecuted in state court.[51]

Under RICO, people are charged with *racketeering* (which could realistically be anything), instead of the actual crime (such as fraud, illegal gambling, etc.). William L. Anderson, an economics professor at Frostburg State University in Maryland, and one of the country's leading authorities on abuse of the criminal law by state and federal prosecutors, points out the difference in standards the prosecutor must meet in RICO cases versus regular criminal prosecutions:

> Because RICO cases are tried in federal courts, U.S. attorneys do not have to prove to juries and judges that the accused engaged in the aforementioned crimes (which as a rule are violations of state criminal law); they must show only that it appears the defendants carried on those activities. Moreover, for a RICO conviction, the prosecutor must meet only the civil standard of "preponderance of the evidence," not the higher standard of "guilt beyond a reasonable doubt" that historically has been required for a criminal conviction.[52]

Moreover, many of the "crimes" being prosecuted at the federal level are plainly not federal in nature, meaning they were meant to be handled by the states. Thus, the misappropriation of RICO violates the constitutional principle of federalism and contributes to the inefficiencies of the federal court system.[53]

Many absurd examples of RICO's use have arisen over the years. Professor Anderson recounted a story about his friend who was charged with racketeering under RICO. The friend's company was raided by a federal SWAT team in 1996, despite evidence that actions taken by company employees were done in good faith and without criminal intent. Anderson explains that his friend's assets were frozen after the SWAT team invasion, and he was therefore forced into using a public defender. Instead of taking the government's plea bargain of four years in prison, he went through with the trial. Then in 2001, a federal judge sentenced him to ten years in prison, and all of his assets were seized.[54]

The federal government can also use RICO to get around statutes of limitations. If the federal government, for example, wants to prosecute someone for fraud, it must do so within five years and prove guilt beyond a reasonable doubt. If successful, the feds get jail time for the defendant and restitution from him for the harm he caused. If the feds cannot prove guilt beyond a reasonable doubt within that time, there's a way out: They can use RICO, which has a *ten*-year statute of limitations and a lower standard of proof. If successful, the government can wipe out the defendant via RICO's treble (or triple) damages provisions.

In October 2007, the United States Supreme Court refused an opportunity to address the overuse of RICO in civil lawsuits against large corporations. This refusal to address the issue came after the U.S. Chamber of Commerce's National Chamber Litigation Center (NCLC) filed a brief asking the justices to review whether the RICO laws were being used properly in civil cases because the expansion of RICO in this capacity would "undermine business partnerships and adversely impact the economy."[55]

It is unfortunate that the Supreme Court failed to address the overuse of RICO because this abuse is impacting our economy in many ways. It forces expensive litigation on behalf of the nation's businesses, expensive prosecutions using government money, and the crowding of jails with long-term sentences often for nonviolent criminals. And why do we have RICO? Because the federal government fanned flames of fear about some aging mob figures whose wealth it wanted to seize, but whose guilt it could not prove.

Don't Give In! Our Democracy Depends on It.

In times when the nation is fearful and hysterical, we are generally willing to give up some rights. Yet, even giving up *some* of our civil liberties sets us up for danger. As with most constitutional rights, there is a slippery slope. Once some rights get taken away, other liberties are more easily curtailed; and then the process repeats a generation later. Soon, more rights are lost, and the entire notion of democracy falls apart.

We cannot acquiesce in the destruction of our liberties; we cannot allow the government to hoodwink us into being an obedient flock of sheep. Fear is a powerful weapon for the government, and it knows it. One of the great thieves of life and fortune in American history, FDR, told us as much when he articulated that "the only thing we have to fear is fear itself." Unfortunately for 2,700 American sailors at Pearl Harbor, he knew exactly what he was talking about.

Do you still think that the rights God gave you and that are *guaranteed* by the Constitution can be exercised in bad times, as well as in good?

243

Lie #14

"Your Boys Are Not Going to Be Sent into Any Foreign Wars"[1]

In 1915, a German U-boat sank the *Lusitania*, a British liner carrying nearly two hundred Americans. It was an event instrumental in bringing the United States into the war in Europe. The sinking of the ship, however, was not a surprise. There is significant evidence pointing to the fact that not only were the British aware there were German submarines in the area, but also that the Americans had knowledge of an impending attack. The British wanted the Americans involved in World War I to strengthen their chances of victory, and President Woodrow Wilson wanted innocent American deaths to justify politically American entry into what he called "the war to end all wars," so that after the war, he could "make the world safe for democracy." The United States fought for about a year and a half in World War I, from April 6th 1917, until the war ended on November 11th 1918, and lost 116,502 lives, 53,402 of which were lost in combat.[2]

It was not the first time, nor the last, that the United States government created fear and hysteria to justify war; and then used war to enhance fear and hysteria. It is commonplace in America for our leaders to lie in order to enter or initiate armed conflicts. Despite this tradition, Americans continue to stand on the sidelines while the government hijacks power, often leading us into imprudent and devastating wars. Less frequently, the government has waged war for good reason, but lied to win our consent. Regardless of their intentions, our leaders do not get elected or appointed or paid to lie to us. They are elected to protect our liberties and our way of life, but not to use their authority to deceive and exploit us. It is the American experience and experiment that the government works for *us*, and not the other way around.

We must not allow the government to continue treating the Constitution, and our natural rights, and our pursuits of happiness as minor speed bumps along its path to unlimited power, especially when its plans involve the sacrifice of American lives. Niccolo Machiavelli, the famous Florentine philosopher and political theorist, stated the following in his treatise entitled *The Prince*: "[M]en are so simple, and so subject to present necessities, that he who seeks to deceive will always find someone who will allow himself to be deceived." Let's stop proving him right; there's just too much at stake. But right he is.

Building a Tradition of Deception

As we learned in an earlier chapter, some of the biggest misconceptions concern President Lincoln and the Civil War. Lincoln was not the "Great Emancipator." He did not oppose slavery. Before the Civil War, he rarely spoke about slavery. When he did, Lincoln stressed that the president was not constitutionally permitted to do anything about slavery, and suggested that if anything was to be done, the blacks should be shipped to Africa; whether forced to come here or born here. While working as a lawyer, Lincoln represented slave owners, and in that capacity he prosecuted fugitive slaves, returned them to their masters, and was paid handsomely for it.

Furthermore, the Civil War initially was not about slavery. It started because the South vehemently opposed the federal government's increasing power at the expense of the states. The tipping point occurred when the federal government, upon Lincoln taking office, passed a high tariff that benefited the North and harmed the South. The high tariff forced the South to purchase higher-priced Northern goods, and cut off its business relationship with Europe. Lincoln did not introduce the abolition of slavery as a goal until two years into the war, and his Emancipation Proclamation was grossly ineffective.

Lincoln did *not* attempt to free the slaves in the "border" States of Delaware, Kentucky, Maryland, Tennessee, and Missouri. His so-called Emancipation Proclamation expressly *permitted slavery* to exist and remain lawful in those states. Nevertheless, Lincoln is viewed as a hero and is falsely recognized by the government and its school systems as the greatest United States president. He was a tyrant.

The point of this story is that the government—and especially our presidents—continually seek to control the news, lie to us in order to reach their objectives, and smother or even prevent dissent. During the Civil War, Lincoln shut down thousands of newspapers and charged thousands of editors and writers with treason. Many of Lincoln's critics were *executed*, and many more were *jailed*, because of their exercise of *free speech*. Our leaders do not employ such drastic measures today, but they lie and instill fear in us to argue for the necessity of war. Unfortunately, we do not discover their true motives until it is too late.

Lincoln's war killed over 650,000 Americans, more than have been killed in all wars in American history combined. He arrested newspaper editors, state legislators, and even a Republican congressman who merely spoke out against him. He suspended the writ of *habeas corpus*. His soldiers robbed American banks, burned American court-houses, raped American women, and killed American civilians—*all with legal impunity.*

In 1898, President William McKinley used the sinking of the USS *Maine* in Havana Harbor, Cuba, to gather American support for the eventual Spanish-American War. President McKinley claimed that the *Maine* had been sunk by a Spanish mine on February 15th 1898, while the American captain of the ship asserted that it was sunk by a coal bin explosion. On April 19th 1898, Congress issued a resolution ordering Spain to give up Cuba. It also authorized the president to use force if Spain did not comply. On April 25th, the United States declared war on Spain. The United States fought for about four months in the Spanish-American War, and it cost us 2,446 American lives, 385 of which were lost in combat.[3]

These events show that when the United States government wants to go to war, it uses certain incidents and circumstances to make the use of force politically palatable to American voters. It happens all the time.

"Your Boys Are Not Going to Be Sent into Any Foreign Wars."

—President Franklin Delano Roosevelt[4]

After World War I, the country was disillusioned by the failure of America's idealistic commitment to make "the world safe for democracy." The overwhelming majority of Americans favored isolationism over fighting another war. In September 1940, a Gallup Poll revealed that 88 percent of Americans opposed war with Germany. This poll was taken after Hitler annexed Austria and occupied Poland and blitzed London. Germany had conquered most of

Europe and was sinking American ships in the Atlantic Ocean, but Americans at home wanted no part of Europe's war.

President Franklin Delano Roosevelt purported to adhere to American public opinion, stating numerous times that he would not enter "Europe's War." Roosevelt, however, wanted to get involved in the war, believing that a Nazi-dominated Europe would execute his bellicose but freedom-preaching second cousin, Winston Churchill, and would prove a difficult trading partner for the United States. Surmising that Americans would only rally to oppose an overt act of war on the United States, Roosevelt and his advisers sought to provoke such an overt act.

Roosevelt targeted Japan, which on September 27th 1940, signed a mutual assistance treaty, known as the Tripartite Pact, with Germany and Italy; the three countries were known collectively as the Axis Powers. If Japan committed an overt act of war on the United States, Americans would certainly not object to attacking Japan. Based on the treaty, Germany would then have to come to Japan's defense, and thus, the United States would be able to sidestep American popular opinion, and get a crack at the Nazis.

On October 7th 1940, just ten days after Japan entered into its Tripartite Pact with Germany and Italy, Lieutenant Commander Arthur McCollum of the Office of Naval Intelligence submitted a memorandum proposal, known as the "McCollum memo," to Navy Captain Walter Anderson, the Director of Naval Intelligence. In an era before the Central Intelligence Agency (CIA), Naval Intelligence ranked high in the President's armament of intelligence-gathering government agencies. The memo outlined options available to the United States in response to Japan's actions in the South Pacific. It included an eight-part plan to counter Japanese hegemony in East Asia. The memo also indicates that at least one individual in the Office of Naval Intelligence promoted the idea of *provoking* Japan into going to war with the United States. The memo states, "It is not believed that in the present state of political opinion the United States government is capable of declaring war against Japan without more ado [. . .] If by [the eight-point plan] Japan could be led to commit an overt act of war, so much the better."[5] From this point on, the Roosevelt administration worked to implement McCollum's plan, showing that it was absolutely committed to going to war.

On October 8th 1940, President Roosevelt called Admiral James O. Richardson, Commander-in-Chief of the U.S. Fleet, to the White House to discuss the provocation plan. Richardson objected to the plan, and Roosevelt subsequently fired him. In his place, Roosevelt installed Rear Admiral Husband E. Kimmel as commander of the fleet in Hawaii on February 1st 1941. Major General William Short was promoted to lieutenant general, and Roosevelt gave him command of the U.S. Army troops in Hawaii. These were two promotions that each of these selfless military men would live to regret. They became pawns in FDR's murderous scheme to provoke the Japanese Navy *to slaughter American sailors.*

For most of 1941, the United States implemented its eight-point plan and gauged Japan's reaction by intercepting and decoding its naval communications. In response, Japan's militarists rose to power and coordinated the military for war against Great Britain, the Netherlands, and the United States. The United States got word of the Pearl Harbor attack in *January* 1941, eleven months prior to the actual event. The United States continued to monitor Japanese communications, but did not actively attempt to prevent the attack.

In fact, Roosevelt and the military implemented the so-called "Vacant Sea" policy in late November 1941 to goad a Japanese attack. Navy officials declared the North Pacific off-limits to all American and allied shipping, military and commercial, forcing ships to use the Torres Strait route in the South Pacific between Australia and

New Guinea. The strategy was simple: Leave the North Pacific free for Japan's attack fleet to approach Hawaiian waters. As explained by Rear Admiral Richmond K. Turner, the War Plans officer for the Navy at the time, "We were prepared to divert traffic when we believed that war was imminent. We sent the traffic down via the Torres Strait, so that the track of the Japanese task force would be clear of any traffic."[6] The order was sent to Admiral Kimmel and San Francisco's 12th Naval District on November 25th 1941, one hour after the Japanese fleet set sail for Pearl Harbor. Following orders, Kimmel pulled his Pacific Fleet back to Pearl Harbor, opening up the entire Pacific Ocean for the Japanese, and leaving Pearl Harbor as the biggest sitting duck in history.

Even more egregious were the orders from naval headquarters when Kimmel attempted to conduct an exercise with his forces to the north of Hawaii in the very same location the Japanese used in early December 1941 to start their attack. Kimmel had scheduled an exercise to prepare for a possible Hawaiian attack for November 21st 1941. Admiral Royal E. Ingersoll, Assistant Chief of Naval Operations, told Kimmel to expect a surprise aggressive movement from the Japanese, but not to place the fleet in a position that would precipitate Japanese action. *President Roosevelt would not allow Admiral Kimmel to stop Japan's advance toward the United States.*

Even when the Japanese attack on Pearl Harbor became a certainty, FDR continued to order Kimmel to exercise restraint. On November 27th and 28th 1941, Roosevelt warned of possible hostile action by Japan, but did not mention Hawaii. He also instructed commanders to "execute appropriate defensive deployment" and "undertake reconnaissance," but stressed that "United States policy calls for Japan to commit the first overt act." President Roosevelt was not concerned with protecting American lives or property; he would and did largely sacrifice them as an excuse for a world war. These messages prevented

Kimmel from taking any active precautions to try to preempt an attack. Furthermore, the government instructed General Short that he should mainly be on the lookout for sabotage and espionage, and that "protective measures should be confined to those essential to security, avoiding unnecessary publicity and alarm."

President Roosevelt finally got his wish. In the Japanese attack on Pearl Harbor, 2,403 American men, women, and children were killed, and 1,178 were wounded. Sunday, December 7th 1941, was "a date which will live in infamy," on more than one level. In response to the attack, and continuing the lie, Roosevelt implored Congress to declare war on Japan, calling the massacre at Pearl Harbor an "unprovoked and dastardly attack by Japan." The attack on Pearl Harbor was secretly provoked, undoubtedly anticipated, and ardently hoped for by the privately lying President who publicly condemned it. The infamy was his.

The shameful and downright cowardly aspect of the Pearl Harbor story is that President Roosevelt did not have to resort to deception. By 1941, Roosevelt had been elected president not once, not twice, but *three* times. He was the boss. He also knew that Nazi Germany represented an incredibly serious threat to American and global freedom and safety; the Nazis were mass murderers who sought to take over the world. If Roosevelt found it prudent to enter World War II, he should have done so. He should have been honest with the American people, instead of lying and sacrificing 2,403 American lives. It is nice to be able to gain your country's support, but we do not live in a true democracy. We elect our representatives, trusting them to make decisions to protect our freedom. The United States' effort in War World II would not have been considered any less heroic if Roosevelt had leveled with us, instead of developing an elaborate, murderous scheme to deceive us. In the end, the United States spent about forty months fighting

World War II, and 405,399 American service personnel were killed, 291,557 of whom died in combat.[7]

Another serious problem with Roosevelt's scheme is that he acted knowing that provoking an "overt act" could result in substantial American deaths. He was willing to trade American lives for a ticket to war with Germany. This is "dastardly." *It is never, under any circumstances, necessary, moral, or lawful for the government intentionally to kill or permit the killing of known innocents.*

President Roosevelt was a lawyer, but he must have been absent during the first week of law school.[8] The famous English case of *The Queen v. Dudley and Stephens* (1884), which is typically taught during a law student's first week of the first-year criminal law course, states that intentional killing of the innocent is never reasonable or lawful or morally justifiable, no matter the circumstances. Tom Dudley, Edwin Stephens, Edmund Brooks, and Richard Parker were in a boat, stranded on the high seas. After having gone seven days without food, and five days without water, Dudley and Stephens decided to kill Parker and feed on his carcass so that they would not starve to death while waiting for assistance. (Brooks was not involved in the decision, but Dudley and Stephens claimed he agreed.) As a result, instead of all four crewmembers succumbing to death, three lives were saved at the expense of just one. Dudley and Stephens, nevertheless, were prosecuted and convicted of murder. According to the English High Court of Justice, "To preserve one's life is generally speaking a duty, but it may be the plainest and the highest duty to sacrifice it."

President Roosevelt did not personally kill 2,403 Americans at Pearl Harbor, but the same principle applies. He welcomed an attack he knew would certainly result in thousands of American casualties. In the long term, he undoubtedly preserved lives by entering World War II, but his murderous offense in starting the war is not morally, legally, or constitutionally justified.

"They Fired at Us First."

For much of the twentieth century, the United States government used the threat of communism and the Cold War to justify armed conflict with numerous Asian nations, and pulled an FDR-like move to enter the Vietnam War in 1964.

Communist movements, supported by the People's Republic of China and the Soviet Union, were sweeping through Southeast Asia. This led to a clash between the national and communist powers in Vietnam and incited the First Indochina War (1946 to 1954), in which the French, supported by the United States, fought against the communist guerrillas. The communists defeated the French, signifying the rise of a revolutionary communist force.

The Geneva Accords (1954) ended the hostilities and stipulated that Indochina was to be independent from French colonial rule. Furthermore, foreign presence was to cease in the region, and Vietnam was temporarily partitioned into northern and southern zones until nationwide elections could be held in 1956. The United States refused to recognize the Accords, as the agreement would limit its involvement in a region infected with communism.

Late in 1954, President Dwight D. Eisenhower advanced the Domino Theory, teaching that once one nation falls to communism, neighboring nations will also succumb to that horrid form of government, one by one. Based on this severely flawed theory, the United States installed a puppet regime in South Vietnam. Ho Chi Minh's communist government controlled North Vietnam, with support from China and the Soviet Union. In 1961, the United States provided direct military and financial support to South Vietnam under President John F. Kennedy. This also violated the Geneva Accords.

Furthermore, the United States initiated covert CIA operations that escalated and intensified American involvement in Vietnam before the outbreak of war. In 1961, the CIA began reconnaissance missions in the North and naval sabotage operations by sending destroyer boats to the northern coast. This program was later transferred in 1964 to the Defense Department and was under the direct control of the Pentagon. The United States military also used Agent Orange along the Ho Chi Minh trail, along which the Vietcong was transporting troops and weapons.

In addition, President Kennedy authorized the CIA to support a coup against Ngo Dinh Diem, the first president of South Vietnam, because Kennedy's administration feared that Diem would be unable to defeat the Communists. In 1963, a local general in the Army of the Republic of Vietnam (ARVN) overthrew and executed Diem and his brother, Ngo Dinh Nhu. The United States, in noble fashion, denied any involvement in the assassination and primarily placed blame on the ARVN.

That brings us to President Lyndon B. Johnson's best impression of FDR. In 1964, Johnson blatantly provoked a Vietnamese attack, but claimed that the United States was attacked first. On July 31st 1964, two American destroyers, the USS *Maddox* and *The Turner Joy*, began an electronic intelligence collection mission in the Gulf of Tonkin. This was a secret mission orchestrated by the Pentagon without any congressional authority. On August 2nd 1964, the *Maddox* reported that it was attacked by three North Vietnamese torpedo boats. The *Maddox* allegedly returned fire, sinking one of the boats and severely damaging the other.

In 2005, a declassified National Security Agency (NSA) report revealed that the *Maddox* actually fired first. There is evidence that the destroyers were, in fact, instructed to open fire to scare off any communist boats that came too close. According to the report, Captain John J. Herrick, the task force commander in the Gulf of

Tonkin, ordered the destroyers to "open fire if the boats approached within ten thousand yards . . . The *Maddox* fired three rounds to warn off the communist boats. This initial action was never reported by the Johnson administration, which insisted that the Vietnamese boats fired first."

Two days later, on August 4th 1964, the Pentagon claimed that North Vietnamese boats launched a second attack in the Gulf of Tonkin. On that date, the U.S. destroyers believed they received radio and radar signals indicating that they were under attack by the North Vietnamese Navy, and opened fire for two hours. A 2005 NSA report revealed, however, that not only was there no North Vietnamese attack on August 4th, but there may not have even been any North Vietnamese boats in the area. Cables from Herrick showed that the signals came from "freak weather effects," "almost total darkness," and an "overeager sonarman" who "was hearing [his] ship's own propeller beat."

Nevertheless, on the night of August 4th, in the midst of a presidential election campaign against Senator Barry M. Goldwater, President Johnson proclaimed on national television that the United States would begin air strikes against North Vietnam to "retaliate" against the (phantom) torpedo attack. In his speech, Johnson announced that "[t]his new act of aggression, aimed directly at our own forces, again brings home to all of us in the United States the importance of the struggle for peace and security in southeast Asia . . . Yet our response, for the present, will be limited and fitting. We Americans know, although others appear to forget, the risks of spreading conflict. We still seek no wider war."

Seeking to protect the United States against the North Vietnamese, Congress passed the Gulf of Tonkin Resolution (H.J. RES 1145), a joint resolution giving Johnson the right to initiate military force in Vietnam without a formal declaration of war.[9] Until late in 1964, after Election Day, Johnson held himself out as the peace candidate and called Goldwater "a war monger."

To say the consequences of starting war with Vietnam were devastating is to be guilty of an egregious understatement. In addition to costing better than $200 million, the Vietnam War resulted in more than 519,000 seriously injured Americans, more than 300,000 wounded Americans, and more than 50,000 *dead* Americans. Furthermore, roughly 2,500 Americans are still missing in action and presumed dead. *Why?* Because Presidents Eisenhower, Kennedy, and Johnson believed that communism, a form of government and political theory that exalts the state over individuals, could somehow be contained on the battlefield.

When in history have ideas been contained via the use of military force? Never! Not even the most powerful military in the world can "draw a line" stopping the expansion of ideas. President Johnson believed that the Vietnam War would be different, however, and he lied to us to get us involved. Johnson also knew that America's major wartime presidents—Lincoln, Wilson, and FDR—were its most powerful and revered. He yearned to be among them. Twenty-five years after the Tonkin deception, Communism fell of its own weight, without a shot being fired. And LBJ's presidency is all but forgotten, except for civil rights and the Medicare and Medicaid bills we are all still paying.

"Grave and Gathering" Deceit

President George W. Bush's use of deception to trick Congress and the American people into authorizing the Iraq War should go down as one of the deadliest, yet most creative marketing jobs in the history of the world.[10] The Bush Administration's goal, from the beginning of its stint at 1600 Pennsylvania Avenue, was to go to war with Iraq. Paul O'Neill, President Bush's first treasury secretary, who attended the first meeting of Bush's National Security Council on January 30th 2001, stated, "Ten days in, and it was about Iraq." According to O'Neill, "From the start, we were building the case against Hussein and looking at how we could take him out and change Iraq into a new country. And, if we did that, it would solve everything. It was all about finding *a way to do it*."

There's certainly nothing wrong with "building a case"; lawyers do it all the time. When advocating, it is important for attorneys to highlight arguments that help their clients, while trying to downplay arguments that hurt them. Lawyers, under no circumstances, are permitted *to lie* to get their way. For some reason, however, we do not hold politicians and presidents to this standard. George W. Bush realized this, and capitalized.

Before September 11th 2001, George W. Bush saw Saddam Hussein as a threat to Middle Eastern and American security, yet did not overtly seek war with Iraq. Even after 9/11, on September 16th 2001, Vice President Dick Cheney told Tim Russert on *Meet the Press* that "Saddam Hussein's bottled up at this point." According to Cheney, there was no evidence linking Iraq to the terrorism and 9/11.

The attacks of September 11th 2001, provided President Bush with an advantage, in that there was overwhelming support for any and all counterterrorism plans put forth by the government. At the time, President Bush was revered and recorded astronomical approval ratings. Yet, public support for a war with Iraq was lacking. In November 2001, 74 percent of Americans favored ousting Saddam Hussein. By the end of Summer 2002, however, only a bare majority of Americans still supported regime change in Iraq. What is striking, though, is that more than 80 percent of Americans believed Iraq supported terrorist organizations poised to attack the United States. Better than 90 percent of Americans believed

Iraq possessed or was developing weapons of mass destruction. A majority of Americans, contrary to Cheney's statement made a year earlier, believed that Saddam was linked to the 9/11 attacks.

Americans felt this way about Iraq because the Bush Administration conducted an intense campaign to "educate" (lie to) the American public about the threat Saddam Hussein posed to the United States. In December 2001, Cheney returned to *Meet the Press* and suggested that Saddam Hussein did, in fact, play a role in 9/11. In early 2002, National Security Advisor Condoleezza Rice was calling for a serious response to regimes that seek to obtain and use weapons of mass destruction (WMDs). Cheney declared that Iraq officials had "a robust set of programs to develop their own weapons of mass destruction," and that "we know [Saddam] has been actively and aggressively doing everything he can to enhance his capabilities." Cheney also continued to discuss Saddam's relationship with the terrorists.

In Summer 2002, Bush created the White House Iraq Group (WHIG), a committee set up to coordinate marketing the war to the public. In August 2002, at the Veterans of Foreign Wars convention in Nashville, Tennessee, Cheney stated that "there is no doubt that Saddam Hussein now has weapons of mass destruction. There is no doubt *he is amassing them to use* against our friends, against our allies, *against us*" (emphasis added). Later, on September 8th 2002, Condoleezza Rice stated the following at the United Nations: "The problem here is that there will always be some uncertainty about how quickly [Saddam] can acquire nuclear weapons. But we don't want the smoking gun to be a mushroom cloud."

The message was clear: Saddam had WMDs, he could use them at any moment, and he was friends with the terrorists. To any American, this was frightening. Might Saddam's WMDs have been the same shipments that the *U.S. sold to him* in 1986 so as to help him defeat

Iran in the Iran-Iraq War? If so, the sales were orchestrated by then-and-future Secretary of Defense Donald Rumsfeld.

In September 2002, the Bush Administration took its marketing campaign to the next level. On September 12th 2002, at the United Nations, Bush reminded the UN that Saddam brutalized his own people and disregarded UN Security Council resolutions. Bush also threw in a few lies, so as not to veer from the theme of his presidency. He stated that Iraq posed a "grave and gathering danger," was pursuing a nuclear weapons program, and supported terrorism. According to Bush, if the UN did not control Iraq, the United States would dispel the threat militarily.

A little over a week later, on September 20th 2002, Bush called a meeting of the Republican governors at the White House to promote war with Iraq. Bush went through all the usual talking points but also emphasized the importance of promoting liberty, individual freedom, and democracy around the world. According to Bush, "Afghanistan and Iraq will lead [the Middle East] to democracy. They are going to be the catalyst to change the Middle East and the world." There is nothing wrong with promoting liberty and individual freedom; in fact, it is encouraged. However, the idea that a country, through the use of military force, can coercively install freedom in a region that had never been exposed to democracy is misguided. Yet, it was clear that Bush wanted to be the first president to deliver freedom to the Middle East and fix a broken region.

Bush, however, did not promote his grand ideas directly to the American people. Instead, Bush continued instilling fear in us and warning of the grave threat that Saddam posed to American security. For example, in a speech in Houston, Texas, on September 27th 2002, Bush stated that Saddam was *the guy who tried to kill my dad*," a former American president. Bush knew that scaring us into going to war with Iraq with statements like these would be much more effective than trying to tell us that installing democracy in Iraq would somehow work and also spill over to the rest of the Middle East.

By late October 2002, Bush's marketing plan was coming to a close. Congress passed a joint resolution authorizing the president to use military force in Iraq. President Bush, however, continued to plug the war by telling more and more lies. This wasn't a problem for the Bush administration, however, so long as it created more and more fear. In December 2002, Secretary of State Colin Powell stated that Iraq sought to import yellowcake uranium from Niger. In his State of the Union Address on January 28th 2003, Bush reiterated Powell's claim, stating that "the British government has learned that Saddam Hussein has recently sought significant quantities of uranium from Africa."

These claims, however, had been proven false long before the administration sought to pass them off as true. The Niger story was based on forged documents, and an investigation done by the Bush administration in March 2002 indicated that Saddam was *not* looking to purchase uranium from Africa. Apparently, the administration felt that every little bit of lying would be worth it in the long run.

On March 19th 2003, the United States invaded Iraq and quickly ousted Saddam Hussein. Unfortunately, the Bush Administration did not plan for the aftermath, or develop a strategy to leave Iraq. Bush claimed that the United States would deal with Iraq in a "logical way," but his approach to Iraq was anything but logical. We are still in Iraq. More than 4,400 Americans are dead, and there have been over 650,000 Iraqi civilian deaths. More than 2,500,000 Iraqis have fled their country since the U.S. invasion and occupation began.

"Wrong, Terribly Wrong"

The American tragedies discussed in this chapter are not entirely the fault of the American people. We hire government officials expecting them to do the right thing. We *want* them to do the right thing. We also trust that the government has credible information at hand and takes threats to our freedom very seriously. Yet, this chapter shows that the government *constantly* lies to us in order to enter and initiate wars. This is a common government practice that we must recognize, and one that must be stopped. It is unacceptable that the government lies to us all the time, about everything. It is dangerous and criminal, however, that the government lies to us in order to send troops into harm's way.

In *The New York Times* on July 7th 2009, Bob Herbert wrote an op-ed piece entitled "After the War Was Over," in the wake of Robert McNamara's death "at the ripe old age of 93." McNamara was the Secretary of Defense under Presidents Kennedy and Johnson, and he assured Johnson that we had solid evidence of a North Vietnamese attack in the Gulf of Tonkin. He was wrong, and long after the war he admitted that he had been "wrong, terribly wrong" about Vietnam.

We were misled to enter the Spanish-American War, World War I and World War II, the Vietnam War, and the ongoing wars in Afghanistan and Iraq. We were "wrong, terribly wrong" about Vietnam and Iraq. Herbert pointed out that apologies after wars are over do not bring soldiers and civilians back to life, and stated his "utter contempt" for such apologies. Implicit in Herbert's view was the necessity to put an end to the lying and to stop nonsensical and irrational wars before it is too late. In terms of war, deception and misinformation kill.

Lie #15

"We Don't Torture"[1]

On June 26th 2003, President George W. Bush asserted, "The United States is committed to the worldwide elimination of torture, and we are leading this fight by example." No surprise here; President Bush lied. The United States of America is not committed to the worldwide elimination of torture; rather, under Bush, it *supported, facilitated, and directly engaged in* torture. The United States has tortured people, and will continue to torture as long as Americans overlook and excuse the crimes committed by our government, and as long as Americans accept government deception on torture.

President George W. Bush's administration used fear mongering to justify its torture policy and restrictions on the due process rights of persons it arrested. Under the cloak of "saving lives" and "dispelling grave threats," our officials have repeatedly condoned policies that violate international conventions (treaties) regarding the treatment of prisoners, as well as the United States Constitution and federal and state statutory law.

This chapter discusses the Bush administration's torture policy, but also explains how the federal government, during times of war, severely restricts the rights of all persons except those in the government.

Detention, *Habeas Corpus*, and the Supreme Court

The Latin phrase *habeas corpus* literally means "you have the body." It is a legal action, usually called a "writ," which means a "right," through which an individual seeks relief from unlawful detention. The *habeas corpus* protection is directly guaranteed in the United States Constitution. Article I, Section 9, Clause 2, provides that "[t]he Privilege of the Writ of Habeas Corpus shall not be suspended, unless when in Cases of Rebellion or Invasion the public Safety may require it." The protection is also codified in the United States Code, under 28 U.S.C. §2242(a), which states the following: "Writs of *habeas corpus* may be granted by the Supreme Court, any justice thereof, the district courts and any circuit judge within their respective jurisdictions." Furthermore, the Supreme Court has held that the right to *habeas corpus* is derived from common law. According to Justice John Paul Stevens, "'. . . *habeas corpus* is . . . a writ antecedent to statute, throwing its root deep into the genius of our common law.'"[2] Indeed, the right to *habeas corpus* has been guaranteed to all persons in Western law since the Magna Carta was signed in 1215.

Since the right to be left alone, thus the right to be free from unlawful restraint, is a natural right, *habeas corpus* is essential to permit the vindication of that natural right: It permits the person who is suffering from the unlawful restraint to require the government that is restraining him to justify the lawfulness of the restraint to a neutral judge. Nevertheless, Congress and the Bush administration, after September 11th 2001, sought to restrict severely this fundamental right. It was up to the Supreme Court of the United States to reinstate it.

On June 28th 2004, the Supreme Court issued three decisions

concerning the detention of so-called "enemy combatants."[3] In the case of *Hamdi v. Rumsfeld*,[4] local Afghan authorities had seized Yaser Esam Hamdi in 2001, and turned him over to the United States military. The military then transferred him to Guantanamo Bay, Cuba. Upon discerning that Hamdi was in fact an American citizen, the military moved Hamdi to the naval brig in Norfolk, Virginia, and designated him as an "illegal enemy combatant." By giving him this title, the government saw fit to deny Hamdi due process or the assistance of counsel.

The government also believed it could detain Hamdi indefinitely. The military treated Hamdi poorly when holding him at Norfolk. Jack Goldsmith of the Justice Department's Office of Legal Counsel (OLC), upon visiting Norfolk, saw Hamdi curled up in a fetal position in his cell and commented that "it seemed unnecessary to hold a twenty-two-year-old foot soldier in a remote wing of a run-down prison in a tiny cell, isolated from almost all human contact."[5] The Pentagon finally permitted Hamdi to communicate with a lawyer in December 2003, more than *two years* after he was initially incarcerated. He was not permitted to meet with his lawyer in person until February 2004.

Hamdi's father managed to file suit on his son's behalf in federal court in 2002. Judge Robert G. Doumar, a United States District judge in the Eastern District of Virginia and a Reagan appointee who understands the Constitution, ruled that Hamdi, a United States citizen designated as an "enemy combatant," was entitled to a lawyer, and that the government must put forth sufficient evidence validating his detention.[6] In his opinion, Judge Doumar offered a brilliant defense of liberty when he ruled:

> We must protect the freedoms of even those who hate us . . . If we
> fail in this task, we become victims of the precedents we create. We

have prided ourselves on being a nation of laws applying equally to all and not a nation of men who have few or no standards . . . We must preserve the rights afforded to us by our Constitution and laws for without it we return to the chaos of a rule of men and not of laws. . . .[7]

After the Fourth Circuit Court of Appeals reversed Judge Doumar's decision, Hamdi appealed to the United States Supreme Court. In a 6 to 3 decision, the Court ruled that the federal courts had *habeas corpus* jurisdiction for an American citizen detained in the United States. Justice Sandra Day O'Connor wrote an inspired majority opinion, in which she stated, "It is during our most challenging and uncertain moments that our Nation's commitment to due process is most severely tested; and it is in those times that we must preserve our commitment at home to the principles for which we fight abroad."[8] O'Connor made it clear that the current Court was far different from the one that decided *Korematsu*. She warned against condensing power into the executive branch and emphasized that "*a state of war is not a blank check for the president* when it comes to the rights of the Nation's citizens"[9] (emphases added).

While he strongly disagreed with the government's detention program, Justice Antonin Scalia, in his concurring opinion in *Hamdi*, went even further than O'Connor and opined that the president's detention scheme, in which he merely declared persons to be "enemy combatants" in order to incarcerate them and rob them of all legal protections, itself was obviously unconstitutional for American citizens.[10]

The Supreme Court's decision in *Rumsfeld v. Padilla*,[11] decided on the same day as *Hamdi*, shows how even bright lawyers can sometimes see only the tree in front of them and not the surrounding forest. Jose Padilla, an American citizen, was apprehended at O'Hare

International Airport in Chicago and detained as an enemy combatant on the suspicion that he was planning to construct and detonate a "dirty bomb."[12] He was taken to New York and held there as a material witness. His incarceration in New York was clearly unlawful, as there was no proceeding or trial pending in which his testimony was needed as a material witness. Padilla filed a *habeas corpus* petition from New York, but was later transferred to a military prison in South Carolina. His *habeas* petition, however, continued to be litigated in the Southern District of New York, and later in the Second Circuit, which ruled for Padilla.

At the Supreme Court, the Justice Department argued that Padilla could not challenge his incarceration, even though he could potentially be imprisoned for the rest of his life.[13] The basis for this argument, according to Paul Clement, the deputy solicitor general, was Congress's granting of permission to the president to "use of all necessary and appropriate force."[14] The Court, 5 to 4, resolved the case on procedural grounds, holding that Padilla's *habeas* petition must have been brought in the judicial district where he was then being detained, in South Carolina, where the government moved him during his incarceration in order to create this procedural default.

After he refiled his *habeas corpus* petition in federal court in South Carolina, Padilla scored an impressive victory. The lawyers in the Bush administration, fearing that the Supreme Court would uphold Judge Doumar's logic in *Hamdi*, advised President Bush to release Padilla from military confinement. *This was done after six years of solitary confinement with no charges pending against him.*

The third case decided on June 28th 2004—and the one most devastating to the torturers in the Bush administration—was *Rasul v. Bush*.[15] The lead plaintiff in the case was Shafiq Rasul,[16] an alien being detained at Guantanamo Bay, Cuba. The Bush administration believed that Guantanamo prisoners were entitled to no due process, and it argued this position at the Supreme Court. To open his oral argument, Ted Olson, the solicitor general, stated:

> Mr. Chief Justice, and may it please the Court: The United States is at war. It is in that context that petitioners ask this Court to assert jurisdiction that is not authorized by Congress, does not arise from the Constitution, has never been exercised by this Court.[17]

Justice Stevens quickly interrupted, and asked Olson whether the United States could continue to detain people on Guantanamo even if the war hypothetically ended.[18] When Olson responded affirmatively, it became clear that the Bush administration was not engaging in a "temporary program." The "War on Terror" was simply the shield it used to protect its extra-constitutional behavior. Thankfully, the Supreme Court held, 6 to 3, that the United States maintained significant control over Guantanamo Bay such that the federal courts have jurisdiction to hear *habeas corpus* petitions filed by those detained there.

In response to *Rasul*, a major blow to the administration, Congress and the President teamed up against the Court. Congress passed the Detainee Treatment Act of 2005, which stated that "No court or judge shall have jurisdiction to . . . consider a *habeas corpus* petition from an alien detained by the Department of Defense at Guantanamo Bay, Cuba." The only route for these detainees was first through military commissions, and then review in the U.S. Court of Appeals for the District of Columbia Circuit.

The Court struck back in the case of *Hamdan v. Rumsfeld*,[19] in which it held that the relevant provision of the Detainee Treatment Act applied only prospectively, not retroactively, to those petitions that were already pending in federal court at the time the law was enacted.

Congress, in turn, became even more specific. Section 7 of the Military Commissions Act of 2006 states the following: "No court or judge has jurisdiction over *habeas corpus* concerning any aspect of the detention, transfer, treatment . . . of an alien who has either been determined to be an enemy combatant or is awaiting such a determination." The Act applies to *all cases without exception*, pending on or after the date of enactment.

On June 12th 2008, the Supreme Court ended the ping-pong match it was having with Congress and the president, and ruled in the case of *Boumediene v. Bush*,[20] that despite the administration's statutory restrictions on the *habeas* protection, Guantánamo detainees have a *constitutional* right to *habeas corpus* under Article I, Section 9, Clause 2. The Bush administration, despite all its efforts to break the law, could not avoid the Constitution. And since the right to *habeas corpus* vindicates a natural right (the right to be free from unlawful restraint), no president or Congress can permanently take it away.

Were Hamdi and Padilla tortured? These two Americans were denied all human contact, for six years in Padilla's case and for two years in Hamdi's. The Bush administration was so fanatical and demonic about denying them human contact that whenever it moved them from place to place in the prison system, their eyes were covered, their ears were blocked, their hands and fingers were covered, and their ankles were chained to each other. All this while no charges were pending. Is it any wonder that they babbled and drooled like babies when they first met their attorneys?

There is simply no authority in any federal statute permitting the government to treat anyone in this manner, much less an American *against whom no charges had been filed*. This psychological torment was torture, and those who authorized its administration knew it. They knew it because they took an oath to uphold the Constitution, the Eighth Amendment of which prohibits the infliction of "cruel and unusual punishments." One member of President Bush's cabinet actually suggested the following nonsensical argument: well, they were not charged with any crimes, so they were not tried or convicted, thus what we did to them was not punishment. Such "logic" would permit the rack and burning at the stake.

"We Tortured"

—Susan J. Crawford, a top Bush administration official[21]

The Bush administration repeatedly claimed that the United States does not support torture. We have just examined one of its arguments.

Then-Vice President Dick Cheney, an avowed proponent of torture, which he preferred to call "enhanced interrogation," has stated that what constitutes torture is in the eye of the beholder, and that "you can get into a debate about what shocks the conscience and what is cruel and inhuman."[22] Debate all you want, Mr. Vice President, but you have laws, international conventions, and the United States Constitution to contend with. The United States Code, for example, defines "torture" quite clearly. Under 18 U.S.C. §2340, "torture" consists of an act committed by a person acting under the color of law, specifically intended to inflict severe physical or mental pain or suffering (other than pain or suffering incidental to lawful sanctions) upon another person within his custody or physical control. According to the statute, "severe mental pain or suffering" is

> the prolonged mental harm caused by or resulting from (a) the
> intentional infliction or threatened infliction of severe physical
> pain or suffering; (b) the administration or application, or threat-
> ened administration or application, of mind-altering substances
> or other procedures calculated to disrupt profoundly the senses or

the personality; (c) the threat of imminent death; or (d) the threat that another person will imminently be subjected to death, severe physical pain or suffering, or the administration or application of mind-altering substances or other procedures calculated to disrupt profoundly the senses or personality.

In addition, the War Crimes Act of 1996 makes it a crime for any United States national to order or engage in the murder, torture *or inhuman treatment* of a detainee.[23] In addition to those who engage in this conduct, any official who authorizes or condones such abuse violates the Act as well. If a detainee dies, the Act imposes the death penalty on those who caused it.

Furthermore, the United States is required by law to operate under the Geneva Conventions, agreed to in 1948 and 1949, which set the standards in international law for treatment of prisoners. A crucial provision within these standards is "Common Article 3," which appears in each of the four conventions. Common Article 3 demands that "[p]ersons taking active part in the hostilities . . . shall in *all circumstances* be treated humanely. . . ."[24] (emphases added). The Article goes on to state that "violence to life and person, in particular murder of all kinds, mutilation, *cruel treatment and torture*" shall be prohibited "at any time and in any place whatsoever"[25] (emphases added). It also specifically prohibits "outrages upon personal dignity," including "humiliating and degrading treatment."[26]

The United States military also takes interrogation tactics very seriously. The main goals of military interrogation are effectiveness and compliance with the law.[27] The *U.S. Army Field Manual* 34-52 (FM 34-52) was once the rulebook for military interrogators, and applied to *all* foreigners, with no exception.[28] A key principle of FM 34-52 was that interrogators will only get results if they create a rapport with the detainees.[29] Based on this principle, FM 34-52 specified the following four propositions: (1) any interrogation must have a specific purpose; (2) it must be based on rapport; (3) every detainee has a breaking point, although it is not typically known until it has been reached; and (4) susceptibility to interrogation diminishes with the passage of time.[30]

FM 34-52 prohibited "physical or mental torture, threats, insults, or exposure to inhuman treatment as a means of or aid to interrogation," regardless of the enemy.[31] The manual provided a broad description of "torture," defining it as "the infliction of intense pain to body or mind to extract a confession or information, or for sadistic pleasure."[32] Physical torture, according to FM 34-52, includes "any form of beating"; forcing a detainee to stand, sit, or kneel in an abnormal position for an extended period of time; and sleep deprivation.[33] According to the manual, abnormal sleep deprivation is an example of mental torture.[34]

Unfortunately, but not surprisingly, the Bush administration intentionally disregarded these provisions, sidestepped well-established law, and essentially created a new legal framework under which it was permissible to humiliate and torture people. As stated above, the administration started by trying to keep the federal judicial system out of Guantanamo Bay; one former Bush administration lawyer called it "the legal equivalent of outer space."[35] As early as January 9th 2002, just four months after September 11th, John Yoo, the go-to lawyer in the Justice Department's Office of Legal Counsel (OLC), on whose ratiocinations the Bush White House relied when it wished to evade or avoid the Constitution and federal law, coauthored a forty-two-page memo concluding that no laws of war, including the Geneva Conventions, applied to the conflict in Afghanistan.[36]

Upon seeing the Yoo memo, one State Department lawyer stated, "We were horrified."[37] The chief legal advisor for the Department of State, Bush appointee William Howard Taft IV, sent a memo to Yoo in response, calling his assessment "seriously flawed."[38]

The Bush administration, as you may have noticed throughout its stint at the White House, did not respond well to criticism, or simply opposing points of view. White House Counsel (and later Attorney General) Alberto Gonzales, in late January 2002, wrote a memo to President Bush, noting Secretary of State Colin Powell's opposition to the Yoo memo.[39] Gonzales then made his case for torture, stating that "[t]he nature of the new war places a high premium on other factors, such as the ability to quickly obtain [sic] information from captured terrorists and their sponsors in order to avoid further atrocities against American civilians."[40] According to Gonzales, "this new paradigm *renders obsolete Geneva's strict limitations on questioning* of enemy prisoners and *renders quaint* some of its provisions"[41] (emphases added).

Furthermore, Attorney General Gonzales believed that stepping outside of the Geneva Conventions would preserve President Bush's "flexibility" during the war.[42] That is, it would protect administration personnel from prosecution under the 1996 War Crimes Act, which defines a war crime as "any grave breach" of the Geneva Conventions.[43] Gonzales's argument is quite disturbing. He advocated breaking the law by suggesting that the law should not apply. And he was President Bush's lawyer, and he became the nation's chief law enforcement officer.

On February 7th 2002, the Bush administration claimed to have conceded to Powell's skepticism by stating that the United States would apply the Geneva Conventions to the Afghan war.[44] However, Taliban and al-Qaeda detainees would still not be protected by the Geneva Conventions.[45] This essentially opened the door for harsh treatment and permitted President Bush to use any method he liked to achieve any goal he wished.

Later, on August 1st 2002, President Bush got more help from Justice Department attorneys, Jay Bybee and again John Yoo. Bybee, like Yoo, was a senior official at the OLC. On August 1st, the OLC issued two memos, which Georgetown Law Professor David Cole later called the "original sin."[46] The memos were written in response to Gonzales's request for an opinion on whether the United States' interrogation policies were banned by federal law. Gonzales knew the answer that Bush wanted, but he needed a second opinion.

In the initial August 1st memo, Bybee and Yoo decided to circumvent the law by defining torture in an extremely narrow way. According to the memo, torture consists of "severe physical or mental pain or suffering" that produces a near occasion of death.[47] It then concluded that in order for pain to be "severe," it must be "equivalent in intensity to the pain accompanying organ failure, impairment of bodily function, or even death."[48] The memo stated that "prolonged mental harm" is harm that must last for "months or years."[49] *The memo also declared that the president had the power to authorize torture, regardless of the federal statute criminalizing it.*[50] Additionally, the memo advised that interrogators could escape liability for engaging in torture by utilizing expanded versions of the doctrines of "self-defense" and "necessity."[51]

The second August 1st 2002 memo, which was not released to the public until April 2009, approved all of the CIA's proposed "interrogation" techniques, including: attention grasp, walling, facial hold, facial slap, cramped confinement, wall standing, stress positions, sleep deprivation, insects placed in a confinement box, and waterboarding.[52] The OLC claimed that none of the techniques were severe enough to constitute its own tailor-made definition of torture.[53]

The OLC concluded, for example, that waterboarding "inflicts no pain or actual harm whatsoever."[54] Yet, the Justice Department did not do its own independent research to analyze the various proposed tactics. Rather, it simply accepted the CIA's positions on these methods.[55] The memo states that "[the CIA has] informed us that . . . [waterboarding] . . . does not inflict actual physical harm."[56] So, basically, the OLC under Jay Bybee took the advice of those who asked for *its* advice on interrogation tactics to determine the lawfulness of those tactics. *Does this make any sense?* Bush, believe it or not, later appointed Bybee to the Ninth Circuit Court of Appeals.

Furthermore, on December 2nd 2002, Secretary of Defense Donald Rumsfeld signed off on a memo, known as the "Haynes memo," which *blatantly* condoned torture.[57] That memo was drafted by William J. Haynes II, the General Counsel at the Defense Department, and was addressed to Rumsfeld.[58] Haynes sought Rumsfeld's approval of various new interrogation techniques, including isolation for up to thirty days, deprivation of light and auditory stimuli, and waterboarding, to name a few.[59] Rumsfeld approved, but questioned a technique in which interrogators forced detainees to stand for a maximum of four hours.[60] At the bottom of the document, Rumsfeld wrote, "I stand for 8–10 hours a day. Why is standing limited to 4 hours?"[61]

The Bush administration, therefore, had managed to sidestep the law, and through the Haynes memo, had more recipes for torture. The horrific incidents at Abu Ghraib, a prison located in Baghdad, Iraq, seem less and less like isolated incidents, despite no hard publicly known proof that they were ordered. During the summer of 2004, photos were released of American soldiers brutalizing and humiliating Iraqi prisoners. These soldiers forced Iraqis to masturbate and sexually assaulted them with chemical light sticks. American military personnel were also captured laughing over dead Iraqis whose bodies were disfigured. Another picture that surfaced was of a hooded Iraqi man standing naked on a box, with his arms outspread, and wires dangling from his fingers, nose, and penis. This is an arcane method of interrogation called "the Vietnam." Many said that the soldiers had to have been taught how to do this, which could lead one to believe that they were ordered to do it. According to Senator Lindsey Graham (R-SC), "The photos clearly demonstrate to me the level of prisoner abuse and mistreatment went far beyond what I expected . . . It seems to have been planned." Planned by whom, Senator?

We know for sure that the Bush administration planned, condoned, and continues to defend a procedure known as waterboarding, and used it against prisoners Khalid Sheikh Mohammed, Abu Zubayda, and Abd al-Rahim al-Nashiri on multiple occasions. Waterboarding is a "stress-and-duress" procedure consisting of immobilizing a person on his back, with his head inclined downward. The "interrogator" then pours water over the face and into the breathing passages. Through forced suffocation, and inhalation of water, the subject experiences the process of drowning. Waterboarding does not always cause lasting physical damage, but it causes extreme pain, damage to the lungs, brain damage caused by oxygen deprivation, physical injuries due to struggling against the restraints, and even death.

Waterboarding nevertheless constitutes torture, even under now-Judge Jay Bybee's narrow definition of the term. As stated above, under the United States Code, torture is defined as "an act . . . specifically intended to inflict severe physical or mental pain or suffering. . . ." The Code defines severe mental pain or suffering as "the prolonged mental harm caused by or resulting from" a predicate act. One qualifying predicate act is "the threat of imminent death." Bybee wrote in the memo that "waterboarding constitutes a threat of imminent death," but found no evidence that the procedure caused prolonged mental harm. Thus even by his own perverse, twisted logic, now life-tenured federal Judge Bybee conceded that waterboarding is torture because it always brings the victim to a near occasion of death.

Allen Keller, M.D., however, found evidence of prolonged mental harm.[62] Dr. Keller, an Associate Professor of Medicine at the New York University School of Medicine, and the Director of the Bellevue/NYU Program for Survivors of Torture, testified before the Senate Select Committee on Intelligence on September 25th 2007.[63] He stated, quite clearly, that waterboarding causes prolonged mental harm.[64] According to Dr. Keller, "[l]ong term effects include panic attacks, depression and [post traumatic stress disorder]."[65] Dr. Keller, who treats torture victims at Bellevue Hospital in New York City, described one patient who "would panic and gasp for breath whenever it rained, even years after his abuse."[66] Another patient panics every time he showers, and yet another victim "panics every time he becomes the least bit short of breath, even during exercise."[67] It is clear, then, that waterboarding does constitute torture, and the Bush administration broke the law.

President Bush, Vice President Cheney, and their colleagues don't care, though. The law is a mere suggestion to these people. Cheney, in a recent speech at the American Enterprise Institute on May 21st 2009, stated that he would not have changed any of the practices the Bush administration implemented.[68]

The Justice Department's actions in response to the leak of the initial August 2002 memo showed this continued objection to the rule of law.[69] When the first August 2002 memo became public in 2004, the Justice Department issued a replacement memo on December 30th 2004, which essentially overruled the August 2002 memo.[70] Nevertheless, the Justice Department could not keep from breaking the law. The OLC issued three secret memos in May 2005, signed by the head of the OLC, Steven Bradbury, which declared that none of the CIA techniques amounted to torture.[71] The OLC based its assessment on two facts that are irrelevant to the lawfulness of the interrogation techniques.[72]

One fact was that American soldiers in the military's counter-terrorism training program had not suffered severe physical pain or prolonged mental harm when the techniques were performed on them.[73] This information has nothing to do with the techniques' lawfulness because American soldiers are not Guantánamo Bay detainees. Our soldiers entered this program voluntarily, the tactics used against them have clearly defined limits, and the soldiers can utter a code word whenever they want to stop the ordeal.[74] Prisoners do not have these luxuries.

The other fact on which Bradbury relied was that CIA-employed physicians would be present during interrogations of prisoners to monitor them.[75] *How can physicians assess the severity of pain being inflicted? How can they know when to stop the process?*[76] *Did they ever stop it? What kind of a physician would facilitate the administration of pain? Don't physicians promise, "First do no harm"?*

The third May 2005 memo, the most disturbing of them all, went even further, stating that the CIA's interrogation techniques did not even amount to "cruel, inhuman, or degrading treatment."[77] Why did the OLC write this memo? The Bush administration knew that Congress would soon vote on President Bush's objections to the Detainee Treatment Act, which prohibited "cruel, inhuman, or degrading treatment" of any person in U.S. custody.[78] Therefore, the Justice Department, in order to continue to permit the Bush administration to use cruel, inhuman, and degrading treatment, was forced to conclude that the enhanced interrogation techniques that Congress thought it was outlawing were neither cruel, nor inhuman, nor degrading. The OLC rationalized its claim, stating that in order for techniques to be considered cruel, inhuman, or degrading, they must "shock the conscience," and the CIA's techniques did not shock the conscience.[79] *Whose conscience?*

Unfortunately, in its memo the OLC conveniently disregarded the

United States Supreme Court case of *Chavez v. Martinez* (2003).[80] In that case, the Supreme Court held that any intentional infliction of pain in the course of interrogation shocks the conscience, even where the statements gathered are not used to prosecute the subject.[81] So, it turns out that intentionally inflicting pain is illegal. I guess our Justice Department, employing some of the most brilliant attorneys in the country, mistakenly skipped over the *Chavez* case, or, it was under pressure to disregard it. Of course, one must possess a conscience in order for it to be shocked, and many in the Bush administration gave all indications of lacking any semblance of a conscience.

The latest public memo from the OLC on the CIA interrogation tactics was the one dated July 2007.[82] This memo contains some remarkable language, considering the time at which it was written. Before the memo was written, the Supreme Court ruled that Common Article 3 of the Geneva Conventions covered al-Qaeda detainees, even though the Bush administration argued that they were not covered.[83] The OLC claimed that al-Qaeda detainees were different, and that the CIA could engage in degrading treatment that did not constitute an "outrage upon personal dignity,"[84] a class of treatment prohibited by Common Article 3. Furthermore, the memo stated that even if the CIA program violated Common Article 3, the president could simply declare that it does not apply.[85]

The Office of Legal Counsel operates as the "constitutional conscience" of the Justice Department.[86] Its job is to exercise independent, objective judgment to make sure the president and the executive branch are working within the law.[87] Its job is not to write one-sided memos ignoring laws and treaties unfavorable to the president's cause. The OLC is important not only because it works for the federal government, and Americans expect that the government will respect the rule of law (*isn't there a mountain of evidence that militates against such an expectation?*), but also the OLC's role is vital because

its work is virtually unchecked.[88] OLC lawyers are not private attorneys who put forth their clients' best argument in an adversarial
setting.[89] No judge or jury reviews the OLC's opinions. Rather, the
OLC is supposed to work as a check on the executive branch, representing a line of defense against unlawful executive activity.

It is clear, then, that the lawyers who wrote the torture memos and
facilitated the Bush administration's torture policy, are not merely
guilty of exercising poor judgment; they disregarded their honorable
role in our government and involved themselves in a criminal conspiracy. The Department of Justice must investigate and prosecute
these lawyers to show that the guidelines they set for the CIA were
illegal and essentially worked as a permission slip for CIA agents to
violate the law. If we have any respect for our laws or any sense of
justice, we must show that this behavior will not be tolerated.

By the way, we also need to prosecute the OLC lawyers. We are
legally bound by the Convention Against Torture to submit any case
alleging torture by a person within our jurisdiction "to . . . compe-
tent authorities for the purpose of prosecution."[90] *Mr. President and
Attorney General Holder, what are you waiting for?*

We Allowed It

Depriving people of natural rights without due process is wrong,
immoral, criminal, and unconstitutional; torture is the same, except
that it can *never* be lawful or moral, since it is even prohibited after or
as a result of due process. Yet, it seems that throughout history, we
continue to restrict the rights of those who scare us. Bush administration personnel believed they were above the law and did horrible
things in the name of "protecting our country." After the atrocities of
September 11th, some people actually agreed with the Bush administration and believed that the terrorists, or even potential terrorists,

or even people the President thinks wanted to be terrorists, somehow deserve this treatment. Dick Cheney believes that "enhanced interrogations" were "essential, justified, successful, and the right thing to do."

Nevertheless, we are country of laws, and not of men. No one in the government can disregard the law because we're living under special circumstances. Depriving people of due process is against the law. Torture is against federal and state law, and it violates the Natural Law and the Constitution. We must recognize this fact, and prevent the government from doing this again. We must be skeptical of the government, *especially* during times of national crisis or fabricated national crisis.

Lie #16

"The Right of the People to Be Secure in Their Persons, Houses, Papers, and Effects, Shall Not Be Violated"

Imagine living in a world where the police can search your home without your knowledge at any time day or night; where the government listens to your telephone calls, and your mail is customarily opened and read; where even the Internet does not provide a safe haven for you to speak out, because every Web site you visit and e-mail you write and keystroke you press is filed away for the police to reference, as is a record of every book you ever buy or borrow from the library; where even your most private records, like your medical or financial or legal records, are subject to prying eyes.

Now imagine that you could be arrested and held indefinitely based on what you wrote or said, or even on the mere suspicion that you were not wholeheartedly supportive of the current regime. Sounds terrifying? Well, do not breathe a sigh of relief that you are lucky enough to have avoided such fate, because what you are imagining is the United States of America *circa* 2010. These imaginings, which invoke memories of Soviet Russia or Nazi Germany or Orwell's *1984*, are all permitted by provisions in the USA Patriot Act, signed into law by President George W. Bush and enforced by President Barack Obama.

The United States of America is the country that most people around the world associate with freedom. The American Dream is the dream of those in the farthest corners of the world, where countries are run by despots and people fear to speak. The Land of the Free calls to those who dream of a country where freedom still reigns. It is the dream of those who are scared that they might at any moment disappear because they said the wrong thing, because they put forth an opinion that might not have pleased those in power.

As we discussed in Lie #13, unbelievable as it may seem, the benignly titled Patriot Act has very little to do with patriotism and protection from terrorism and much to do with the grasp for power that the federal government is so fond of. It is perhaps not surprising that the government would miss the irony of entitling this atrocity, which the ultimate patriots, our Founding Fathers, would have revolted against. The American Revolution, after all, was caused by the high rate of taxation imposed on the colonies by England. If taxes incited the Founding Fathers to tarring and feathering, I can only imagine what the agents of the government would be subjected to if they had proposed such a thing as the Patriot Act.

Well, the America of today is quite different than the Founding Fathers would have ever imagined. And it is quite different than what the citizens of this country imagine today. Benjamin Franklin once said, "They who can give up essential liberty to obtain a little temporary safety, deserve neither liberty nor safety." And if he were to take a look at the America of today, he would say that we deserve none of the liberties, which we so easily surrendered in fear, through deception, in the stated purposes of a search for national security.

The government found it so easy to deceive us, found that when we were scared, we would throw ourselves at its mercy, in order to feel safe. National security, they claimed, was attainable and the Patriot Act, which of course would require our patriotism and sacrifice, would help them attain it, never explaining that it would be at the cost of individual fundamental liberties that once made America the dream of the oppressed.

All We Have to Fear Is Fear Itself
(and, of Course, Those Scheming Frenchmen)

Many assume that the power grab and ensuing denials of people's rights brought by the Patriot Act have no precedents in American history. Sadly, that is not the case. The federal government has used fear to grasp our rights since the dawn of this country, and even John Adams, a Founding Father, used that fear after he became president and signed the Alien and Sedition Acts of 1798 into law. The fear was caused by what is now known as the XYZ affair, a French-American diplomatic incident.

> "Fear is the Foundation of Most Governments."
> —President John Adams

The United States government has developed a rich tradition of restricting the freedoms of groups of people that it believes or wants the public to believe pose a security threat, especially during times of war and national crisis. In 1798, the United States was nearing war with France. The Federalists (Washington, Adams, Hamilton, to name a few) controlled the executive and legislative branches of government, but felt threatened by the ideas emanating from the French Revolution. They believed that the Democratic-Republicans, also called anti-Federalists (Jefferson, Madison, and Monroe, to name a few) who espoused these "French" views, would motivate aliens living in the United States to support the French.[1] To suppress these ideas, Congress enacted the Alien and Sedition Acts over the summer of 1798.

The Sedition Act victimized Matthew Lyon, a Republican congressman from Vermont, during his reelection campaign.[2] Lyon published an article attacking the Adams administration and declaring that "every consideration of the public welfare [was] swallowed up in a continual grasp for power, in an unbounded thirst for ridiculous pomp, foolish adulation, and selfish avarice." The government made it impossible for Lyon to prevail at his trial. The trial judge instructed the jury that it must find "malicious intent," an element of the crime, *unless* the statement "could have been uttered with any other intent than that of making odious or contemptible the President and the government, and bringing them both into disrepute." Lyon could have defended himself by proving the *truth* of his statements, but this was quite the difficult task, as his statement was an *opinion*.

The jury convicted the Congressman and the judge sentenced Lyon to a $1,000 fine and four months in jail. It can be said that Lyon got the last laugh, however, as he was reelected while in prison! The Sedition Act proved to be a disaster for the Federalists politically, as the nation elected a Democratic-Republican by the name of Thomas Jefferson as our third president.

The United States also suppressed the freedom of speech during both the Civil War and World War I. During the Civil War, the Union as well as the Confederacy suppressed opposition newspapers and jailed critics.[3] During World War I, the government passed laws, such as the Espionage Act of 1917, and the Sedition Act of 1918, which criminalized public criticism of the war. German-Americans, labor leaders, and socialists were also subject to government persecution.

Moreover, during the Red Scare that followed the Great War, thousands of radicals were arrested, and many aliens were deported.

The Oxymoron of the "Secret" Court of Justice

Following the uproar surrounding the Alien and Sedition Acts, Presidents tended to avoid any public scrutiny of their unconstitutional actions. Rather than attempting to pass unconstitutional laws so that their actions would appear to be legal, some were reckless enough to impair the civil liberties of the people without their knowledge and without the need of Congressional approval and therefore criticisms. Presidents Kennedy and Lyndon B. Johnson routinely wiretapped the telephone calls of those they feared, without search warrants. The most famous example of such action was in the form of President Richard Nixon and the wiretapping of almost anyone of import in Washington, DC. Then he got caught, and his Presidency came to a crashing halt. The permanently upsetting result of JFK's, LBJ's, and Nixon's chicanery is that these illegal actions led to the passage of one of the most intrusive laws in America, the Foreign Intelligence Surveillance Act of 1978, better known as FISA.

The stated purpose of the Act was to protect the citizens of the United States from wiretapping, and it attempted to do this by requiring warrants for any wiretaps. But the warrants were no ordinary warrants from the courts established under the Constitution. Instead, FISA created a new court authorized to approve these wiretap warrants, both the applications for which and orders from would be "maintained under security measures established by the Chief Justice in consultation with the Attorney General and the Director of Central Intelligence."[4] So, the secret court was created to review secret applications and issue secret decisions. And this was supposed to protect the liberties of the citizens of the United States.

Also, the Act was supposed to be limited to foreign powers and agents of foreign powers, and the primary purpose was to gather foreign intelligence. Well, at least that is how the government sold it, claiming it would protect American citizens from JFK/LBJ/Nixon-like warrantless wiretapping, which would now only be used against foreigners. And it was supposed to provide judicial oversight of the federal government's surveillance activities while maintaining the confidential nature needed to ensure national security.

The emphasis on oversight and protection of liberties was some-what tenuous considering that the Act permitted surveillance in the United States without a court order for one year unless the "surveil-lance will acquire the contents of any communication to which a United States person is a party."[5] When an American citizen was to be involved, then the government was required to obtain judicial autho-rization within seventy-two hours *after* the start of surveillance.

So, not only does the Act purport to give the government permis-sion to initiate surveillance against an American citizen without a court order for three days, but once they start surveillance, govern-ment agents are not required to provide any federal district court with probable cause of a crime, as the Fourth Amendment requires. Rather, all that is required is that the government go to this secret court and explain that it suspected the American citizen of being involved with a foreigner in potential espionage. The court, which was not required to disclose its records and which would never be open to public scrutiny, was a rubber stamp; a rubber stamp that, between the years of 1979 to 2007, rejected only *nine* of the *25,361* warrant applications submitted to it.[6]

Aside from the secrecy granted these FISA courts, the ease with which warrants were granted also stemmed from the much lower threshold for proof that FISA required. Rather than, as in a typical warrant, containing a requirement of probable cause to believe that *the target possesses* evidence of a crime, FISA only requires that there be probable cause to believe that *the target is an agent of a foreign power* and that the place where the surveillance will be taking place is being used by the foreign power. This means that the only thing the government needs to show is *probable cause* that the target of the surveillance is foreign, not that there is evidence to induce a judicial conclusion that the target is involved in any activity which could be a threat to national security.

The Act also provided the same requirements for physical as well as electronic surveillance. If the requirements for a criminal case were based on FISA, this would mean that if the police wanted to search your house because they suspected you of criminal conduct, all that the officers would have to establish is that there was probable cause to believe that you were you and your house was your house. It would not even have to be certain, just probable, that they were right. Yet somehow, the federal government in the administration of President Jimmy Carter successfully sold the idea to the country that the Act would protect liberties and ensure privacy. And we believed it because of the Cold War, because of the fear of the Soviet Union, because we wanted to be safe, and because we wanted to believe that the government could protect us. We forgot about the right to be left alone.

Good-bye Liberty, Hello Tyranny

While the Sedition Acts and FISA claimed to protect Americans and provide us with both liberty and security, they were just the prologue to our current debacle. And it all began, as do most roads to tyranny, with a terrible disaster, a horrible action that spawned the government-hoped-for reaction. On September 11th 2001, New York City, Washington, D.C., and Shankville, Pennsylvania, were the scenes of one of the most horrific tragedies of our history. We were attacked by those who resented our presence in their countries and while our country stood still, sadness and shock emanating throughout, the federal government chose to help terrorists cause more American suffering by diminishing the liberty that makes America so great. The Bush Administration, within only weeks of the tragedy, had drafted the Patriot Act of 2001.

The Patriot Act sailed through Congress with little opposition. It was a well-contrived acronym that inspired visions of the Founding Fathers fighting for freedom. And so nobody seemed to notice or care that it actually takes from the people each of the cherished freedoms for which so many fought and died. The Act tramples the constitutional rights of law-abiding American citizens by snooping into their private communications and personal records. It also expands the power of federal agencies, allowing searches and seizures without a warrant and without any probable cause. It allows for the detainment of people without lawyers for indefinite periods, often solely on the baseless suspicions of one or another federal agent. And it can do all this in secret, without public or judicial scrutiny.

Sadly, considering the constitutional impact of the Patriot Act, one would think that Congress would have spent a little more time debating its various provisions. And maybe it would have, if any congressperson had bothered to read it and consider the implications. But while claiming to be working for the people and asserting that it protects us from unconstitutional laws, Congress did not fight it even a little.

The Patriot Act was introduced on October 23rd and in two days passed both the House and the Senate and was signed into law on October 26th. Considering that the Act was 342 pages in very small print, it was amazing that it took less than two days for most to read it. The more amazing thing was that later most of Congress admitted never having read the Act. Our representatives passed a law that they failed to read, a law that was drafted by the top law enforcement agency, the Department of Justice. Apparently, Congress would like us to believe that it did not need to read the law it was approving, because it assumed that the top law enforcement agency would never attempt to increase its influence or power.

Probable Farce

Most of the Patriot Act amended preexisting laws, one of them being FISA. With its amendments, the Act quickly and easily rid FISA of the few protections it contained against total government interference in our personal liberties. Prior to the amendment, the FISA secret courts could only grant a warrant when the "primary purpose" of the search was to gather intelligence from foreign powers. Now, the secret courts can grant warrants when the purpose of foreign intelligence gathering is a "significant purpose"[7] of the surveillance. And "foreign power" was amended to "foreign person." Never mind that the Constitution protects the liberties of all *persons*, citizens and aliens, domestic and foreign, residents and strangers, saints and thugs; the Patriot Act purports to change that.

So anyone who the government decides might at some point yield information that will link the government to foreign intelligence can be snooped on, without their knowledge, and without even a shred of evidence to link them to criminal activity. The best part is that if any evidence of criminal activity not linked to foreign intelligence is discovered during these fishing expeditions, the government *must* pass that information on to another agency permitted to use it in criminal prosecution.[8]

Basically, if the federal government is wrong, and you have absolutely no connection to any foreign power, at least the resources are not wasted if they can find some other criminal activity to pin on you; too bad for your constitutional rights. Even if we believe that it is only the so-called War on Terror that is keeping us safe, we cannot keep letting the government tell us that it is okay for us to give up the Constitution in exchange for the promise of security.

The Supreme Court held in the case of *Texas v. Stanford* (1965) that the government may not constitutionally issue general warrants that do not describe with particularity the place to be searched or the things to be seized.[9] This requirement of specificity is an inherent part of the Fourth Amendment and protects against fishing expeditions by the local or state police or federal agents. Or at least it did, until a section of the Patriot Act amended FISA to authorize roving wiretaps. Roving wiretaps are in essence warrants that are not required to specify each common carrier or third party involved in the court order. The roving wiretaps allow for taps on a multitude of computers or telephones, rather than requiring that the secret court "warrant" specify the computer or telephone.[10] So, the government can request that all of the computers at the New York Public Library be put under surveillance, and that would be more than specific enough for the FISA "court."

Another tragic aspect of the Patriot Act is that it grants federal judges powers outside their geographic jurisdictions and permits them to authorize wiretaps on a national level.[11] How can judges have power in geographic areas where they do not sit and thus do not have lawful jurisdiction? The whole purpose of geographic jurisdiction (a federal judge in Newark generally lacks jurisdiction over persons in Los Angeles) is to facilitate access to courts. If the judge in Newark authorizes a wiretap in Los Angeles, should the targets of the wiretap need to travel three thousand miles to challenge it? No; before the Patriot Act. Yes; since it became law.

Sneaking Away from Liberty

As if the almost complete reduction of a probable cause requirement were not enough, the new secret court FISA warrants also breach another constitutional requirement, that of notice. Fourth Amendment jurisprudence has had a long-standing practice of serving the warrant before a search could begin. The notice requirement ensured that an innocent person could look over the warrant and point out any mistakes so that wrong houses were not searched as well as assuring that only those things that were permitted to be searched were searched and the police did not expand their boundaries. The Patriot Act changes that, permitting the government to avoid notifying the owner for a month after the search, through showing only that there is "reasonable cause to believe" that notice could potentially "seriously jeopardize an investigation."[12]

These are called sneak-and-peak warrants, and the Patriot Act is the first "express statutory authorization" for this type of warrant.[13] The Patriot Act requirement in essence then dismisses notice without a second thought, as any four-year-old could come up with a reason that giving notice to a criminal suspect could maybe put the investigation in jeopardy.

A federal district court judge once warned that sneak-and-peek warrants "constitute . . . a dangerous and radical threat to civil rights and to the security of all our homes and persons."[14] This was in 1986, when sneak-and-peek warrants were only permitted by the courts in limited and distinct situations where the danger was extreme, palpable, and imminent. With the changes made by the Patriot Act, sneak-and-peak warrants will soon become standard issue. And because the records for these FISA court warrants are confidential, the public cannot scrutinize them. Even when the ACLU sued under the Freedom of Information Act to compel the federal government to reveal statistical information with regard to various Patriot Act provisions, including sneak-and peek-warrants, the court held that such information could be withheld on the grounds of national security.[15]

And it was on grounds of that ever-comforting phrase, national security, that an American attorney was detained for over two weeks by the federal government *by mistake*. Brandon Mayfield was an attorney who performed *pro bono* work with the Modest Means Program, which provided attorneys at reduced-rates for low-income clients. Brandon had had the misfortune to fall in love and marry an Egyptian woman, and, thereafter, he converted to Islam. Life was going well, and the happy couple had three children.

Then disaster struck when the federal government made a giant mistake and thought it matched the fingerprints found on a backpack in the rubble of the 2004 Madrid train bombing to Brandon. After the FBI *authorized itself* to enter his house and wiretap his phones, he was arrested on a material witness warrant, all based on a faulty fingerprint match whose accuracy the FBI lied about.

Brandon was held for two weeks, without access to his family and only limited access to an attorney. Only when multiple efforts by Spanish authorities to alert the FBI that they did not think the fingerprints were Brandon's did he get his day in court, where the case against him was dismissed. The FBI apologized for its mistake but never admitted to any misuse of the Patriot Act. Brandon filed a lawsuit, and U.S. District Judge Ann Aiken in Eugene, Oregon, held that certain provisions of the Act were unconstitutional. The federal government has of course appealed and continues to enforce the provisions found unconstitutional.

National Security Letters:
The New Judge-Proof Warrant

How did the FBI bypass the Fourth Amendment to the Constitution its agents swore to uphold and *authorize itself* to break into Brandon Mayfield's home and wiretap his telephones and eventually arrest him based on a lie? Well, another aspect of the Patriot Act that has been horrific in application is the National Security Letter or NSL. Though it may not sound threatening, the NSL is in essence a search warrant, but one that requires no probable cause or judicial oversight and that allows for any federal agent to request any and all of your personal records.[16] Prior to the enactment of the Patriot Act, NSLs were only authorized to be used to investigate those suspected of being spies and had to be issued by very senior officials. Now almost every federal agent can use them against aliens and citizens alike without showing probable cause of crime to a federal district judge and without showing probable cause to believe that the target is suspicious and a foreigner to the secret FISA court.

It does not matter whether the target of the NSL has ever even been suspected of terrorist or simply criminal activity. So think about the people you have lived next door to, attended school with, worked with or in any other way met for any period of time. If any one of those people have since then been—whether wrongfully or rightfully—considered a suspicious foreigner by a single federal agent, which might even be a question of donating money to a foreign charity, then you can be the next target of an NSL.

Now originally, National Security Letters were only to be used to obtain information from financial institutions, like banks and credit unions. Those institutions were required to provide financial data in order to aid federal agencies in gathering information to prevent terrorism. And, of course, originally these records would be provided without a warrant, only for those who were the *target* of a terrorism investigation. Then the Patriot Act amended this and allowed these to be the *financial* records of someone "sought for" a terrorism investigation, meaning that anyone who the government decides is worth investigating can be investigated, and the government can get records without a constitutional search warrant. And, of course, the Bush administration stressed that there was nothing to worry about, that this involved only financial institutions and would not affect the average American citizen.

But Republicans who ran the Congress in 2003 were not finished and decided to enact the Intelligence Authorization Act for the Fiscal Year 2004. This type of Act is passed every year and typically involves budgeting decisions for the coming year. President Bush signed this version of the Act into law on December 13th 2003, with no public notice, as it was "coincidentally" signed the same day that news of Saddam Hussein's capture was made public.[17] Unfortunately for the American people, one section of this Act amended the definition of "financial institution" in the Right to Financial Privacy Act of 1978. The definition of "financial institution" as amended includes pawnbrokers, jewelry stores, car dealers, casinos, travel agents, physicians, health care officials, lawyers, and finally "any business . . . which engages in *any* activity which the Secretary of Treasury determines . . . to be an activity which is similar to . . . any business described in this paragraph is authorized to engage,"[18] and that great financial institution to which we would all "eagerly" repose our savings, the U.S. Post Office.

Basically, this opened the door to any business that the federal government wanted the records of, including medical records, telephone records, computer keystrokes, legal records, and records from your corner bodega.[19] And, as one Congressman noted, the language in the Act "only vaguely limits this expanded definition to financial information."[20]

The government can compel all your records, and *needs only to satisfy itself* that the information it is gathering is sought in connection with an investigation into terrorism or foreign intelligence gathering. That's all; the agents are not even required to show to a superior that the information they collect is relevant to that investigation, just that they are in the process of an investigation. Anyone who receives an NSL cannot reveal that fact to anybody, even you as the target, for fear of criminal prosecution.

In 2005 it was uncovered that during one investigation of Las Vegas businesses, the FBI had issued tens of thousands of NSLs and obtained over a million financial, employment, and medical records of the customers of the target of the investigation. So your medical records, your financial records, and any other records that the government deems necessary will be opened for the world. And there will be not a thing you can do about it. All this, perhaps, because you spoke with the person sitting next to you on an airplane who was deemed suspicious by the government.

Be Careful What You Read

*Dear reader, since you have actually picked up and read this book, it might be a little late for a warning. Just in case you thought you were safe to read whatever you choose, I want to warn you that your reading habits may be monitored for "suspicious" behavior. Considering the title of this book, your name might now be on a list authorized by the Patriot Act, which permits the FBI to review any tangible record, including reading habits. And the targets of these reading habit investigations need not be terrorists; the government does not even have to show the secret FISA court that the person is linked in any way to terrorism. Instead, all **agents are required to show to themselves** is that the records are required for an investigation of terrorism.*

Even now, the Department of Justice has actually claimed that the secret FISA court has no authority to reject requests for FISA orders because all of them are acceptable, even when the *primary* purpose has nothing whatsoever to do with terrorism.[21] The libraries and bookstores required to provide the surveillance information cannot reveal or notify anyone of that fact. And, like with National Security Letters, there is no judicial oversight of the secret warrants permitting access to such records.[22] The only limitation on access to such records is that the investigation cannot be launched *solely* if its basis is a First Amendment–protected activity; but if there is *any other* "unprotected" reason for the investigation, then that trumps the First Amendment.

The only bright light at the end of the tunnel is that librarians, after realizing the implications of the Act, have begun shredding records at the earliest possible time, so that they would not be able to provide the requested information under an NSL. But all that stands between what we choose to read and the government are the abilities of the librarians to shred faster than the government can collect.

No End in Sight

Democrats have admitted that the Patriot Act is unconstitutional, but they were willing to reauthorize the Act for four years, this coming from the party that is meant to stand for civil liberties and freedom.[23] Even if the government admits to taking our liberties, trying to justify it by stating that it is necessary for our safety and security, would still be fallacious. No matter how often the government can claim to be able to protect us, and blame any of its inadequacies on lack of power, the argument is a lie. There is only one reason that the government takes away freedoms: Freedom is an obstacle to dominance, and almost everyone in government possesses what St. Augustine called *libido dominandi*, the lust to dominate.

The ruse that most persons fall for is that this is done for our safety. People want to feel secure, and their belief that the government can provide us with such security ensures that many are willing to sacrifice their safety. Yet, there is a reason that the Constitution exists in this country. As Congressman Ron Paul has stated, "These are not the most dangerous times in American history, despite the self-flattery of our politicians and media."[24]

Rather, as he so aptly noted, America has survived the burning down of the White House, a Civil War, involvement in two World Wars, and has won a forty-year Cold War with the Soviet Union, a time where spying was rampant through the federal agencies and where citizens drawn by the rhetoric of Communism defected to the Soviet Union, and most notably, fingers were poised to press the nuclear launch button. Yet, somehow, America not only survived but flourished without the Patriot Act. It is in periods of crisis that we should strive to protect our liberties, not sacrifice them on the altar of a false sense of security.

During the reauthorization of the Patriot Act and an extension of its sunset provisions in 2005, many proponents made mention of the then-recent subway bombings in London as an argument in favor of the Patriot Act. They argued that government spying on Americans without judicially issued search warrants could prevent such actions here. But as Congressman Paul points out, London is "the most heavily monitored city in the world" and the British are "not hampered by our 4th Amendment or our due process requirements," yet they were unable to protect themselves, proving that "even a wholesale surveillance society cannot be made completely safe against determined terrorists."[25] If the freedomless British cannot protect their cities from attack, why do politicians attempt to argue that stripping us of our liberties will work here at home?

There is no reason to believe that any of the actions taken under the Patriot Act can make us safer. All the justifications and endless explanations for the need of a Patriot Act have no support in reality and are just lies created by the government to lull us into acquiescence, to enhance the government's power over us, and to make it appear to fearful or gullible Americans that because the government is curtailing our freedoms it must be making us safer by doing so. Be ashamed for accepting such arrant nonsense.

It is no surprise, considering the unconstitutional atrocities permitted by the Patriot Act, that seven states have passed resolutions condemning the Act. Each day, more fight to force President Obama to repeal it. But once it has managed to deceive us into granting it more power, the federal government is loath to return it. Unremarkably, therefore, even President Obama, who ran for office as a defender of civil liberties, now supports maintaining the existing law.

This Is America

The cynically named Patriot Act is a revolting and unconstitutional example of the federal government taking advantage of people during times of crisis. To pass the Act in the wake of September 11th 2001, was one thing; to reauthorize it after it has proven to be wildly unconstitutional and phenomenally ineffective is quite another. How do we expect to be the example of democracy in the Middle East and around the world when our government doesn't even trust us, and goes out of its way to lie to us in order to strip us of our freedoms? As a result of the tragedy that was September 11th 2001, it is important to take terrorist threats seriously, but under no circumstances should we have to fear what we say, write, or type. This is America, isn't it?

Lie #17

"America Has a Free Market"

As hue and cry abound around the current economic crisis, and blame is passed from Wall Street to Main Street and back again, it is strange to note that we hear so little about the blame that should rest in Washington, D.C. And the blame that does come to rest on the shoulders of the government seems largely focused on "too little government intervention," which permitted "too much capitalism."[1] Apparently, all those acronyms that the government is so famous for producing and the regulations it enforces are not considered intervention.

The government has managed to convince most Americans not only that they are living in a country whose economy is based on laissez-faire capitalism but also that the free market is to blame for all our problems. And until those myths are rebutted and the truth of the matter is revealed, we will continue on the path forged by the Great Depression, and ending with central economic planning in Washington, privately owned entities under government control, and nationalization of businesses that are "too big to fail."

The Unaffordable Cost of "Affordable Housing"[2]

Ever since FDR and his New Deal policies in the 1930s, the federal government has inserted itself into housing policy in order to ensure—it contends—that everyone has access to affordable housing. Beginning with rent control, the trend continued with encouraging homeownership, with the establishment of Fannie Mae and Freddie Mac to the Community Reinvestment Act of 1977 (CRA), forcing banks to make loans to those they would normally reject as dangerous credit risks. Somehow, the Reinvestment Act claimed that is was unfair for banks to reject certain parts of the community based on credit, because everyone deserved to own a house, whether he or she could actually afford it or not. Basically, Fannie and Freddie, capitalized with taxpayer dollars, took the underperforming mortgages, that the CRA forced the banks to make, off the banks' balance sheets. So, credit-risky owners got homes they couldn't afford, banks got fees for lending to risky borrowers, and taxpayers got stuck with the risks and the eventual losses.

Yet, even with all the laws and regulations around, the government continues to blame deregulation and the "free" market. How it can do so with a straight face, considering that we have *seventy-three thousand* pages of detailed government [economic] regulations,"[3] is beyond me. And the regulations and government intervention are directly to blame for the mess we are in now, no matter how hard the government tries to lie to us and blame Wall Street or Main Street or deregulation. It was the government that encouraged, enticed, and compelled banks to loan to people whom they would usually deny as bad credit risks.

It was the government that created the Department of Housing and Urban Development (HUD), which guaranteed billions of dollars in loans. And, of course, if a loan is guaranteed by the government, there is no reason for a bank to look at the borrower's ability to return the money.[4] Slowly, too, HUD lowered its standards, and the government's approval for granting mortgage insurance became almost automatic. Such guarantees brought about new banks, like

Countrywide Financial, which were opened around the nation, centered on serving that portion of the population that could not get "prime" loans because of poor credit history, and providing them with "sub-prime" mortgages, sometimes with no money down, to buy houses they could ill afford.

Many were expecting house prices to continue to rise and therefore bought million-dollar houses on incomes of less than $30,000, with no money down. So when the housing bubble burst, as all bubbles eventually do, these people had mortgage payments due that they could not afford, and their houses were worth less than the mortgage that they had to pay. So the banks foreclosed on homes that were not worth the money that had been loaned in order to purchase them.

These same mortgages had also been wrapped up into securities, called mortgage-backed securities, which were then sold by the banks to investors, which provided the banks with additional money to make more loans. Sometimes Fannie and Freddie were the investors. But the value of these securities depended on the mortgage payments being paid in full and on time. When the housing boom collapsed and people stopped paying, these securities became worthless, and losses of billions accumulated in those who had invested.

Many of those who had invested were investment banks, which then had losses of billions, and they collapsed as well. The market went into free fall, largely because the government induced and forced banks to loan to people with poor credit, because it felt that everyone deserved affordable housing and so it had to provide it, through any means necessary. But what the government tends to forget is that there is no such thing as a free lunch. So now, we will soon be paying in higher taxes and inflation for the so-called "affordable housing" that the government was desperate to provide.

The Bailout: Free Money for the Incompetent

By bailing out banks and related companies, the government has essentially ensured what it claimed it was trying to prevent, market instability. Now that certain firms are aware that they are too big to fail, they will be much more likely to engage in riskier investment schemes. They are aware that if their risky investment fails, the government will ensure their survival, and if it succeeds, there will be a large payout, as there is with any risky investment that succeeds. But the payout will be theirs and theirs alone. As the *Wall Street Journal* so aptly described the process, "[t]heir profit is privatized but their risk is socialized."[5]

Economists often state that the Great Depression was inordinately long, due in large part to the inflexibility of wages and other forms of government intervention.[6] The government responded by printing money, artificially stabilizing prices, employing the population on worthless projects, and thereby, according to the Austrian economists, expanding the Great Depression by around fifteen years.[7] The Great Depression was "great" because of its duration (from 1929 to 1946) and its duration was assured by FDR's central planning.

On the other hand, when the stock market crashed on October 19th 1987—a day known as Black Monday—and the Dow Jones dropped 508 points in one day,[8] while 205 banks failed that year,[9] President Reagan ignored the cries for help and did nothing. The government took not one step to intervene in the markets, though panic was widespread. Within a few months, the market stabilized and prosperity came slinking back. It has now been nearly eighteen months since the markets had their September 2008 collapse, and as much as the Federal Reserve is claiming that things are looking up, the markets are unstable and unemployment, even with the Bush and Obama bailouts, is over 10 percent.

Everyone claims that the bailout of the system is necessary in order to prevent another Great Depression. Yet, as Llewellyn Rockwell has pointed out, "[it] makes no sense to warn that we will repeat the past if we fail to do the things that actually made the past as bad as it was."[10] Maybe, rather than emulating a government that prolonged the Great Depression, we might think about emulating the administration that managed to allow Black Monday to be only a three-month-long affair.

President Reagan's chief economist, Arthur Laffer, has explained that the Obama $780 billion February 2009 stimulus plan, just like the Bush February 2008 $200 billion stimulus and the Bush October 2008 $700 billion TARP plans, will drive the country to economic ruin.[11] Laffer argues that these stimulus packages will have the same result as the $85 billion bailout of AIG, most of which money has ended up with the banks as beneficiaries and the taxpayers as the payees.[12] The bailout plan is essentially Robin Hood, except he is taking from the rich and poor alike to give to the extraordinarily wealthy. As Laffer notes, "There is no tooth fairy. Every dollar given to someone comes from someone else."

Since the government does not *produce* wealth, it only *transfers* resources and *consumes* wealth, that someone else who had the money will be driven to spend less. So the only gain is for those who receive that money, who, as has already been aptly proven, are not too good at knowing how to spend it. And an examination of the wish list received from cities around the country illustrates that no one seems to know where it will go. Requests include two million dollars for more neon signs in Las Vegas (of all places), three million for an environmentally friendly clubhouse, six million for waterslides, almost one million for a Frisbee golf course, and even Harley Davidson motorcycles for the police.[13] The money and how it is to be allocated are still in question. Some of the various projects that have been proposed will create jobs, as did the digging and filling of ditches during the reign of FDR, but whether they can create prosperity is out of the question.

It is the capitalist market that has proven to be the best allocator of resources. Many considered Lehman Brothers, one of New York's largest investment banks, too big too fail. Yet fail it did. In January 2008, the bank had assets of $639 billion and over twenty-six thousand employees, but the government let it go. Within a few days, the market had allowed the viable Lehman pieces to survive, and the rest were washed away.[14] That is how the market works, and the only way to ensure that the rest of the available resources are allocated to end this bust as quickly as possible is to stop any government intervention, allowing any firms that must fail to fail, and to do so quickly.

Any bailout, as in the case of AIG (where currently, executives largely responsible for its near-bankruptcy are to receive $165 million in bonuses),[15] will only result in creating a monster that will have a terrible impact on the future of the economy. If the executives are getting paid the big bucks to fail, why would they make any attempts to succeed? The longer a business that squanders money and profits is allowed to stay open, the more damage will be visited to the market and therefore to viable and profitable companies, which could otherwise fill in the gap that would be left by the closing of such companies.

From Too Big to Fail, to Too Public to Succeed

The claims by the government that the companies it bails out will return to private ownership after they stabilize is a well-known government deception. History has many such stories of companies in trouble that the government "rescues." Once government bureaucrats get their hands on a certain industry, they cannot let it go.

The strange thing is that Americans really do believe that the government can fix the problems in the private sector, because they believe that it is the greed of capitalistic businessmen that brings the market down, and so only the forces of a not-for-profit government can bring the market back up. People seem to have forgotten the disastrous result of a centrally controlled economy that was the Soviet Union. This government deception has been fed to us for so long that it has become an accepted fact, without any basis in actual reality.

This pervasive myth leads to the situation in which a libertarian may argue for the privatization of some part of the public sector, for example, utility companies, and the general population is shocked and awed that anyone would even contemplate such a thing. Professor Murray Rothbard once made a great analogy, noting that if the government had a monopoly on shoe manufacture and sale and had been providing shoes for everyone from tax revenues, then anyone who proposed that shoe production be privatized would get the same reaction. People would cry:

How could you? You are opposed to the public, to the poor people, wearing shoes! And who would supply shoes to the public if the government got out of the business? How many shoes would be available in each city and town? How would the shoe firm be capitalized? What material would they use? What would be the pricing arrangements? Wouldn't regulation of the shoe industry be needed to see to it the product is sound? And who would supply the poor with shoes?[16]

Because the government's own mythology has become so predominant in our time, most really do believe that if the government has been providing a monopolized service, no one else could or would want to do it, unless the new producer charged exorbitant amounts. Yet, all Professor Rothbard was attempting to prove was that the capitalist economy can handle itself, and it can do so better than the government because businesspeople have to answer to their customers and investors, and if they do not provide the product that customers want and bring a return to investors, then competition will wipe them out.

The government has no such worries. For one, since there is no relationship between product and payment, the government needn't worry about not getting paid for the product. It also does not have to worry about competition, because it has effectively banned anyone from competing with it. And, of course, the government never needs to impress investors when it wants cash. It just raises taxes, which we pay like sheep, or it prints money, which devalues all previously printed money.

Government Motors

There are many who argue that the Bush and Obama bailouts were the only possible solutions to ensuring that the economy did not collapse. On the other hand, as former British Prime Minister Margaret Thatcher once said, "The problem with socialism is that sooner or later, you run out of other people's money," so some firms need to go down because they are no longer functioning effectively in the market, and the government is just throwing good money after bad.

Some of these are lucky, like General Motors, which has now become Government Motors, with the federal government purchasing a huge stake in the company. General Motors initially received $20 billion as a bailout, but that did not save the company. So the government decided to give the company another $30 billion, but this time with a 60 percent controlling stake in the company. The result has been that government agents are making financing and business decisions, including President Obama effectively firing the long-time CEO, Richard Wagoner, and Congressman Barney Frank deciding where at least one GM warehouse should be (hint: in his congressional district).

Finally, rather than following well-established securities law, where secured creditors and bondholders get paid first when a corporation liquidates, the government paid out the United Auto Workers union, an unsecured creditor meant to get paid last in a bankruptcy. Instead, the union got almost double the amount of what the secured creditors did. Of course, the government continues to placate the public with assurances of the temporary nature of the fix and how GM will soon become profitable again.

So there it is; the government has acquired yet another corporation that it thinks it will be able to run more successfully than the private sector did. Of course, nationalizing an automobile maker sounds very much like something from Communist Russia, or Socialist Venezuela; and we know how successful those governments have been at earning profits. So now our government has spent billions of dollars of taxpayer money so that it can keep open a company, General Motors, that the market was on the brink of closing. And, if the history of Amtrak and the Post Office has anything to say, the government will continue to pour billions into GM well into the next century, without a thought for profit but always with the justifications of employment and public welfare.

Reagan once said that "[g]overnment's view of the economy could be summed up in a few short phrases: If it moves, tax it. If it keeps moving, regulate it. And if it stops moving, subsidize it." Well, the government has just done that with General Motors, because it will never be able to run it profitably, so instead it will just keep pumping taxpayer money into it.

Government Railroad

The story of Amtrak begins in 1971 during the Nixon Administration, as it was then that Congress established Amtrak as a federally owned passenger railroad. Originally, the government claimed that such a passenger railroad was important and also claimed that it expected "the corporation would experience financial losses for three years and then become a self-sustaining enterprise."[17] Well, it has now been forty years, and Amtrak has yet to make a profit. Instead, it has survived on government subsidies, grants, and loans of enormous proportions, totaling *over $25 billion throughout its existence.*[18]

At the same time, while airline travel has increased from 191.3 million passengers in 1972 to 665.6 million in 2000, Amtrak passengers went from 16.6 million in 1972 to 22.5 million in 2000.[19] This increase of 6 million passengers, considering the intense population growth in the U.S. during that time, exhibits the minimal need for train travel, and the fact that if there were a demand for such travel, the private market could handle it more efficiently. And if it could not, Amtrak would have been closed many years ago.

Privatization in other countries has illustrated that the private industry is much more efficient than anything the public sector can do. For example, privately owned Virgin Rail took over publicly owned British Rail and sparked such a traffic boom that the company has now placed an order for $3 billion in new trains.[20] While Amtrak's survival depends not on its ability to generate profits but solely on political hay, it will keep losing money and costing billions of dollars. The government has given multiple deadlines for Amtrak to reach profitability or face closure, and such deadlines have never been met, yet Amtrak continues its operations.[21]

One could argue that Amtrak, rather than an illustration of government inefficiency, is an illustration of the lack of demand for rail transport. For those there is the example of the United States Postal Service (USPS). Currently the USPS is facing extraordinary deficits. From January to July 2009, *the USPS lost over $7 billion*, and the government is attempting to figure out a resolution, including stopping Saturday delivery.[22]

Because the government consumes wealth, rather than produces wealth, the government can only save money by shutting down (so as to stop the consumption). In this respect (consumption versus production) the government and private enterprise are literally opposites. When private enterprise wants more income, it works overtime and produces more goods. When the government wants to save money, as the government of the City of Chicago did for a few days in the summer of 2009, it shuts down.

The Father of the Three-Cent Stamp

For some reason, we have become so indoctrinated to the need for a government-run monopoly on mail delivery that many have forgotten the story of Lysander Spooner. Though not many today know the name, he was a lawyer and author of *The Unconstitutionality of Slavery*, which was cited by Supreme Court Justice Antonin Scalia in his opinion in *District of Columbia v. Heller*. Another of his achievements was his establishment of the American Mail Company in 1844, a challenge to the monopoly of the Post Office, which was charging exorbitant rates.

By early 1843, mail prices had soared, and the government charged nearly nineteen cents to deliver a letter from Boston to New York.[23] In setting up his company, Spooner set up service to run between New York, Boston, Philadelphia, and Baltimore, which were also some of the main Post Office routes. He then announced that he would be charging a little over six cents per half-ounce letter and that there would be daily delivery in the cities. Initially, the government ignored his new company, but soon it was losing customers to the American Letter Mail Company.

Because of the competition from his business, the government filed suit to have him barred from invading the postal monopoly. "A 'not guilty' verdict was sustained by the U.S. District Court . . . [t]he court expressed doubt that the U.S. had the right to monopolize transportation of mail."[24] Still, Post Office revenues continued to drop until Congress was forced to give the Post Office permission to drop prices to five cents a letter. And later, Spooner was responsible for Congress agreeing to drop the price once again, which earned him the name "Father of the Three-Cent Stamp."[25] This entrepreneur had been able to create a successful and profitable company that charged almost one-third the price that the government charged for its mail delivery and created a situation where the government was forced to compete and reach prices that people were willing to pay.

Of course, once the government regained its monopoly, the price of mail increased constantly with no end in sight, and the Post Office is no longer even profitable, running massive deficits. Still the government claims that it would not be possible to provide mail service through a private company. Today, it is unlawful to charge the same or less than the Post Office to deliver any mail—unlawful to compete with the government.

R.I.P., Personal Responsibility

The magic of this idea of affordable housing, cheap automobiles, mail, and railroads, the idea that everyone deserves something from another, has resulted in a total depreciation of the idea of personal responsibility, an idea that is at the basis of America's values. The government does not have its own money to give away, but it loves to reallocate resources. So when the government is using taxes to pay for mistakes made by big businesses as well as by the little guys, it is only taking from those who have managed not to make gigantic mistakes and giving it to save those who have. And, of course, the government justifies its actions, blaming the big businesses and deflecting blame from itself and the little taxpayers who bought houses they could ill afford. And this is where personal responsibility has lost itself.

President George W. Bush asked for, received, and signed the American Dream Downpayment Act in 2005. Though I have always believed that the American Dream involves hard work and dedication, apparently in 2005, it was for sale to the lowest bidder. This Act in essence gave the government the authority to provide those in the lowest income brackets with down payments on homes that they could not afford. No longer did people have to save for the American Dream; the government decided to give it away, but of course only to those who had *not* worked hard and *not* saved from their incomes until they could afford to buy. That is perhaps the most stupefying consequence of this Act, because free down payments meant more people could buy, which in turn meant more demand, which in turn meant housing prices soared. So those who had saved enough to buy a house no longer had enough, because prices had climbed, and therefore so did the amount required for a down payment from those who did not qualify for the American Dream.

Still, once the housing bubble burst and the system collapsed, no one wanted to take the blame. Those who had bought houses they could not afford ran to the government for help, clamoring about the unfairness of the system. Those who invested in mortgage-backed securities and lost billions cried that they needed money from the government or else they would collapse, and the market would spiral out of control. The government blamed laissez-faire capitalists and the greedy bankers with their grubby hands. There was blame to go around, but no one would take it. And not only would they not accept it, but they also wanted payment from the taxpayers—from those who could still afford to pay the taxes. Of course, the government gave them all money.

The lesson learned was that as long as you did not take responsibility for your actions, then you would receive more money. The government bailed out the banks, it bailed out the people who could not afford their mortgages, and it continues to bail them out. The American Dream, which once rested on personal responsibility and hard work, now rests on getting the most for the least amount of work. And if the climate continues this way, pretty soon there will be nothing left of America or the Dream.

Conclusion

Before you finish reading this book, return to those quotations at the beginning. Did I prove my case? If you believe in God, you believe He is Truth. But a Roman governor asks if anyone can know the truth, and a modern-day American vice president marvels at its debasement by the government. And two philosophers claim we are ripe for being plucked into the baskets of the deceivers.

As I finish writing this book, the country is consumed with a great public debate over proposals for the federal government to take over and manage the delivery of health care to every person in America.

During that debate, Congressman Joe Wilson (R-SC) was disciplined by his colleagues in the House of Representatives because he called President Obama a liar during the President's address to a joint session of Congress. The statement that the President made, which provoked the Congressman's ill-timed outburst, claimed that illegal aliens would not receive health care benefits under the President's government option proposal, which essentially establishes a Medicare-type program for everyone in America under the age of sixty-five.

When the Supreme Court last looked at government attempts to deny social benefits to certain groups, the Court held that the Constitution protects all "persons"; persons are citizens as well as strangers, people born here and people who end up here, people here lawfully and people here unlawfully; and in the area of social services, whatever benefits the government makes available to the general public cannot be kept away from a class of persons based on their immigration status or that of their parents.

Did the President know this when he stated the contrary to the Congress? Did he lie? And if he did lie, wasn't that lie in the tradition of his forebears?

We know where his forebears' lies have brought us: war, fear, power, loss of innocent life, loss of liberty, and loss of property. My friend Llewellyn Rockwell, an astute philosopher and commentator whose Web site, LewRockwell.com, is the best monitor of government excess in America today, is fond of reminding me that we are all susceptible to temptation; we all have lusts within us that we must suppress. And the most pernicious of those lusts is *libido dominandi*, the lust to dominate.

This lust is in the heart of all in government who lie, who break the laws they have sworn to uphold, and who violate the Constitution they are committed to preserve. They lie to enhance and retain their power over us. Justice Antonin Scalia has commented that courts should refrain from reading what members of the legislative branch have publicly stated about a law when the courts are endeavoring to interpret the meaning of that law. It doesn't matter, he has argued many times, why they say they voted for any given law. They only do so, he maintains, for one reason: To get reelected— the Natural Law, the Constitution, the laws of the land be damned. They want to dominate us.

I don't personally know this lust, but it must be overpowering. My own lust is to challenge illicit authority, to break the chains of slavery with which the government has bound us, and to liberate all persons to fulfill their lives as they see fit, by pursuing happiness.

How can we do this?

We will need a major political transformation in this country to rid ourselves of persons in government who kill, lie, cheat, and steal in our names. We will need to recognize some painful truths.

First, we must acknowledge that through the actions of the government we have lost much of the freedom that we once all thought was guaranteed by the Constitution, our laws, and our values. The lost freedoms have been cataloged in this book and need not be restated here. In sum, they are the loss of the primacy of the individual's inalienable rights and the concept that government is limited in its powers. We have lost the diffusion of power between the states and the federal government. We have lost a federal government that stays within the confines of the Constitution.

Second, we must recognize that we do not have a two-party system in this country; we have one party, the Big Government Party. There is a Republican version that assaults our civil liberties and loves deficits and war, and a Democratic version that assaults our commercial liberties and loves wealth transfers and taxes.

Third, we must acknowledge that there is a fire in the bellies of millions of young people who reject both wretched visions of the Big Government Party. These millions of young folks need either to form a Liberty Party or to build on the libertarian base in the Republican Party by banishing Big Government conservatives, neocons, and so-called social conservatives who want to use government to tell others how to live their lives back to the Democratic Party from whence they came.

Then we need a political fever that consumes the careers of all in government who voted for the Patriot Act, the illegal wars in Iraq and Afghanistan, the TARP and stimulus programs, the federal takeover of education, spying on Americans without warrants, and all other unconstitutional monstrosities that have tethered lovers of liberty to Washington, D.C.

We should abolish the federal income tax, prohibit eminent domain, impose term congressional limits, make Congress part-time, return the power to elect senators to State legislatures, abolish the Federal Reserve system, and prosecute for malfeasance any member of Congress who cannot articulate where the Constitution authorizes whatever he or she is voting for or who has voted for any law that he has or she has not certified under oath that he or she read and fully understands. And we must reject the nice smiles and easy ways and seductive promises of anyone in government who lies to us.

The Big Government Party crowd is obviously not afraid of lying or being caught in a lie. Its members do not fear their own lawlessness or our loss of freedom. They only fear the loss of their own power. So let's use that fear against them. Jefferson understood and articulated this best when he wrote: "When the people fear the government, there is tyranny. When the government fears the people, there is liberty."

If we fear our own government, if we accept its deceptions, its lies to us, if we take no action to redress them, our freedoms are doomed.

Acknowledgments

Though my name is on the cover and title page of this book, it has actually been a collaborative effort. My personal producer at Fox, George Szucs, Jr., who runs my professional life, ran it so that I had the time and temperament to work on this book. My researchers, Magda Hanebach and Jaclyn Sakow, provided terrific material from which this book grew. My researcher and intern, James Spithogiannis, was tireless as a sounding board who refined much of my work. My friend James Conley Sheil, who has edited all my published works, and did so very skillfully on this book as well, has provided invaluable and irreplaceable assistance. And to my boss at Fox, Roger Ailes, who created out of whole cloth a media network that has become a voice for those who sought one and a balance in the national discourse and a home for freedom—and who found a place in that home for me—I owe much for whatever good I may have done in my public work.

Notes

Lie #1

1. Today, the word *unalienable* has the same meaning as the word *inalienable*. Jefferson's draft of the Declaration of Independence used the word *inalienable*, but the Continental Congress chose to use *unalienable* in the final draft.
2. Floor Statement of Senator Barack Obama on the Nomination of Alberto Gonzales for Attorney General, Feb. 3, 2005.
3. Gordon S. Wood, "Never Forget: They Kept Lots of Slaves," *New York Times*, http://www.nytimes.com/2003/12/14/books/review/14WOODLT.html?scp=3&sq=never%20forget%20they%20kept%20lots%20of%20slaves&st=cse (Dec. 14, 2003).
4. Matthew Spalding, "How to Understand Slavery and the American Founding," The Heritage Foundation, http://www.heritage.org/research/americanfoundingandhistory/wp01.cfm (Aug. 26, 2002).
5. Wood, "Never Forget: They Kept Lots of Slaves."
6. Spalding, "How to Understand Slavery and the American Founding."
7. Ibid.
8. Denis Henderson, and Frederic W. Henderson, "How the Founding Fathers Fought For an End to Slavery," *The American Almanac*, http://american_almanac.tripod.com/ffslave.htm (Mar. 15, 1993).
9. Spalding, "How to Understand Slavery and the American Founding."
10. Ibid.
11. The Northwest Ordinance of 1787, Article 6.
12. Spalding, "How to Understand Slavery and the American Founding."
13. Alan Dershowitz, *America Declares Independence* (Hoboken, NJ: John Wiley & Sons, Inc., 2003), 124.
14. Ibid.
15. Ibid., 127.
16. Ibid., 128.
17. Ibid.
18. Ibid., 129.
19. Ibid., 130–31.
20. Ibid., 135.

21. Ibid., 135–36.
22. Ibid., 125.
23. Ibid.
24. Ibid., 126.
25. "Legacy—Thomas Jefferson," Library of Congress, www.loc.gov/exhibits/jefferson/jeffleg.html (Jan. 26, 2007).
26. Ibid.
27. Wood, "Never Forget: They Kept Lots of Slaves."
28. Ibid.
29. Ibid.
30. Ulrich Boser, "The Sorry Legacy of the Founders," *U.S. News and World Report*, http://www.usnews.com/usnews/culture/articles/040112/12slave.htm (Jan. 4, 2004).
31. Wood, "Never Forget: They Kept Lots of Slaves."
32. Ibid.
33. Ibid.
34. Ibid.
35. Spalding, "How to Understand Slavery and the American Founding."
36. Ibid.
37. Ibid.
38. Ibid.
39. Ibid.
40. *The Federalist*, No. 54.
41. Spalding, "How to Understand Slavery and the American Founding."
42. Ibid.
43. Ibid.
44. Ibid.
45. Ibid.
46. Aside from the debate with Garrison, libertarians today consider Frederick Douglass a hero. In a well-known speech, "What to the Slave Is the Fourth of July?," Douglass, a former slave, proclaimed that "interpreted as it ought to be interpreted, the Constitution is a *Glorious Liberty Document*" (emphases in original). Douglass was also a staunch proponent of the free market, as well as private property. Furthermore, Douglass condemned government affirmative action programs, believing that government aid to blacks after slavery merely showed African-American inferiority. (The source of the information contained in this endnote is Ronald Hamowy's *The Encyclopedia of Libertarianism* (2008), published by SAGE Publications, Inc., at pages 127–28.)
47. . . . though some have tried. For a collection of essays supporting the institution of slavery, see *Defending Slavery: Proslavery Thought in the Old South*, by Paul Finkelman.
48. Michael Knox Beran, "'Never Forget: They Kept Lots of Slaves,'" *The National Review Online*, http://www.nationalreview.com/comment/beran200312290000.asp (Dec. 29, 2003).
49. Paul M. Angle, and Miers, Earl Schenck, eds., *The Living Lincoln: The Man in His Times, in His Own Words* (Fall River, MA: Fall River Press, 1992), 203.
50. Ibid.
51. Ibid.
52. Letter to Horace Greely, editor of the *New York Tribune*, Aug. 22, 1862.

53. *Civil Rights Cases*, 109 U.S. 3, 13 (1883).

54. *Plessy v. Ferguson*, 163 U.S. 537 (1896).

55. *Plessy*, 163 U.S. at 551.

56. *Plessy*, 163 U.S. at 552. The fascinating part of the Plessy case, however, is that regardless of the railroad companies' feelings toward African-Americans, they believed that it was way too costly to purchase additional cars for African-Americans, so as to segregate the two races. Therefore, if the legislature had not passed the race-based law at issue in Plessy, the free market would have ensured racial equality in this area.

57. *Plessy*, 163 U.S. at 559.

58. *Brown v. Board of Education of Topeka*, 347 U.S. 483 (1954).

59. *Regents of Univ. of California v. Bakke*, 438 U.S. 265 (1978).

60. *Grutter v. Bollinger*, 539 U.S. 306 (2003).

61. *Grutter*, 539 U.S. at 341.

62. *Adarand Constructors, Inc. v. Pena*, 515 U.S. 200, 240 (1995).

63. *Grutter*, 539 U.S. at 351.

Lie #2

1. Jeff Benedict, *Little Pink House: A True Story of Defiance and Courage* (New York: Grand Central Publishing, 2009), 88.

2. Ibid., 324.

3. Ibid., 357.

4. Ibid., 330.

5. See my book *Constitutional Chaos: What Happens When the Government Breaks Its Own Laws* (Nashville: Thomas Nelson, 2004), Introduction.

6. Henry David Thoreau, *Civil Disobedience* (1849), http://thoreau.eserver.org/civil .html.

7. *S. Burlington County NAACP v. Mt. Laurel*, 92 NJ 158, 209 (1983).

8. A newspaper, the *Star Ledger*, quoted him.

9. Anastasia C. Sheffler-Wood, "Where Do We Go from Here? States Revise Eminent Domain Legislation in Response to Kelo," 79 Temp. L. Rev. 617 (2006), 618.

10. *Kelo*, 545 U.S. 469 (2005).

11. Patrick McGeehan, "Pfizer to Leave City That Won Land-Use Case," *New York Times*, http://www.nytimes.com/2009/11/13/nyregion/13pfizer .html?scp=2&sq=pfizer&st=cse (Nov. 13, 2009).

12. Ibid.

13. Ibid.

14. *Kelo*, 545 U.S. at 503.

15. 545 U.S. at 522.

16. See my book *Constitutional Chaos: What Happens When the Government Breaks Its Own Laws*, 65–78.

17. Patrick McGeehan, "Pfizer to Leave City That Won Land-Use Case."

18. Ibid.

19. Ibid.

20. Ibid.

21. Brian A. Blum and Juliana B. Wellman, "Participation, Assent and Liberty in Contract Formation," Ariz. St. L.J. (1982), 901, 907–08.

22. It is important to note that in discussing a "valid police purpose," the Court was referring to the government's "police power," which is the power of *state governments* to protect the health, safety, welfare, and morality of its people. The police power has nothing to do with the policing of criminals, but rather with government interference with the rights and dealings of the common people.

23. See my book *The Constitution in Exile* (Nashville: Thomas Nelson, 2006), 89–101.

24. This is my favorite line from among all U.S. Supreme Court decisions and best crystallizes an originalist interpretation of the Constitution.

25. Karen De Coster, "Obama to Government Motors: 'Let's Roll'," Ludwig von Mises Institute, http://mises.org/story/3484 (May 22, 2009).

26. See my book *The Constitution in Exile*.

27. "Europe's Solution: Take More Time Off," a post on "Room for Debate," a blog from the editors of the *New York Times*, http://roomfordebate.blogs.nytimes.com/2009/03/29/europes-solution-take-more-time-off/ (Mar. 29, 2009).

Lie #3

1. Then Judge John G. Roberts, at his Senate confirmation hearing (Sept. 12, 2005).

2. "Obama's Primetime Press Conference," Real Clear Politics, http://www.realclearpolitics.com/articles/2009/03/obama_primetime_press_transcript.html (Mar. 24, 2009).

3. Kermit Roosevelt, "Why Judicial 'Activism' Explains Little," *CBS News*, http://www.cbsnews.com/stories/2009/07/08/opinion/main5144440.shtml (Jul. 8, 2009).

4. Bryan A. Garner, *Black's Law Dictionary*, Third Pocket Edition (2006).

5. Ibid.

6. Kermit Roosevelt, *The Myth of Judicial Activism* (New Haven: Yale University Press, 2006), 1–2.

7. Ibid., 2.

8. Then Judge John G. Roberts, at his Senate confirmation hearing (Sept. 12, 2005).

9. Ibid.

10. Ibid.

11. Ibid.

12. Susan Page, "Sessions vows third GOP vote against Sotomayor," *USA Today*, http://www.usatoday.com/news/washington/judicial/2009-07-27-sessions_N.htm?csp=34 (Jul. 27, 2009).

13. David Stout, "McCain Will Vote Against Sotomayor," a post on "The Caucus," a blog from the *New York Times*, http://thecaucus.blogs.nytimes.com/2009/08/03/mccain-will-vote-against-sotomayor/?scp=1&sq=august%203,%202009%20mccain%20opposes%20sotomayor&st=cse (Aug. 3, 2009).

14. Then Judge Sonia Sotomayor's Lecture entitled "A Latina Judge's Life," given at the University of California–Berkeley, in 2001.

15. Sam Stein, "'Where Policy Is Made': Sotomayor's Court Comment Explained," *Huffington Post*, http://www.huffingtonpost.com/2009/05/26/where-policy-is-made-soto_n_207570.html (May 26, 2009).

16. Alexander Hamilton, *The Federalist*, No. 78.

17. Ibid.
18. Hon. Richard B. Sanders, "Do State Constitutions and Courts Still Protect Liberty?" http://www.justicesanders.com/20030803CatoInst.htm.
19. *Marbury v. Madison*, 5 U.S. 137 (1803).
20. Erwin Chemerinsky, *Federal Jurisdiction*, 5th Ed. (New York: Aspen Publishers, 2007), 12.
21. Ibid.
22. Chemerinsky, *Federal Jurisdiction*, 12.
23. Laurence Tribe, *Abortion: The Clash of Absolutes* (New York: W. W. Norton, 1992), 80.
24. Ibid.
25. *Plessy v. Ferguson*, 163 U.S. 537 (1896).
26. *Strauder v. West Virginia*, 100 U.S. 303 (1880).
27. *Strauder*, 100 U.S. at 308.
28. *Roe v. Wade*, 410 U.S. 113, 153 (1973).
29. "The court as interior decorator – Judge Russell Clark orders capital improvements for Kansas City schools," *National Review* (Jan. 22, 1990).
30. John Taylor Gatto, "A Billion, Six for KC," The Odysseus Group, http://www.johntaylorgatto.com/chapters/17f.htm.
31. "The court as interior decorator," *National Review*.
32. Ibid.
33. Ibid.
34. Ibid.
35. George Will, "More Judicial Activism, Please," *Washington Post*, http://www.washingtonpost.com/wp-dyn/content/article/2009/06/12/AR2009061202755.html (Jun. 14, 2009).
36. Ibid.
37. Ibid.

Lie #4

1. Vincent Bugliosi, *The Betrayal of America* (New York: Thunder Mouth's Press / Nation Books, 2001), 16.
2. James Madison, The Federalist, No. 57.
3. "Full Text of the Iraqi Constitution," *Washington Post*, http://www.washingtonpost.com/wp-dyn/content/article/2005/10/12/AR2005101201450.html (Oct. 12, 2005).
4. Ibid.
5. "President George W. Bush's Address Regarding Iraqi Elections," www.johnstonarchive.net/terroirism/bushiraqelection.html (Jan. 30, 2005).
6. Ibid.
7. Kenneth P. Vogel, "Will Afghanistan's election be fair?," *Politico*, http://www.politico.com/news/stories/0609/24105.html (Jun. 23, 2009).
8. Fisher Ames, United States Congressman from 1st District of Massachusetts, 1789–1797, in "The Debates in the Several State Conventions on the Adoption of the Federal Constitution (Source: DiLorenzo, Thomas J., "Repeal the Seventeenth Amendment," LewRockwell.com, http://www.lewrockwell.com/dilorenzo/dilorenzo93.html (May 17, 2005).
9. Thomas J. DiLorenzo, "Repeal the Seventeenth Amendment."
10. Ibid.

11. Ibid.
12. Ibid.
13. Ibid.
14. Ralph A. Rossum, *Federalism, The Supreme Court, and The Seventeenth Amendment* (Maryland: Lexington Books, 2001), 183.
15. Ibid.
16. Ibid., 183–84.
17. Ibid.
18. Ibid., 185.
19. Ibid., 187–90.
20. Ibid., 190–91.
21. Ibid.
22. Ibid.
23. Ibid., 191.
24. Ibid.
25. Ibid.
26. Ibid.
27. Jerry O'Neil (Montana State Senator), "Q. Why should we repeal the 17th Amendment and forfeit our right to vote for U.S. senators?" www.liberty-ca.org/repeal17/states/montana2003oneil.htm (2003).
28. Ibid.
29. Ibid.
30. Ibid.
31. Maraleen D. Shields, "Racial Gerrymandering: Enfranchisement or Political Apartheid," http://www.drury.edu/ess/irconf/MShields.html.
32. Ibid.
33. Ibid.
34. Ibid.
35. Ibid.
36. Ibid.
37. Ibid.
38. Ibid.
39. *Shaw v. Reno*, 509 U.S. 630 (1993).
40. Shields, "Racial Gerrymandering: Enfranchisement or Political Apartheid."
41. Ibid.
42. Ibid.
43. Abigail Thernstrom, and Stephan Thernstrom, "Racial Gerrymandering Is Unnecessary," *Wall Street Journal*, http://online.wsj.com/article/SB122637373937516543.html (Nov. 11, 2008).
44. Ibid.
45. Ibid.
46. Ibid.
47. Ibid.
48. Ibid.
49. Shields, "Racial Gerrymandering: Enfranchisement or Political Apartheid."
50. Private recounts conducted after President Bush was inaugurated indicated that he did, in fact, win the 2000 election. In April 2001, the *Miami Herald* and *USA Today*

reported that if Florida went ahead with the recounts, George W. Bush would have widened his lead by 1,665 votes. The *New York Times* also conducted a recount, and reported on November 12, 2001, that George W. Bush would have prevailed. (Sources: "Media Recount: Bush Won the 2000 Election," *PBS Online NewsHour*, http://www .pbs.org/newshour/media/media_watch/jan-june01/recount_4-3.html (Apr. 3, 2001); Ford, Fessenden, and John M. Broder, "Study of Disputed Florida Ballots Finds Justices Did Not Cast the Deciding Vote," *New York Times*, http://www.nytimes .com/2001/11/12/politics/12VOTE.html?scp=1&sq=november%2012,%202001%20 florida%20ballots&st=cse (Nov. 12, 2001)).

51. Summary of proceedings from *The Nine*, by Jeffrey Toobin (New York: Anchor Books, 2008), chapters 11–13.

52. Toobin, *The Nine*, 165–66.

53. Bugliosi, *The Betrayal of America*, 26.

54. Toobin, *The Nine*, 166.

55. Ibid.

56. Ibid., 167.

57. Ibid., 168.

58. Bugliosi, *The Betrayal of America*, 25.

59. Ibid., 26–27.

60. Ibid., 50.

61. Ibid.

62. William O. Douglas, *The Court Years, 1939-1975: The Autobiography of William O. Douglas* (Vintage Books, 1981).

63. Toobin, *The Nine*, 201.

64. *Bush v. Gore*, 531 U.S. 98, 109 (2000).

65. Steven LaTulippe, "Ron Paul and the Empire," LewRockwell.com, http://www .lewrockwell.com/latulippe/latulippe80.html (Jul. 31, 2007).

66. "Obama-McCain Comparisons," www.obama-mccain.info

67. Ibid.

68. "Andrea Mitchell: John McCain Only Met Sarah Palin Once," *Huffington Post*, www.huffingtonpost.com/2008/08/29/andrea-mitchell-john-mcca_n_122517.html (first posted: Aug. 29, 2008; updated: Sept. 29, 2008).

69. Ibid.

70. "Ron Paul's Opening Statement at National Press Club," The LRC Blog, http://www .lewrockwell.com/blog/lewrw/archives/022773.html (Sept. 10, 2008).

71. Butler Shaffer, "The Voting Ritual," LewRockwell.com, http://www.lewrockwell .com/shaffer/shaffer147.html (Oct. 24, 2006).

72. *David Leip's Atlas of U.S. Presidential Elections*, http://uselectionatlas.org/RESULTS.

73. Ibid.

74. Ibid.

Lie #5

1. Justice William Brennan's majority opinion in *New York Times v. Sullivan*, 376 U.S. 254, 270 (1964).

2. Geoffrey R. Stone, et al., *The First Amendment*, 3rd. ed. (New York: Wolters Kluwer, 2008), 20.

3. *Schenck v. United States*, 249 U.S. 47 (1919).

4. *Frohwerk*, 249 U.S. 204 (1919); Debs, 249 U.S. 211 (1919).

5. Stone, *The First Amendment*, 30.

6. Ibid., 31.

7. Charles Paul Freund, "Dixiecrats Triumphant: The Menacing Mr. Wilson," reason
.com, http://reason.com/archives/2002/12/18/dixiecrats-triumphant (Dec. 18, 2002).

8. Ibid.

9. Ibid.

10. *Abrams v. United States*, 250 U.S. 616 (1919).

11. *Whitney v. California*, 274 U.S. 357 (1927).

12. Stone, *The First Amendment*, 41.

13. Ibid.

14. *Brandenburg v. Ohio*, 395 U.S. 444 (1969).

15. *Virginia Board*, 425 U.S. 748 (1976).

16. *Central Hudson*, 447 U.S. 557 (1980).

17. *Edenfield*, 507 U.S. 761, 700 (1993).

18. *44 Liquormart*, 517 U.S. 484 (1996).

19. *44 Liquormart*, 517 U.S. at 503 (citations omitted).

20. *Lorillard*, 533 U.S. 525 (2001).

21. *Lorillard*, 533 U.S. at 564.

22. Duff Wilson, "Senate Approves Tight Regulation over Cigarettes," *New York Times*
(June 12, 2009).

23. Duff Wilson, "Tobacco Regulation Is Expected to Face a Free-Speech Challenge,"
New York Times, http://www.nytimes.com/2009/06/12/business/12tobacco
.html?_r=1&scp=1&sq=senate%20approves%20tight%20regulation%20over%20
cigarettes&st=cse (June 16, 2009).

24. Ibid.

25. Ibid.

26. Ibid.

27. *Erznoznik*, 422 U.S. 205 (1975).

28. *Sable Communications, Inc. v. FCC*, 492 U.S. 115 (1989).

29. *Sable Communications*, 492 U.S. 115 at 131.

30. Val E. Limburg, "Fairness Doctrine," the Museum of Broadcast Communications,
http://www.museum.tv/archives/etc/F/htmlF/fairnessdoct/fairnessdoct.htm.

31. Ibid.

32. Ibid.

33. *Red Lion*, 395 U.S. 367 (1969).

34. Brian Jennings, *Censorship: The Threat To Silence Talk Radio* (New York: Threshold
Editions, 2009), 15–17.

35. Ibid.

36. Limburg, "Fairness Doctrine."

37. Ibid.

38. Jennings, *Censorship*, 28.

39. "Talk Show Hosts May Be Accomplices Under Hate Bill," *Examiner.com*, http://www
.examiner.com/x-9462-LA-Nonpartisan-Examiner~y2009m6d26-Talk-show-host-can-
be-prosecuted-as-accomplices-under-new-senate-hate-bill?cid=exrss-LA-Nonpartisan-
Examiner (June 26, 2009).

Lie #6

1. "The Right to Keep and Bear Arms," Report of the Senate Subcommittee on the Constitution, February 1982, preface by Orrin G. Hatch.

2. Adapted from John Twelve Hawks's *The Traveler*: "If privacy had a tombstone, it would read this was for your own good."

3. "Experience should teach us to be most on our guard to protect liberty when the Government's purposes are beneficent. Men born to freedom are naturally alert to repel invasion of their liberty by evil-minded rulers. The greatest dangers to liberty lurk in insidious encroachment by men of zeal, well-meaning but without understanding."—Justice Louis Brandeis, dissenting in *Olmstead v. United States*, 277 U.S. 438, 479 (1928).

4. 26 U.S.C. ch. 53, available at http://www.atf.gov/pub/fire-explo_pub/nfa.htm.

5. Lawrence H. Officer and Samuel H. Williamson, "Purchasing Power of Money in the United States from 1774 to 2008," MeasuringWorth, http://www.measuringworth.com/ppowerus/index.php (2009).

6. *Sonzinsky v. United States*, 300 U.S. 506 (1937).

7. *Child Labor Tax Cases.*

8. Interestingly, armies in the past had often used the short-barreled rifle as part of their military equipment. Therefore, whether intentionally or inadvertently, the federal government lied to the Supreme Court.

9. The Supreme Court avoided the Second Amendment issue until 2008 and the Heller case. There were some cases that addressed the Second Amendment in dicta, but none set precedent regarding the Amendment's meaning.

10. Stephen P. Holbrook, "Nazi Firearms Laws and the Disarming of the German Jews," *Arizona Journal of International and Comparitive Law* 17, no. 3, 483–535 (2000).

11. "The Right to Keep and Bear Arms."

12.. Earl R. Kruschke, *Gun Control: A Reference Handbook* (Santa Barbara: ABC–CLIO, 1994).

13. Gregg Lee Carter, *Gun Control in the United States: A Reference Handbook* (Santa Barbara: ABL–CLIO, 2006), 150.

14. John R. Lott Jr., "More 'Assault Weapons,' Less Crime," LewRockwell.com, http://www.lewrockwell.com/lott/lott42.html (Jun. 29, 2005).

15. Ibid.

16. John Ross, *Self-Defense Laws and Violent Crime Rates in the United States.*

17. Gary Kleck, *Point Blank: Guns and Violence in America* (Aldine Transaction, 1991).

18. Don B. Kates Jr., "Supreme Court Affirms Individual Right: What's Next?" the Independent Institute, http://www.independent.org/newsroom/article.asp?id=2247 (Jun. 26, 2008).

19. Robert A. Levy, "Pistol Whipped: Baseless Lawsuits, Foolish Laws," Cato Institute Policy Analysis, No. 400, www.cato.org/pub_display.php?pub_id=1259 (May 9, 2001).

20. Though typically attributed to Benjamin Franklin by a wide variety of sources, others have claimed that it was developed by a newspaper journalist in the twentieth century. The opinions and accuracies of such attribution vary. Since it sounds like Ben Franklin, I attribute it to him.

21. This may sound unbelievable but it appears in the Congressional Record-House on February 8, 1995, at page H1381, along with a long list of other BATF transgressions.

22. "The Right to Keep and Bear Arms."

23. Bill Miller, "Twist of Fate Turns Teacher's Source of Protection into Tormentor," *Washington Post*, November 19, 1992, as cited in "H.R. 666 and the Assault on the Bill of Rights," available at http://gunowners.org/fs9506.htm.

24. David Weigel, "Dick Heller Get Your Gun," http://www.reason.com/blog/show/127643.html.

25. For a detailed exposition of the applicability of the "state interest of the highest order" doctrine to First Amendment rights, as well as the way that it has been largely ignored and put on a back burner, see my article, "Whatever Happened to Freedom of Speech? A Defense of 'State Interest of the Highest Order' as a Unifying Standard for Erratic First Amendment Jurisprudence," Published in *Seton Hall Law Review*, 29, 1999.

26. *Maloney v. Cuomo*, 554 F.3d 56 (2d Cir. 2009).

27. "Obama explains his support of the assault weapons ban," John Lott's Blogspot, http:johnrlott.blogspot.com/2008/09/obama-explains-his-support-of-assault.html.

28. John Lott, "The new assault weapons ban will not reduce crime in this country," Fox Forum at foxnews.com (Feb. 26, 2009).

29. Joshua Rhett Miller, "Gun Advocates Ready for Battle on Federal Assault Weapons Ban," foxnews.com (Mar. 17, 2009).

30. This comparison is taken from Stephen P. Halbrook's "What the Framer's Intended: A Linguistic Analysis of the Right to 'Bear Arms,'" Part IV, available at http://www.stephenhalbrook.com/law_review_articles/linguistic-analysis.pdf.

Lie #7

1. Murray N. Rothbard, *For A New Liberty: The Libertarian Manifesto* (San Francisco: Fox & Wilkes, 1996), 111.

2. John Tierney, "Health Halo Can Hide the Calories," *New York Times*, http://www.nytimes.com/2008/12/02/science/02tier.html?_r=2 (Dec. 1, 2008).

3. Anemolla Hartocollis, "Restaurants Prepare for Big Switch: No Trans Fat," *New York Times*, http://www.nytimes.com/2008/06/21/nyregion/21trans.html (Jun. 21, 2008).

4. "Obama Selects Frieden as CDC Director," http://www.foxnews.com/politics/2009/05/15/report-obama-selects-frieden-cdc-director (May 15, 2009).

5. Niv Elis, "FDA Regulates Tobacco, And Phillip Morris Cheers," *Forbes.com*, http://www.forbes.com/2009/06/11/fda-smoking-cigarettes-business-healthcare-tobacco.html (Jun. 11, 2009).

6. Gardiner Harris, "F.D.A. Bans Sale of Flavored Cigarettes," *New York Times* (Sept. 23, 2009).

7. Ibid.

8. Chris Conrad, *Hemp: Lifeline to the Future* (Sacramento: FS Book Company, 1994), 192–203.

9. Claire Suddath, "The War on Drugs," *Time*, http://www.time.com/time/world/article/0,8599,1887488,00.htm (Mar. 25, 2009).

10. Ibid.

11. The information on the Marihuana Tax Act comes from Paul Armentano's article, "How the Feds Got Into the Pot Prohibition Business," LewRockwell.com, http://www.lewrockwell.com/armentano-p/armentano-p43.1.html (Sept. 4, 2009).

12. *Gonzales v. Raich*, 545 U.S. 1, 7 (2005).

13. *Raich*, 545 U.S. at 17.

14. *Raich*, 545 U.S. at 57–58.

15. "'To Allow or Deny?: Opposing Views on Access to Experimental Drugs," Stanford Scientific, http://www.stanfordscientific.org/index.php?option=com_content&view=article&id=72:a-passion-for-service&catid=42:volume-6-issue-2&Itemid=59 (Feb. 23, 2008).

16. Ibid.

17. Ibid.

18. Kerry Howley, "Dying for Lifesaving Drugs," *Reason* Magazine, http://www.reason.com/news/show/120763.html (August/September 2007).

19. Steven Walker and Dan Popeo, "Trends," *Milken Institute Review*, http://site03.sequoia.fuzint.com/upload/MilkenReviewArticle.pdf (First Quarter, 2004).

20. Howley, "Dying for Lifesaving Drugs."

21. Ibid.

22. *Abigail Alliance*, 445 F.3d 470 (D.C. Cir. 2006).

23. 445 F.3d at 480.

24. 445 F.3d at 486.

25. Bill Sardi, "Manhunt Medicine: Forced Cancer Treatment," LewRockwell.com, http://www.lewrockwell.com/sardi/sardi110.html (May 26, 2009).

26. "Daniel Hauser angry over continuing chemo," http://www.news.com.au/story/0,27574,25683954-401,00.html (Jun. 24, 2009).

27. Sardi, "Manhunt Medicine: Forced Cancer Treatment."

28. Radley Balko, "Who's in Charge of Your Health?" reason.com, http://www.reason.com/news/show/133689.html (May 26, 2009).

Lie #8

1. Murray Rothbard, *The Case Against the Fed* (Auburn, AL: Ludwig von Mises Institute, 1994), 116. See http://mises.org/books/fed.pdf.

2. Ibid.

3. Rexford G. Tugwell, "A Center Report: Rewriting the Constitution," *Center magazine* (March 1968), 18–20.

4. Telephone Interview with Larry Parks (Jul. 15, 2009).

5. John Rubino and Jim Quinn, "It Started with Ron Paul," LewRockwell.com, http://www.lewrockwell.com/quinn/quinn14.1.html (Sept. 5, 2009).

6. Murray Rothbard, *The Case Against the Fed*, 74.

7. This quote is attributed to Mayer Amschel Rothschild (1790). See http://thinkexist.com/quotes/mayer_amschel_rothschild.

8. Upon the eve of the creation of the Federal Reserve Board, Congressman Charles Lindberg Sr. (the grandfather of the famous aviator of the same name) said, "The money trust deliberately caused the 1907 money panic and thereby forced Congress to create a

National Monetary Commission which led to the ultimate creation of the privately owned Federal Reserve Bank. The Federal Reserve Act establishes the most gigantic monetary trust on earth. When the President signs the bill, the invisible government of the Monetary Powers will be legalized. The people must make a declaration of independence to relieve themselves from the Monetary Powers, by taking control of Congress! . . . The worst legislative crime of the ages is perpetrated by this banking bill. The caucus and the party bosses have again operated and prevented the people from getting the benefit of their own government!" (Available at http://www.dailypaul.com/node/56117).

9. Ron Paul, *Freedom Under Siege: The U.S. Constitution After 200 Years* (Auburn, AL: Ludvig von Mises Institute, 1988), 113. See http://mises.org/books/fed.pdf.

10. Ibid.

11. Eustace Mullins, *The Secrets of the Federal Reserve* (John McLaughlin, 1993), chap. 2.

12. Ibid.

13. The Freedom of Information Act (FOIA) is applicable to all government agencies.

14. A. Ralph Epperson, *The Unseen Hand* (Tucson, AZ: Publius Press, 1985), 175.

15. "Executive Orders Disposition Tables: John F. Kennedy—1963," http://www.archives.gov/federal-register/executive-orders/1963-kennedy.html.

16. "JFK vs. Federal Reserve," http://foundationfortruthinlaw.org/jfk-vs-fed.html; July 25, 2008 post on *Daily Paul* entitled, "JFK & Executive Order 11110," http://www.dailypaul.com/node/56117.

17. Friedrich A. Hayek, "A Free-Market Monetary System," lecture delivered at the Gold and Monetary Conference in New Orleans, on November 19, 1977 (available at http://mises.org/story/3204).

18. Murray Rothbard, "Economic Depressions: Their Cause and Cure," Ludvig von Mises Institute, http://mises.org/story/3127, 26.

19. This chapter is based on explanations provided by G. Edward Griffin, "A Talk by G. Edward Griffin," www.bigeye.com/griffin.htm.

20. Mike Ziegler, "Good as Gold," *Liberty Watch*, www.libertywatch.com/volume03/issue08/coverstory.php.

21. Ibid.

22. Ibid.

23. Joan Whitley, "Four Month Trial Ends with No Convictions," *Las Vegas Review-Journal*, http://www.lvrj.com/news/9893062.html (Sept. 20, 2007).

24. Statement by Alan Greenspan, Chairman, Board of Governors of the Federal Reserve System, before the Committee on Banking, Finance and Urban Affairs, U.S. House of Representatives, October 19, 1993, http://findarticles.com/p/articles/mi_m4126/is_n12_v79/ai_14725422/pg_4/.

25. Noted by Congressman Ron Paul in a July 20, 1979, speech to the House of Representatives. Ron Paul, *Pillars of Prosperity: Free Markets, Honest Money, Private Property*, (Auburn, AL: Ludvig von Mises Institute, 2008), 105.

26. Vin Suprynowicz, "Not Worth A Continental," LewRockwell.com, http://www.lewrockwell.com/suprynowicz/suprynowicz88.html (Aug. 8, 2008).

27. Gene Epstein, "Freedom from the Fed Fix," *Barron's*, http://online.barrons.com/article/SB121702626696486253.html?mod=9_0031_b_this_weeks_magazine_columns (Jul. 28, 2008).

28. Patrice Hill, "Federal Reserve to Gain Power Under Plan," *Washington Times* (Jun.16, 2009).

Lie #9

1. http://thinkexist.com/quotation/nothing_is_so_permanent_as_a_temporary_government/191475.html.
2. http://www.dictionary-quotes.com/the-government-solution-to-a-problem-is-usually-as-bad-as-the-problem-milton-friedman/.
3. Timothy J. Gillis, *Taxation & National Destiny: A Tax Systems Analysis and Proposal*, (San Diego: Maximus Profectus, 1999), 17.
4. "Fact Sheets: Taxes," from the United States Department of the Treasury, http://www.treasury.gov/education/fact-sheets/taxes/ustax.shtml.
5. Gillis, *Taxation & National Destiny*, 32.
6. Mark Schmidt, "Income Tax Withholding: Why 'First Dibs' for Uncle Sam Leaves Taxpayers Finishing Last," National Taxpayers Union, http://www.ntu.org/main/press.php?PressID=256&org_name=NTU (Jul. 29, 2002).
7. Ibid.
8. Ibid.
9. Ibid.
10. Ibid.
11. Ibid.
12. Ibid.
13. Ibid.
14. Brian Doherty, "Best of Both Worlds: Milton Friedman reminisces about his career as an economist and his lifetime 'avocation' as a spokesman for freedom," *Reason magazine*, http://reason.com/archives/1995/06/01/best-of-both-worlds (June 1995).
15. Ibid.
16. Ibid.
17. David Henderson, "Government Greed," *Reason magazine*, http://reason.com/archives/1999/04/01/government-greed (April 1999).
18. Doherty, "Best of Both Worlds."
19. Daniel J. Mitchell, "Defending Ron Paul's Tax Plan," Cato @ Liberty (a Cato Institute blog), http://www.cato-at-liberty.org/2007/11/09/defending-ron-pauls-tax-plan (Nov. 9, 2007).
20. glassbooth, http://glassbooth.org/explore/index/bob-barr/19/taxes-and-budget/13.
21. Frank Chodorov, "Taxation Is Robbery," Ludvig von Mises Institute, http://mises.org/etexts/taxrob.asp.
22. Gregory Bresiger, "Housing Socialism," LewRockwell.com, http://www.lewrockwell.com/bresiger/bresiger20.html (Sept. 14, 2006).
23. Ibid.
24. "Rent Control," a message from Malcolm Gladwell to Jacob Weisberg, *Slate* http://www.slate.com/id/3651/entry/11183 (May 20, 1997).
25. Becky Akers, "Wretched Rangel's Angles and Wrangles," LewRockwell.com, http://www.lewrockwell.com/akers/akers89.html (Jul. 19, 2008).
26. Ibid.

27. Ibid.
28. Thomas Sowell, "Social Security: The Enron That Politicians Have In the Closet," *Capitalism Magazine*, http://www.capmag.com/article.asp?ID=1505 (Mar. 23, 2002).
29. Ibid.
30. Office of Management and Budget's Mid-Session Review, Fiscal Year 2009, http://www.whitehouse.gov/omb/budget/fy2009/pdf/09msr.pdf.
31. Dale Steinreich, "Social Security Reform: True and False," Ludvig von Mises Institute, http://mises.org/freemarket_detail.aspx?control=160&sortorder=articledate (Oct. 1996).
32. Ibid.

Lie #10

1. Ronald Reagan's Remarks to Representatives of the Future Farmers of America, July 28, 1988, http://www.reagan.utexas.edu/archives/speeches/1988/072888c.htm.
2. Ibid.
3. Tiffany Sharples, "A Brief History of: FEMA," *Time.com*, http://www.time.com/time/magazine/article/0,9171,1837231,00.html (Aug. 28, 2008).
4. See my article entitled "Franklin Delano Bush," LewRockwell.com, http://www.lewrockwell.com/orig6/napolitano1.html (Sept. 24, 2005).
5. William L. Anderson, "Katrina and the Never-Ending Scandal of State Management," Ludvig von Mises Institute, http://mises.org/story/1909 (Sept. 13, 2005).
6. Sheila Kaplan, "FEMA covered up cancer risks to Katrina victims," *Salon.com*, http://archive.salon.com/news/feature/2008/01/29/fema_coverup/index.html (Jan. 29, 2008).
7. Rick Jervis, "Thousands still in FEMA trailers," *USA Today*, http://www.usatoday.com/news/nation/2009-06-28-fema-trailers_N.htm (Jun. 29, 2009).
8. http://www.cbsnews.com/stories/2009/02/25/cbsnews_investigates/main4828884.shtml?tag=contentMain;contentBody.
9. "FEMA Dissolves Gulf Coast Recovery Office," CBSNews.com, http://www.cbsnews.com/stories/2009/04/09/cbsnews_investigates/main4932321.shtml (Apr. 9, 2009).
10. "Hurricane Ike—Hotline Calls—Gaps—Summary 9/14/08," Disaster Accountability Blog, http://blog.disasteraccountability.com/2008/09/15/hurricane-ike-hotline-calls-gaps-summary-91408 (Sept. 15, 2008).
11. "Information Limited, Frustrations Grow," Disaster Accountability Blog http://blog.disasteraccountability.com/2008/09/18/information-limited-frustrations-grow (Sept. 18, 2008).
12. John Whitehead, "More on rebuilding New Orleans: Lessons from Princeville, NC," *Environmental Economics*, http://www.env-econ.net/2005/09/more_on_rebuild.html (Sept. 6, 2005).
13. Amy Liu and Nigel Holmes, "The State of New Orleans: An Update," *New York Times* (Aug. 28, 2009).
14. Ibid.
15. Ibid.
16. Ibid.
17. Ibid.

18. Ibid.
19. Ibid.
20. Ibid.
21. "FEMA public affairs team wins 'prize'," Disaster Accountability Blog, http://blog .disasteraccountability.com/2007/12/11/femas-prize-winning-public-affairs-team (Dec. 11, 2007).
22. Jim Grichar, "Abolish the FDA!!" LewRockwell.com, http://www.lewrockwell.com/ grichar/grichar17.html (May 19, 2003).
23. "FDA to Require Chantix, Zyban to Carry 'Strongest' Suicide, Depression Warning," Associated Press, http://www.foxnews.com/story/0,2933,529738,00.html (Jul. 1, 2009).
24. Grichar, "Abolish the Fed!!"
25. Jane Zhang, Julie Jargon, and A. J. Miranda, "Tomato industry stews amid salmonella outbreak," San Diego Union-Tribune, http://www.signonsandiego.com/ uniontrib/20080702/news_1n2tomatoes.html (Wall Street Journal, Jul. 2, 2008).
26. Ibid.

Lie #11

1. Brian Doherty, "Prohibition = Violence," reason.com, http://www.reason.com/news/ show/34755.html (Jan. 29, 2003).
2. Ibid.
3. Ibid.
4. Ethan Nadelmann, "Can We Really Afford a (Failed) War on Drugs?" commonwealthclub.org, http://www.commonwealthclub.org/archive/03/03- 07nadelmann-speech.html (Jul. 24, 2003).
5. Ethan Nadelmann, "Canada Must Not Follow the U.S. on Drug Policy," Drug Policy Alliance, http://www.drugpolicy.org/library/ottawa022207.cfm (Ottawa Citizen, Feb. 22, 2007).
6. Nadelmann, "Can We Really Afford a (Failed) War on Drugs?".
7. Anthony Gregory, "The Evil War on Drugs," LewRockwell.com, http://www .lewrockwell.com/gregory/gregory106.html (Feb. 1, 2006).
8. "Drug raids gone bad," Philadelphia Daily News, http://www.philly.com/dailynews/ local/20090320_DRUG_RAIDS_GONE_BAD.html?page=2&c=y (Mar. 20, 2009).
9. http://www.startribune.com/nation/59045917.html?elr=KArks:DCiUMEaPc:UiacyK UzyaP37D_MDua_eyD5PcOiUr.
10. https://www.cato.org/realaudio/drugwar/papers/duke.html.
11. Ibid.
12. Radley Balko and Joel Berger, "Wrong Door," Cato Institute, http://www.cato.org/ pub_display.php?pub_id=6651 (Wall Street Journal, Sept. 2, 2006).
13. Ibid.
14. Radley Balko, "No SWAT," Slate, http://www.slate.com/id/2139458 (Apr. 6, 2006).
15. Jacob G. Hornberger, "Why Does America Have a Drug War?" LewRockwell.com, http://www.lewrockwell.com/hornberger/hornberger159.html (Apr. 22, 2009).
16. "Police: Shooting of Elderly Woman 'Tragic, Unfortunate'," wsbtv.com, http://www .wsbtv.com/news/10374909/detail.html (Nov. 21, 2006).

17. "Terrorism," Drug Policy Alliance Network, http://www.drugpolicy.org/global/terrorism (last updated on July 19, 2004).

18. "Mexico Under Siege: 'It's a War'," *Los Angeles Times*, http://projects.latimes.com/mexico-drug-war/#/its-a-war.

19. Richard Marosi, "Mexico Under Siege: For Tijuana children, drug war gore is part of their school day," *Los Angeles Times*, http://www.latimes.com/news/printedition/front/la-fg-tijuana25-2008oct25,0,2076621.story (Oct. 25, 2008).

20. Ibid.

21. Murray Rothbard, *For A New Liberty: The Libertarian Manifesto*, http://mises.org/rothbard/newlibertywhole.asp#p94, 112.

22. Quote can be found at http://www.freedomkeys.com/kneejerk1.htm.

23. Written in the *Wall Street Journal*, Sept. 7, 1989, and can be found at http://www.freedomkeys.com/kneejerk1.htm.

Lie #12

1. *Hedgepeth v. Washington Metro Area Transit Authority*, 386 F.3d 1148 (D.C. Cir. 2004).

2. Alexander Volokh, "n Guilty Men," 146 U. Pa. L. Rev., 173 (1997) (quoting from *Blackstone's Commentaries on the Laws of England*, 1765–1769).

3. Noting that the Book of Exodus commands, "The innocent and righteous slay thou not," Alexander Volokh, "n Guilty Men."

4. *Coffin v. U.S.*, 156 U.S. 432, 453 (1895).

5. *Stack v. Boyle*, 342 U.S. 1, 4 (1951).

6. Francois Quintard-Morenas, "The Presumption of Innocence in the French and Anglo-American Legal Traditions," (*American Journal of Comparative Law*, forthcoming January 2010), p. 34, available at http://works.bepress.com/francois_quintard_morenas/1/.

7. Ibid., 35.

8. *Wolfish v. Levi*, 573 F.2d 118, 124 (2nd Cir. 1978).

9. *Bell v. Wolfish*, 441 U.S. 520 (1979).

10. Quintard-Morenas, "The Presumption of Innocence in the Civil and Common Law Traditions," 36.

11. *Buzynski v. Oliver*, 538 F. 2d 6 (1st Cir. 1976).

12. *Davis v. United States*, 160 U.S. 469, 486 (1895).

13. *Leland v. Oregon*, 343 U.S. 790 (1952).

14. *Herrera v. Collins*, 506 U.S. 390 (1993).

15. *Herrera*, 506 U.S. at 417.

16. "Government Misconduct," The Innocence Project, http://www.innocenceproject.org/understand/Government-Misconduct.php.

17. *Addington v. Texas*, 441 U.S. 418, 429 (1979).

18. http://blog.mises.org.archives/007037.asp; "DEA Returns Tucker's Cash," ACLU, www.aclu-nm.org/News_Events/news_10_3_07.html.

19. *U.S. v. $124,700*, 05-3295 (8th Cir. 2006).

20. See my article entitled "The Case Against Military Tribunals," November 29, 2009, http://www.latimes.com/news/opinion/la-oe-napolitano29-2009nov29,0,6594004.story.

21. Richard M. Salsman, "The Three Myths of Antitrust, Part 4: 'Arbitrary Law'," *Capitalism Magazine*, http://www.capmag.com/article.asp?ID=616 (Jul. 16, 2000).

22. Ayn Rand, *Capitalism: The Unknown Ideal*, Centennial ed. (Signet, 1986), 51.

23. Thomas E. Woods, Jr., *The Politically Incorrect Guide to American History* (Regnery Publishing, 2004), 105.

24. Thomas J. DiLorenzo, "The Antitrust Economists' Paradox," *Austrian Economics Newsletter* (Summer 1991), available at http://mises.org/journals/scholar/DiLorenzo. PDF.

25. Ibid.

26. D. T. Armentano, "A Politically Incorrect Guide to Antitrust Policy," Ludvig von Mises Institute, http://mises.org/story/2694 (Sept. 15, 2007).

27. Ibid.

28. Ibid.

29. *United States v. Aluminum Co. of America*, 148 F.2d 416 (2d Cir. 1945).

Lie #13

1. John Cochran, "New Gun Control Law Is Killer's Legacy," *ABC News,* http://www.abcnews.go.com/Politics/story?id=4126152 (Jan. 12, 2008).

2. Ibid.

3. Ibid.

4. Ibid.

5. Terence Hunt, "School violence stuns nation," *Boulder Daily Camera* (May 21, 1999).

6. Ibid.

7. Ibid.

8. Marc Lacey, "Clinton Recalls Columbine and Pushes for Gun Control," *New York Times*, http://www.nytimes.com/2000/04/13/us/clinton-recalls-columbine-and-pushes-for-gun-control.html?scp=1&sq=clinton%20recalls%20columbine%20april%2013,%202000&st=cse (Apr. 13, 2000).

9. Joel Roberts, "University of Texas Tower Sniper Recalled," *CBS News,* http://www.cbsnews.com/stories/2007/04/16/national/main2689785.shtml (Apr. 16, 2007).

10. Ibid.

11. Ibid.

12. Buck Wroten, "University of Texas Tower Shooting, 1966, Buck Wroten," Memory Archive, http://www.memoryarchive.org/en/University_of_Texas_Tower_Shooting,_1966,_Buck_Wroten.

13. Pamela Colloff, "96 Minutes," *TexasMonthly*, http://www.texasmonthly.com/preview/2006-08-01/feature (August 2006).

14. Ibid.

15. Joshunda Sanders, "UT students protest gun bill," statesman.com, http://www.statesman.com/blogs/content/shared-gen/blogs/austin/politics/entries/2009/04/16/ut_students_protest_gun_bill.html (Apr. 16, 2009).

16. "World War II Rationing," http://www.ameshistoricalsociety.org/exhibits/events/rationing.htm.

17. Ibid.

18. Ibid.

19. "World War II Rationing," http://www.u-s-history.com/pages/h1674.html.

20. William H. Rehnquist, *All the Laws but One* (New York: Knopf, 1998), 192.

21. Ibid.

22. Ibid.

23. Ibid.
24. Ibid.
25. Ibid.
26. Ibid.
27. *Hirabayashi v. U.S.*, 320 U.S. 81 (1943).
28. Rehnquist, *All the Laws but One*, 198.
29. Ibid.
30. Ibid., 200.
31. Ibid.
32. Ibid.
33. Frank H. Wu, "Profiling in the Wake of September 11: The Precedent of the Japanese American Internment," *Criminal Justice Magazine*, 17, Issue 2 (Summer 2002), available at http://www.abanet.org/crimjust/cjmag/17-2/japanese.html.
34. Ibid.
35. Sue Blevins, "The Model State Emergency Health Powers Act: An Assault on Civil Liberties in the Name of Homeland Security," The Heritage Foundation, http://www.heritage.org/Research/HomelandSecurity/HL748.cfm (Jun. 10, 2002).
36. "The Model State Emergency Powers Act," as of December 21, 2001, http://www.publichealthlaw.net/MSEHPA/MSEHPA2.pdf.
37. Blevins, "The Model State Emergency Health Powers Act."
38. "Model Emergency Health Powers Act (MEHPA) Turns Governors into Dictators," Association of American Physicians and Surgeons, Inc., http://www.aapsonline.org/testimony/emerpower.htm (Dec. 3, 2001).
39. "The Model State Emergency Powers Act," as of December 21, 2001, http://www.publichealthlaw.net/MSEHPA/MSEHPA2.pdf.
40. Ibid.
41. Ibid.
42. Amitai Etzioni, *How Patriotic Is the Patriot Act?*, (New York: Routledge, 2005), 89.
43. "Questions and Answers: Travel and Quarantine," Centers for Disease Control and Prevention, http://www.cdc.gov/ncidod/sars/qa/travel.htm (May 3, 2005).
44. Etzioni, *How Patriotic Is the Patriot Act?*, 89–90.
45. Ibid., 90.
46. Ron Paul, "International Bailout Brings Us Closer to Economic Collapse," Inforwars, http://www.infowars.com/international-bailout-brings-us-closer-to-economic-collapse (Jun. 24, 2009).
47. L. Gordon Crovitz, *RICO Racket* (Washington D.C.: National Legal Center for the Public Interest, 1989), 18.
48. Ibid., 20.
49. Samuel A. Alito in Crovitz, *RICO Racket*, 1–2.
50. Ibid., 3.
51. William Anderson and Candice E. Jackson, "Washington's Biggest Crime Problem," *Reason* magazine, http://www.reason.com/news/show/29099.html (April 2004).
52. William Anderson, "Mick Vick and the Feds," LewRockwell.com, http://www.lewrockwell.com/anderson/anderson194.html (Aug. 20, 2007).
53. Anderson and Jackson, "Washington's Biggest Crime Problem."
54. William Anderson, "Aschroft and Justice: Mutual Exclusives," LewRockwell.com, http://www.lewrockwell.com/anderson/anderson55.html (Aug. 30, 2002).

55. "High court won't hear charges of RICO-misuse in suits," LegalNewsLine.com, http://www.legalnewsline.com/news/202624-high-court-wont-hear-charges-of-rico-misuse-in-suits (Oct. 16, 2007).

Lie #14

1. President Franklin D. Roosevelt, prior to sending American troops to fight in World War II.
2. Ibid.
3. Anne Leland and Mari-Jana Oboroceanu, "American War and Military Operations Casualties: Lists and Statistics," Congressional Research Service, http://www.fas.org/sgp/crs/natsec/RL32492.pdf (Sept. 15, 2009).
4. This section of the chapter is largely based on the book entitled *Day of Deceit: The Truth About FDR and Pearl Harbor*, Robert B. Stinnett (New York: Touchstone, 2000).
5. "The McCollum Memo" (Oct. 7, 1940), which can be found at http://whatreallyhappened.com/WRHARTICLES/McCollum/index.html.
6. Donald E. Schmidt, *The Folly of War: American Foreign Policy, 1898–2005* (Algora Publishing: 2005), 144.
7. "American War and Military Operations Casualties: Lists and Statistics."
8. President Roosevelt attended Columbia Law School, but passed the New York State Bar Exam before completing his studies, and never graduated.
9. According to Article I, Section 8, of the United States Constitution, "The Congress has the Power To . . . declare War" (emphasis added). The Constitution nowhere grants such authority to the President, or any other government official or entity.
10. This section of the chapter is largely based on Scott McClellan's *What Happened?* (New York: Public Affairs, 2008). McClellan was one of President George W. Bush's press secretaries. His book recounts his experiences at the Bush White House and Washington's culture of deception.

Lie #15

1. President George W. Bush.
2. *Rasul v. Bush*, 542 U.S. 466, 473 (2004) (citations omitted).
3. Doernberg, et al., *Federal Courts, Federalism and Separation of Powers*, 4th ed. (St. Paul, MN: Thomson/West, 2008), 1064.
4. *Hamdi*, 542 U.S. 507 (2004).
5. Jane Mayer, *The Dark Side: The Inside Story of How the War on Terror Turned Into a War on American Ideals* (New York: Random House, 2008), 199.
6. *Hamdi v. Rumsfeld*, 243 F. Supp. 2d 527 (E.D. Va. 2002).
7. Ibid., 243 F. Supp. 2d at 536.
8. *Hamdi*, 542 U.S. at 532.
9. Ibid., 542 U.S. at 536.
10. Toobin, *The Nine*, 275.
11. *Rumsfeld v. Padilla*, 542 U.S. 426 (2004).
12. Chemerinsky, Federal Jurisdiction, 906–7.
13. Toobin, *The Nine*, 270.
14. Ibid.

15. *Rasul*, 542 U.S. 466 (2004).

16. Shafiq Rasul was actually released before the decision was handed down, but remained as lead plaintiff.

17. Toobin, *The Nine*, 269.

18. Ibid.

19. *Hamdan*, 548 U.S. 557 (2006).

20. *Boumediene*, 128 U.S. 2229 (2008).

21. In January 2009, Susan J. Crawford, a top Bush administration official, stated that the United States tortured Mohammed al-Qahtani. According to Crawford, Qahtani was subjected to nudity, sleep deprivation, sustained isolation, and prolonged exposure to cold. Qahtani currently has an action pending in federal court, challenging his confinement. (Source: Del Quentin Wilber and Julie Tate, "Detainee's Lawyers to Get Interrogation Tapes," *Washington Post* [Oct. 6, 2009]).

22. Vice President Cheney, in an interview with *Nightline*, http://abcnews.go.com/Nightline/IraqCoverage/story?id=1419206 (Dec. 18, 2005).

23. Elizabeth Holtzman, "The Impeachment of George W. Bush," *The Nation*, http://www.thenation.com/doc/20060130/holtzman (Jan. 11, 2006).

24. Common Article 3 of the Geneva Conventions.

25. Ibid.

26. Ibid.

27. Philippe Sands, *Torture Team*, (New York: Palgrave Macmillan 2009), 8.

28. Ibid., 7–8.

29. Ibid., 7.

30. Ibid., 8.

31. Ibid., 9.

32. Ibid., 13.

33. Ibid.

34. Ibid.

35. John Barry, Michael Hirsh, and Michael Isikoff, "The Roots of Torture," *Newsweek*, http://www.newsweek.com/id/105387 (May 24, 2004).

36. Ibid.

37. Ibid.

38. Ibid.

39. Ibid.

40. Ibid.

41. Ibid.

42. Ibid.

43. Ibid.

44. Ibid.

45. Ibid.

46. David Cole, "The Torture Memos: The Case Against the Lawyers," *New York Review* (Oct. 8, 2009) (written Sept. 10, 2009).

47. Ibid.

48. Ibid.

49. Ibid.

50. Ibid.

51. Ibid.

52. Ibid.
53. Ibid.
54. Ibid.
55. Ibid.
56. Ibid.
57. Sands, Torture Team, 3.
58. Ibid.
59. Ibid., 3–4.
60. Ibid., 5.
61. Ibid.
62. Bryan Walsh, "Waterboarding: A Mental and Physical Trauma," Time.com, http://www.time.com/time/nation/article/0,8599,1892721,00.html (Apr. 20, 2009).
63. Ibid.
64. Ibid.
65. Ibid.
66. Ibid.
67. Ibid.
68. It is interesting to note that Cheney and his general counsel, David Addington, theorized that torture could not actually be considered torture unless the subject suffered a near-death experience. A CIA doctor, however, noted that torture always constitutes a near-death experience. Therefore, Cheney and the Bush administration had actually been violating their own rationale.
69. Cole, "The Torture Memos: The Case Against the Lawyers."
70. Ibid.
71. Ibid.
72. Ibid.
73. Ibid.
74. Ibid.
75. Ibid.
76. Ibid.
77. Ibid.
78. Ibid.
79. Ibid.
80. *Chavez v. Martinez*, 538 U.S. 760 (2003).
81. Ibid.
82. Ibid.
83. Ibid.
84. Ibid.
85. Ibid.
86. Ibid.
87. Ibid.
88. Ibid.
89. Ibid.
90. Ibid.

Lie #16

1. Stone, et al., *The First Amendment*, 7.
2. Ibid., 8.
3. Eric Foner, "The Most Patriotic Act," *The Nation*, http://www.thenation.com/doc/20011008/foner (Sept. 20, 2001).
4. FISA §1803(a).
5. FISA 50 U.S.C. §1802(a)(1)(B).
6. Others were split or refilled with further information. Electronic Privacy Information Centre, table of Foreign Intelligence Surveillance Act Orders 1979–2007, available at http://epic.org/privacy/wiretap/stats/fisa_stats.html.
7. Section 218 of the Patriot Act (50 U.S.C. 1804 of FISA).
8. Pen American Center—Discussion of Patriot Act provisions available at http://www.pen.org/printmedia.php/prmMediaID/64.
9. *Stanford v. Texas*, 379 U.S. 476 (1965).
10. http://www.pen.org/printmedia.php/prmMediaID/64.
11. Ibid.
12. Section 213 amending 18 U.S.C. 3103(a).
13. "Sneak and Peek Search Warrants and the Patriot Act," *Georgia Defender*, 1, http://www.lawsch.uga.edu/academics/profiles/dwilkes_more/37patriot.html (Sept. 2002).
14. *United States v. Freitas*, 800 F. 2d 1451, 1458 (9th Cir. 1986) (Poole, J., dissenting).
15. *ACLU v. U.S. Dep't of Justice*, 265 F. Supp. 2d 20 (D.D.C. 2003).
16. http://www.pen.org/printmedia.php/prmMediaID/64.
17. Kim Zetter, "Bush Grabs New Power for FBI," Wired.com, http://www.wired.com/politics/security/news/2004/01/61792 (Jan. 6, 2004).
18. 31 U.S.C. §5312.
19. The bodega was rationalized on the basis that some provided money-wiring services.
20. Speech of Hon. Mark Udall of Colorado in the House of Representatives, November 20, 2003, at congressional record page E2399.
21. Pen American Center – Analysis of Section 215—available at http://www.pen.org/printmedia.php/prmMediaID/63.
22. Ibid.
23. Ron Paul, "The Police State: A Report," LewRockwell.com, http://www.lewrockwell.com/paul/paul265.html (Jul. 26, 2005).
24. Ron Paul, "Domestic Surveillance and the Patriot Act," LewRockwell.com, http://www.lewrockwell.com/paul/paul295.html (Dec. 27, 2005).
25. Ron Paul, "The Police State: A Report."

Lie #17

1. George Reisman, "The Myth That Laissez Faire is responsible for Our Present Crisis," Ludvig von Mises Institute, http://mises.org/story/3165 (Oct. 23, 2008).
2. Thomas Sowell, *The Housing Boom and Bust* (New York: Basic Books, 2009) (inspired the chapter).
3. Reisman, "The Myth That Laissez Faire is responsible for Our Present Crisis."
4. Ibid.
5. Sowell, *The Housing Boom and Bust*, 5.

6. Mark Skousen, "Why the U.S. Economy is Not Depression Proof, *Review of Austrian Economics*, 3, 81.

7. Llewellyn H. Rockwell, "Don't Bail Them Out," Ludvig von Mises Institute, http://mises.org/story/3104 (Sept. 10, 2008).

8. Annelena Lobb, "Looking Back at Black Monday: A Discussion with Richard Sylla," *Wall Street Journal* (Oct. 15, 2007).

9. Skousen, "Why the U.S. Economy is Not Depression Proof," 80.

10. Rockwell, "Don't Bail Them Out."

11. Arthur Laffer, "A Warning from Reagan's Economist," *Daily Beast*, http://www.thedailybeast.com/blogs-and-stories/2008-11-24/reagans-economist-bashes-obama/1/ (Nov. 24, 2008).

12. "Timeline: AIG Developments Since US Bailout," *Insurance Journal*, http://www.insurancejournal.com/news/national/2009/03/16/98729.htm (Mar. 16, 2009).

13. Jennifer Levitz and Philip Shishkin, "Stimulus Brings Out City Wish Lists: Neon for Vegas, Harleys for Shreveport," *Wall Street Journal*, http://online.wsj.com/article/SB123369271403544637.html (Feb. 4, 2009).

14. Frank Shostak, "The Rescue Package Will Delay Recovery," Ludvig von Mises Institute, http://www.mises.org/story/3131 (Sept. 29, 2008).

15. Edmund L. Andrews and Peter Barker, "AIG Planning Huge Bonuses After $170 Billion Bailout," *New York Times*, http://www.nytimes.com/2009/03/15/business/15AIG.html (Mar. 15, 2009).

16. Murray Rothbard, *For a New Liberty: The Libertarian Manifesto* (San Francisco: Fox & Wilkes, 1996), 195.

17. Joseph Vranich, and Edward L. Hudgins, "Help Passenger Rail by Privatizing Amtrak," Cato Institute, Policy Analysis, http://www.cato.org/pubs/pas/pa419.pdf (Nov. 1, 2001), 6.

18. Ibid., 25.

19. Ibid., 13.

20. Ibid., 29.

21. Ibid., 6.

22. Andrea Fuller, "Increasing Postal Deficits Intensify Talks on Solution," *Wall Street Journal* (July 30, 2009).

23. Michael Billy, Lysander Spooner and the United States Postal Monopoly, *"Digital Journal"*, http://www.digitaljournal.com/article/271139 (Apr. 18, 2009).

24. "'Father of 3-cent Stamp' Spooner Fought Post Office," *Linn's Weekly Stamp News*, Feb.–Mar. 1983, http://www.lysanderspooner.org/STAMP2.htm.

25. Billy, "Lysander Spooner and the United States Postal Monopoly."

About the Author

Andrew P. Napolitano joined Fox News Channel (FNC) in January 1998 and currently serves as the Senior Judicial Analyst. He provides on-air legal analysis throughout the day weekdays on both FNC and Fox Business Network (FBN) daily. He is the host of *Freedom Watch* on Foxnews.com weekdays and on FBN on weekends, and he is the regular fill-in host on *The Glenn Beck Program*.

Judge Napolitano is the youngest life-tenured Superior Court judge in the history of the State of New Jersey. While on the bench from 1987 to 1995, Judge Napolitano tried more than 150 jury trials and sat in all parts of the Superior Court—criminal, civil, general equity, and family. He has handled thousands of sentencings, motions, hearings, and divorces. For eleven years, he served as an adjunct professor of constitutional law at Seton Hall Law School, where he provided instruction in constitutional law and jurisprudence. Judge Napolitano returned to private law practice in 1995 and began television broadcasting in the same year.

Judge Napolitano is the author of five books on the U.S. Constitution: *Constitutional Chaos: What Happens When the Government Breaks Its Own Laws*; a *New York Times* bestseller, *The Constitution in Exile: How the Federal Government Has Seized Power by Rewriting the Supreme Law of the Land*; *A Nation of Sheep*; *Dred Scott's*

Revenge: A Legal History of Race and Freedom in America; and *Lies the Government Told You: Myth, Power, and Deception in American History*. His writings have also been published in *The New York Times*, *The Wall Street Journal*, *The Los Angeles Times*, *The St. Louis Post-Dispatch*, *The New York Sun*, *The Baltimore Sun*, *The (New London) Day*, *The Seton Hall Law Review*, *The New Jersey Law Journal*, and *The Newark Star-Ledger*. He is a nationally recognized expert on the U.S. Constitution, and he lectures nationally on the Constitution and human freedom.

Judge Napolitano received his undergraduate degree from Princeton University in 1972, and received his Juris Doctor from the University of Notre Dame in 1975.

Index

Also by Andrew P. Napolitano